FOREIGN AFFAIRS

Special Collection

Foreign Affairs Special Collection: Tiananmen and After

Editor Gideon Rose Introduces the Collection

A decade after the crackdown at Tiananmen Square, we at *Foreign Affairs* were able to publish, for the first time, a trove of secret documents showing why China's leaders opted for violence. Now, 25 years after the protests, we are delighted to bring you this collection, which includes expert commentary on what happened back in June 1989, what it meant, and how China has—and hasn't—changed since then.

ON THE PAPERS:
Andrew Nathan, the political science professor who first secured and translated the Tiananmen Papers, reflects on the 25th anniversary of the protests.

ON POLITICAL DEVELOPMENT:
Eric Li, a venture capitalist and political scientist in China, explains why the Chinese Communist Party will continue to thrive for years to come. Yasheng Huang, a professor of political economy, rebuts.

ON ECONOMIC DEVELOPMENT:
CFR Senior Fellow Elizabeth Economy explains why China's increasing economic clout will lead it to seek international political clout as well.

ON THE CHALLENGES AHEAD:
Lynette Ong, an associate professor of political science, warns of China's coming debt crisis, and John Deluy, an assistant professor of international studies, looks at China's new austerity policies.

Visit ForeignAffairs.com for more on these topics—and all our other great content.

Modern China's Original Sin

Tiananmen Square's Legacy of Repression

Andrew J. Nathan

On May 3, 2014, about a dozen rights activists met in a private apartment in Beijing, where they held a seminar marking the 25th anniversary of the protests and crackdown in Tiananmen Square. Since that night, most of the activists have disappeared. One of them, Pu Zhiqiang, a human rights lawyer, has been formally detained (the prelude to a criminal charge) for "picking quarrels and provoking trouble."

In a way, none of this is surprising. China is an authoritarian regime. Whoever challenges it takes a risk. But what is surprising is that this small group of activists had held the same kind of meeting for several years without getting into trouble. The fact that they weren't as lucky this year is one sign among many that repression in China has not only not eased in recent years but is getting worse.

But why? As the rights activists argued, it all goes back to June 4, 1989. The regime's attack on the pro-democracy movement in Tiananmen Square was an inflection point, one at which it could have chosen liberalization or repression. Zhao Ziyang, who was the leader of the Chinese Communist Party (CCP), favored dialogue with the students. He argued that they were patriotic, that they shared the

ANDREW J. NATHAN is Class of 1919 Professor of Political Science at Columbia University.

1

regime's goal of opposing corruption, and that if the leadership told the students that it accepted their demands the students would peacefully leave the square. Li Peng, the prime minister, countered that if the CCP legitimized opposition voices by negotiating with them, the party's political rule, based on a monopoly of power, would crumble. In the end, Chinese leader Deng Xiaoping sided with Li.

Having picked the path of repression in 1989, the regime has had to steadily step it up. Here, too, the May 3 meeting is emblematic. The participants were calling for the regime to acknowledge that the student demonstrations were not dongluan, "a turmoil"—the official term for the demonstrations, which implies that they were a violent rebellion. They also requested that the government acknowledge that its killing of people in the square was a mistake, absolve those who had been convicted in connection with the protests, and identify those killed and offer compensation to their families. Such demands are not exactly radical, but they fly in the face of the government's preferred method for dealing with 1989: forgetting it. Even today, the regime is unable to hold a dialogue with citizens on this or any other topic for fear of losing control.

To be sure, the regime is still widely accepted in society for several reasons, including economic growth, nationalism, and what is still a quite effective system of information control. But repression remains a key pillar of its rule, because people keep searching for facts, keep wanting to speak, keep wanting to communicate. And the more repression is used, the more is needed.

Accordingly, China's security apparatus has grown. It includes the Ministry of Public Security, with a recently added special branch for national security, the political police or guobao. Then there are the relatively new Internet police, the paramilitary People's Armed Police, which has been strengthened since Tiananmen, the Ministry of State Security, and, backing these up if necessary, the People's Liberation Army. According to official figures, the budgets for all these units have steadily grown, to the point where the official budget for the domestic security agencies is larger than the budget for the military, although the openly published figures for both are probably close to meaningless.

The security apparatus is unconstrained by legal procedures and enjoys the use of a wide range of flexible measures. The political police may start by "inviting [dissidents] to drink tea," to warn them politely that their behavior has begun to exceed the regime's ill-defined red lines. If the message is not heeded, the police can follow up with 24-hour surveillance. And if that doesn't work, security officials can disappear people for weeks or months. A dissenter who is still stubborn can be subjected to a trumped-up criminal charge, trial, and a jail sentence, such as the 11-year sentence meted out to Nobel Peace Prize winner Liu Xiaobo or the four-year sentence given to Xu Zhiyong, the leader of a protest group called the New Citizens Movement. Despite the rise of social media, the police can carry out these acts inconspicuously, because censorship keeps the news from all but the most attentive members of the public.

These measures have prevented political dissenters from forming a strong movement or reaching out for broader social support. Meanwhile, local governments use arrests and tactical concessions to deal effectively with the tens of thousands of small-scale protests that break out all over China every year over issues such as land seizure, pollution, labor conditions, and corruption. Another challenge to the security agencies is rising opposition among some of the ethnic groups that China labels "national minorities," especially the Uighurs in Xinjiang and the Tibetans in the Tibetan Autonomous Republic and in the provinces adjoining Tibet. In the last five years there have been over 130 Tibetan self-immolations; a wave of Uighur refugees has tried to flee to other countries (and then been sent back from Pakistan, Cambodia, and Malaysia in violation of international norms against refoulement); and Uighurs have been involved in a growing number of violent incidents, which the regime has labeled terrorist incidents.

With each new generation of leaders since Tiananmen, outside observers and many Chinese have hoped for a period of liberalizing political reform, meaning some kind of movement toward democracy—not American-style, but a Chinese version, having at least the minimal attributes of political freedom, rule of law, and governmental accountability. Instead, each successive head of state—Jiang Zemin, Hu Jintao, and now Xi Jinping—has restricted freedom further. China will likely eventually democratize.

But with every passing year, doing so gets more dangerous for the regime because the bottled-up social pressure has only increased. And so democratization is postponed again and again.

SKELETONS IN THE CLOSET

Political repression is not the only legacy of Tiananmen. The last 25 years have also been a period of rapid economic growth. The crisis of 1989 grew out of the problems produced by ten years of economic reform—inflation, corruption, and ideological confusion—and out of the divisions in the leadership between so-called reformers and conservatives over how to move forward with reform. The violent resolution of the crisis produced a momentary victory for the conservatives, who believed that reform had gone too fast and far enough. But in 1992, Deng restarted reform, effectively arguing that, just as in 1978, only economic growth could save China (meaning in part, the regime) because the Chinese people would no longer accept living in poverty as a form of socialist utopia. As a result of the reforms, between the early 1990s and last year, China's economy grew at double-digit rates each year, producing the fastest and biggest upsurge in wealth in world history, lifting hundreds of millions out of poverty, and creating a huge middle class—and a new world power.

Regime apologists give the government's decision to crack down on the students in Tiananmen Square credit for this economic growth, arguing that it produced the political stability necessary to attract investment and win export contracts. In fact, the credit for growth should go to China's land, resources, industrious labor force, and entrepreneurship—its economic potential—and to Deng's decision to unlock that potential by integrating China into the globalizing world economy. Had the country opted for political liberalization in 1989, it would likely have still enjoyed economic growth—and what economists call better "quality" growth, with less repressed wages, a more consumption-driven model, more equity, less pollution, and less corruption.

What the Tiananmen crackdown did do was to create the conditions for the specific model of growth that a globalizing China pursued, a form of authoritarian crony capitalism. The state controls the main factors of production: land, labor, credit, transportation, energy. It fosters "national champion" companies that are nominally private but are controlled by the CCP. It allows the political elite to get rich through influence and access. As GDP goes up, so does economic inequality, pollution, land seizures, and labor repression.

The point of leverage in this model of growth—the hinge between politics and economics, between government above and society below, and (to use human rights terminology) between rising economic, social, and cultural rights and declining civil and political rights—is the local CCP secretary, especially at the municipal level. There are about 600 municipalities in China, and it is at this level of government that most of the policy action happens. These party secretaries are given specific tasks—the three main ones are economic development, control of population growth, and "social stability maintenance"—and their careers depend on completing them. To do so, they are given full power over the local economy, media, courts, police, the women's federation, and all other local party and state agencies. In this way, strong-arm tactics have come to foster economic growth, and economic growth legitimates strong-arm tactics. Economic, social, and cultural rights have increased as civil and political rights wane.

And this, too, is testimony to the abiding importance of Tiananmen. A population with robust civil and political rights would be a population that the CCP could no longer manage with its current style of rule. The idea—hard for outsiders to grasp—that the award of a Nobel Peace Prize to Liu Xiaobo is an existential threat to such a strong, successful, and resilient regime shows how fragile the system is at its core. The regime suffers from what we might call the fragility of repression. A regime that cannot allow people to discuss Tiananmen is a regime that is afraid of its own history and what that history can do to it. It is trying to outrun history, but history cannot be outrun. It can only be confronted.

When that finally happens, it will be a sign that long postponed political changes are imminent—civil freedom, press freedom, academic freedom—changes that will help a more democratic China to control corruption, pollution, and inequality, that will bring China more stability rather than less, and that will make China an easier neighbor for other countries to live with.

The Tiananmen Papers

Andrew J. Nathan

INSIDE CHINA'S POLITBURO

For the first time ever, reports and minutes have surfaced that provide a revealing and potentially explosive view of decision-making at the highest levels of the government and party in the People's Republic of China (PRC). The materials paint a vivid picture of the battles between hard-liners and reformers on how to handle the student protests that swept China in the spring of 1989. The protests were ultimately ended by force, including the bloody clearing of Beijing streets by troops using live ammunition. The tragic event was one of the most important in the history of communist China, and its consequences are still being felt.

The materials were spirited out of China by a sympathizer of Communist Party members who are seeking a resumption of political reform. They believe that challenging the official picture of Tiananmen as a legitimate suppression of a violent antigovernment riot will help unfreeze the political process. The extensive and dramatic documentary picture of how China's leaders reacted to the student protests is revealed in The Tiananmen Papers: The Chinese Leadership's Decision to Use Force Against Their Own People—In Their Own Words. This article is adapted from the extensive narrative and documents in that book.

ANDREW J. NATHAN is Professor of Political Science at Columbia University and the author of numerous books, including *China's Transition*. He is co-editor with Perry Link, Professor of Chinese language and literature at Princeton University, of *The Tiananmen Papers*, to be published around the world this month by *PublicAffairs* and in a Chinese version later this year. Documents in the book were compiled by Zhang Liang (a pseudonym).

Andrew J. Nathan

THE STUDENTS' CHALLENGE

The 1989 demonstrations were begun by Beijing students to encourage continued economic reform and liberalization. The students did not set out to pose a mortal challenge to what they knew was a dangerous regime. Nor did the regime relish the use of force against the students. The two sides shared many goals and much common language. Yet, through miscommunication and misjudgment, they pushed one another into positions where options for compromise became less and less available.

The spark for the student movement was a desire to commemorate the reformer Hu Yaobang, who had died on April 15. He had been replaced two years earlier as general secretary (party leader) by another moderate, Zhao Ziyang, after student demonstrations in December 1986.

Although there was a provocative edge to the behavior of students in the spring of 1989, most of them stayed within the bounds of certain pieties, acknowledging party leadership and positioning themselves as respectful, if disappointed, supporters of the party's long-term reform project.

Once begun, however, the commemoration quickly evolved into a protest for far-reaching change. On May 4, a student declaration was read in Tiananmen Square calling on the government to accelerate political and economic reform, guarantee constitutional freedoms, fight corruption, adopt a press law, and allow the establishment of privately run newspapers. The declaration said important first steps would include institutionalizing the democratic practices that the students themselves had begun to initiate on their campuses, conducting dialogue between students and the government, promoting democratic reforms of the government system, opposing corruption, and accelerating the adoption of a press law.

Zhao struggled to achieve consensus within the leadership around a conciliatory line toward the students. Senior leader Deng Xiaoping seemed willing to consider anything, so long as the students were somehow cleared from the square in time for Soviet leader Mikhail Gorbachev's upcoming summit visit. But disaster struck for Zhao's moderate strategy on May 13, when the protesting students announced a hunger strike. During the next few days, the intellectuals joined in, incidents in the provinces began to erupt, and the summit that the authorities envisioned as a triumphant climax to years of diplomacy with the Soviet Union was thrown into the shadows. The huge foreign press contingent that had come to Beijing for the summit turned its main attention to the student movement.

Over the course of several weeks, the hunger strikers gained the support of tens of millions of other citizens, who took to the streets in scores of cities to demand a response from the government. The government at first tried to wait out the hunger strikers, then engaged them in limited dialogue, and finally issued orders to force them from the square. In reaching that decision, the party suffered its worst high-level split since the Cultural Revolution. Those favoring political reform lost out and their cause has been in the deep freeze ever since.

The regime has, to be sure, diminished the range of social activities it purports to control in comparison with the totalitarian ambitions of its Maoist years. It has fitted its goals of control more to its means and no longer aspires to change human nature. It has learned that many arenas of freedom are inessential to the monopoly of political power.

Several noteworthy books and an important documentary film have told the story of the Tiananmen events from the viewpoint of students and citizens in Beijing. The book from which this article is adapted provides the first view from Zhongnanhai—the former imperial park at the center of Beijing that houses the Party Central Office, the State Council Office, and the residences of some top leaders. Although the leaders occupied distinct official posts in a triad of organizations—the ruling Chinese Communist Party, the State Council (government cabinet), and the Central Military Commission—behind those red walls they acted as a small and often informal community of perhaps ten decision-makers and their staffs.

Andrew J. Nathan

The eight "elders," retired senior officials who together amounted to China's extraconstitutional final court of appeal, joined their deliberations at crucial moments. (Bo Yibo is the only one of these elders still alive, and he is no longer politically active.)

Three of the elders were most influential, and among these the final voice belonged to Deng Xiaoping, who was retired from all government posts except one and lived outside Zhongnanhai in a private mansion with his own office staff. It was at this house that the most crucial meetings of these tormented months took place.

THE PAPER TRAIL

Into Zhongnanhai flowed a river of documentation from the agencies charged with monitoring and controlling the capital city of Beijing and the vast nation beyond it. On a daily and hourly basis Party Central received classified reports from government, military, and party agencies and diplomatic missions abroad. The material included reports on the state of mind of students, professors, party officials, military officers and troops, workers, farmers, shop clerks, street peddlers, and others around the country. Also captured in these reports is the thinking of provincial and central leaders on policy issues; the traffic on railways; discussions in private meetings; man-in-the-street interviews; and press, academic, and political opinion from abroad.

Often such materials were distributed only to the top forty or so leaders, and many were limited even more sharply to the five-man Politburo Standing Committee plus the eight elders (The Communist Party's Political Bureau—or Politburo-Standing Committee—is the highest organ of formal political power in China, despite constitutional provisions that legally give that role to the National People's Congress.) Certain documents went to only one or a few leaders. Taken as a whole, these reports tell us in extraordinary detail what the central decision-makers saw as they looked out from their compound on the events unfolding around them, and how they evaluated the threat to their rule.

Added to these are minutes of the leaders' formal and informal meetings and accounts of some of their private conversations. In these we observe the conflict among a handful of strong-willed leaders. We learn what the ultimate decision-makers said among themselves as they discussed the unfolding events—how they debated the motives of the students, whom they identified as their main enemies; which considerations dominated their search for a solution; why they waited as long as they did and no longer before ordering the troops to move on Tiananmen Square; and what they ordered the troops to do. Perhaps most dramatic of all, we have definitive evidence of who voted how on key issues, and their reasons for those votes, in their own words.

The records reveal that if left to their own preferences the three-man majority of the Politburo Standing Committee would have voted to persist in dialogue with the students instead of declaring martial law. At the crucial Politburo Standing Committee meeting of May 17, two of the five members, Zhao Ziyang and Hu Qili, voted against martial law. The third-ranking member, Qiao Shi, abstained. We can see from his remarks that he was not in favor of using force. But Qiao, by abstaining, and Zhao, by offering his resignation, deferred to the elders' decision in favor of martial law.

Such seeming weakness was no doubt explained by the knowledge that resistance to Deng Xiaoping would have been futile. The Tiananmen papers reveal that the Politburo Standing Committee was obligated by a secret intra-party resolution to refer any stalemate to Deng and the elders. The documents further show that Deng exercised absolute control over the military through his associate Yang Shangkun, who was president of the PRC and standing vice chair of the Central Military Commission. Had the Standing Committee refused to honor the elders' wishes, Deng had ample means to exert his authority.

Had the Standing Committee majority had its way, China's recent history and its relations with the West would have been very different. Dialogue with the students would have tipped the balance toward political reform. Instead, China has experienced more than a decade of political stasis at home and strained relations with the West.

Andrew J. Nathan

In 1989 Jiang Zemin was party secretary in Shanghai. He committed no heinous act at that time, although his closing of the World Economic Herald newspaper for being too sympathetic to the student cause is still widely resented by intellectuals. What The Tiananmen Papers reveals is that his accession to supreme power came about through a constitutionally irregular procedure—the vote of the elders on May 27—and that the elders chose him because he was a pliable and cautious figure who was outside the paralyzing factional fray that had created the crisis in the first place. This accession route was widely suspected, but the details have never been known before. Although Jiang is not necessarily a committed political conservative, he has paid deference to the concerns of conservatives as a way of balancing contending forces and maintaining his own power.

Today's second-ranking member of the party hierarchy, Li Peng, was premier in 1989. Not only did he advocate a hard line against the students and go on television to declare martial law, as is already known, but the papers show that he manipulated information to lead Deng and the other elders to see the demonstrations as an attack on them personally and on the political structure they had devoted their careers to creating. The Tiananmen Papers also reveals his use of the intelligence and police agencies to collect information that was used to persecute liberal officials and intellectuals after the crackdown.

Both Li Peng and Jiang Zemin are scheduled to step down from their high-level party and state offices in 2002 and 2003. Some commentators expect Jiang will try to retain his third post, that of chairman of the Central Military Commission, thus enabling him to exert influence as a party elder from behind the scenes, as Deng did in the period described in The Tiananmen Papers.

WHAT'S IN A NAME

Throughout the subsequent years, the issue of how to label the student movement has remained alive. Just before ordering the troops to move, the leadership made an official determination that the incident was a fan'geming baoluan (counterrevolutionary riot), an even more severe label than that of "turmoil," which the authorities had applied up to then, and one that implied (falsely) that the demonstrators were armed and had shed blood. Neither designation has ever been officially withdrawn. But in deference to opinion at home and abroad, informal official usage has gravitated to the softer term "political storm" (zhengzhi fengbo, equivalent to "political flap"), a term first introduced by Deng a few days after the crackdown.

Since 1989, there has been a constant stream of appeals for formal reconsideration of the official determination. Ding Zilin, the mother of a student who died on June 4, has led a movement to demand an accounting. In 1999, former high-ranking Zhao Ziyang aide Bao Tong circulated a letter urging the party leaders to acknowledge the mistakes made ten years earlier, calling the opportunity to reverse the verdict the current regime's "greatest political resource" for reviving its legitimacy. On a broader canvas, the party has faced constant demands for political reform. It has responded with arrests and purges of dissidents outside the party who demanded reform. But a sharp debate over reform has also developed within the party. In the course of this debate participants on both sides started to use a technique that had previously been rare in PRC history: that of leaking documents to the outside world—a technique of which The Tiananmen Papers is a spectacular extension.

The party believes it has learned from Tiananmen that democratization is not an irresistible force. There is a widespread view in the West that where globalization and modernization occur, fundamental changes in the party-state system are inevitable, leading to the rise of civil society and some form of democracy. Whether this is right or wrong, the leaders in power in China do not believe it. For them, the lesson of Tiananmen is that at its core, politics is about force.

The events of 1989 left the regime positioned for its responses to later challenges, such as the Chinese Democratic Party in 1998–99 and the Falun Gong religious movement since 1999. In both of these incidents and others, the key to the party's behavior was its

Andrew J. Nathan

fear of independent organizations, whether of religious followers or students, workers or farmers, with or without a broad social base, and with or without party members as constituents. The core political issue has remained what it was in 1989, even if the sociology has been different: the party believes that as soon as it gives in to any demand from any group that it does not control, then the power monopoly that it views as the indispensable organizational principle of the political system will be destroyed.

Many in China, however, share the view held widely overseas that this kind of political rigidity cannot persist in the face of rapid social and ideological change. Can the regime muddle through and survive, or will it implode? This is the choice the backers of this book are trying to avoid. By reopening the issues that were closed in 1989, they seem to want to open a breach in the power monopoly without causing a collapse.

Documents of the sort quoted in this article and in the book from which it is adapted are available to only a tiny handful of people in China. The compiler, who brought the contents of the documents out of China, can be publicly identified only by the pseudonym Zhang Liang. Issues of safety for the compiler and his associates do not allow for public disclosure of the extensive efforts at authentication taken by co-editor Perry Link and myself. China scholar Orville Schell, dean of the Graduate School of Journalism at the University of California, Berkeley, wrote the book's afterword, which explores the issue of authentication of such documents. Schell concurs that there are convincing grounds to assume that the compiler's motivations were honest and that the documents were credible despite the impossibility of making an absolute judgment about material in a closed society like China's.

Following are excerpts from some of the key documents: THE TIANANMEN PAPERS

DENG XIAOPING AND THE APRIL 26 EDITORIAL
On April 25, Li Peng and other officials went to Deng Xiaoping's home to report on the student demonstrations in Beijing and 20

other cities. Deng's response formed the basis of an April 26 editorial that became the party's verdict on the student movement.

Excerpts from Party Central Office Secretariat, "Important meeting minutes," April 25:

> **Li Peng:** Some of the protest posters and the slogans that students shout during the marches are anti-Party and antisocialist. They're clamoring for a reversal of the verdicts on bourgeois liberalization and spiritual pollution [Communist Party jargon for Western cultural influences].
>
> The spear is now pointed directly at you and the others of the elder generation of proletarian revolutionaries.
>
> **Deng Xiaoping:** Saying I'm the mastermind behind the scenes, are they?
>
> **Li Peng:** There are open calls for the government to step down, appeals for nonsense like "open investigations into and discussions of the question of China's governance and power," and calls to institute broader elections and revise the Constitution, to lift restrictions on political parties and newspapers, and to get rid of the category of "counterrevolutionary" crimes. Illegal student organizations have already sprung up in Beijing and Tianjin. . . . The small number of leaders of these illegal organizations have other people behind them calling the shots.
>
> In Beijing there have been two attacks on Xinhua Gate in quick succession; in Changsha and Xi'an there was looting and arson on April 22, and in Wuhan students have demonstrated on the Yangtze River Bridge, blocking the vital artery between Beijing and Guangzhou. These actions seriously harm social stability and unity, and they disrupt social order. Those of us on the Standing Committee all believe that this is turmoil and that we must rely on law to bring a halt to it as soon as possible.
>
> **Deng Xiaoping:** I completely agree with the Standing Committee's decision. This is no ordinary student movement. The students have been raising a ruckus for ten days now, and we've been tolerant and restrained. But things haven't gone our way. A tiny minority is exploiting the students; they want to confuse the people and throw the country into chaos. This is a well-planned plot whose real aim is to reject the Chinese Communist Party and the socialist system at the most fundamental level. We must explain to the whole Party and

nation that we are facing a most serious political struggle. We've got to be explicit and clear in opposing this turmoil.

Li Peng: . . . Shouldn't we organize an editorial in the People's Daily right away, in order to get the word out on what Comrade Xiaoping has said?

That afternoon the Chinese Communist Party (CCP) Central Committee General Office telegraphed the decision to Zhao Ziyang, party general secretary, who was on an ill-timed official visit to North Korea. Zhao wired back: "I completely agree with the policy decision of Comrade Xiaoping with regard to the present problem of turmoil."

Excerpt from the People's Daily, April 26, 1989, editorial, "The necessity for a clear stand against turmoil":

> This is a well-planned plot to confuse the people and throw the country into "turmoil." Its real aim is to reject the Chinese Communist Party and the socialist system at the most fundamental level. This is a most serious political struggle that concerns the whole Party and nation.

The editorial re-ignited the waning student movement, which mounted huge next-day demonstrations in major cities. In Beijing, 50 thousand students from many campuses marched, carrying banners, including one bearing quotations from Deng Xiaoping and Lenin favoring democracy. With irony, they sang the song "Without the Chinese Communist Party There Would Be No New China," and they elicited tears from bystanders when they shouted, "Mama, we haven't done anything wrong."

In the three days after publication the State Security Ministry and Xinhua News Agency sent 36 reports to Zhongnanhai on the reactions of various social strata. Many citizens felt that the editorial was too harsh—that it "defined the nature of the incident at too high a level of seriousness" and that it was not helpful for resolving the problem. The reports described widespread sympathy and protective feelings for the students among university presidents and other high-ranking party and administrative officials. One official revealed that on his campus, two-thirds of faculty members were refusing to attend meetings to study the editorial. Others pointed out that the blame for the demonstrations ultimately lay in the failings of the party itself, without which the students would have no need to protest.

STRAINS AMONG THE LEADERS

On the morning of May 13 Party General Secretary Zhao Zi-yang and PRC President Yang Shangkun went to Deng Xiaoping's home and reported on their recent work. Yang was Deng Xiaoping's closest confidant and business manager within the leadership. Zhao explained the positions he had taken at several Politburo meetings.

Excerpts from memoranda of conversations supplied by a friend of Yang Shangkun who cannot be further identified:

Zhao Ziyang: . . . I've noticed that this movement has two particular features we need to pay attention to: First, the student slogans all support the Constitution; they favor democracy and oppose corruption. These demands are basically in line with what the Party and government advocate, so we cannot reject them out of hand. Second, the number of demonstrators and supporters is enormous, and they include people from all parts of society. So I think we have to keep an eye on the majority and give approval to the mainstream view of the majority if we want to calm this thing down.

Deng Xiaoping: It was obvious from the start that a tiny minority was stirring up the majority, fanning the emotions of the great majority.

Zhao Ziyang: That's why I think we have to separate the broad masses of students and their supporters from the tiny minority [who are] using the movement to fish in troubled waters, stir up trouble, and attack the Party and socialism. We have to rely on guidance. We have to pursue multilevel, multichannel dialogue, get in touch with people, and build understanding. We mustn't let the conflicts get nasty if we expect things to settle down quickly.

Deng Xiaoping: Dialogue is fine, but the point is to solve the problem. We can't be led around by the nose. This movement's dragged on too long, almost a month now. The senior comrades are getting worried. . . . We have to be decisive. I've said over and over that we need stability if we're going to develop. How can we progress if things are in an utter mess?

Yang Shangkun: Gorbachev will be here in two days, and today I hear that the students are going to announce a hunger strike. They obviously want to turn up the heat and get a lot of international attention.

Deng Xiaoping: Tiananmen is the symbol of the People's Republic of China. The Square has to be in order when Gorbachev comes. We have to maintain our international image. What do we look like if the Square's a mess?

Zhao Ziyang: I'll stress the importance of the Gorbachev visit one more time in the media this afternoon.

Deng Xiaoping: As I've said before, the origins of this incident are not so simple. The opposition is not just some students but a bunch of rebels and a lot of riffraff, and a tiny minority who are utterly against opposing bourgeois liberalization. . . . This is not just between the students and the government.

Zhao Ziyang: The consensus in the Politburo has been to use the policies of guiding and dividing, winning over the great majority of students and intellectuals while isolating the tiny minority of anti-communist troublemakers, thereby stilling the movement through democratic and legal means.

Deng Xiaoping: What do the ordinary people in society think?

Zhao Ziyang: The protests are widespread but limited to cities that have universities. The rural areas aren't affected, and the farmers are docile. So are urban workers, basically. The workers are unhappy about certain social conditions and like to let off steam from time to time, so they sympathize with the protesters. But they go to work as usual and they aren't striking, demonstrating, or traveling around like the students.

Deng Xiaoping: . . . We must not give an inch on the basic principle of upholding Communist Party rule and rejecting a Western multi-party system. At the same time, the Party must resolve the issue of democracy and address the problems that arise when corruption pops up in the Party or government.

Zhao Ziyang: . . . When we allow some democracy, things might look "chaotic" on the surface; but these little "troubles" are normal inside a democratic and legal framework. They prevent major upheavals and actually make for stability and peace in the long run.

ZHAO ZIYANG AND JIANG ZEMIN CLASH

On May 10, the full Politburo clashed over how to handle the student movement. Members agreed on the danger of the situation but disagreed over Zhao's line on how it should be handled. Zhao criticized Jiang Zemin for mishandling the World Economic Herald incident, and Jiang stoutly defended himself. (In a private conversation a day later, Yang Shangkun and Deng Xiaoping agreed that Jiang's handling of this incident struck the right balance between discipline and reform-mindedness.)

The student movement was also divided. Although some students returned to classes, others advocated continuing the strike. New leaders emerged, and various groups presented various demands. Journalists and intellectuals spoke out, new issues were added to old ones, and demonstrations burgeoned in the provinces.

Despite the now clear divisions on strategy, the Politburo at its May 10 meeting decided to make further efforts at dialogue with the students. Dialogue had been attempted a number of times in April and May. Some efforts were rebuffed, as when student leaders during the memorial service for Hu Yaobang mounted the steps of the Great Hall of the People with a seven-item petition. No officials would meet with them.

At other times, meetings between student representatives and mid-level government officials were exercises in avoidance. An April 29 meeting between government officials and 45 student representatives was marked mostly by the officials evading questions by changing the subject.

On May 13, the students announced their hunger strike. Excerpts from State Security Ministry, "Trends in Tiananmen Square," fax to Party Central and State Council duty offices, 11:58 pm, May 14:

> Today, more than one thousand students began a hunger strike in the Square. About twenty thousand students and citizens looked on during the day, and this number grew to one hundred thousand in the evening. . . . The striking students were regularly supplied with drinking water, soda, sugar, and medicine. By 10 pm more than a dozen of

them had fainted or suffered stomach cramps and were rushed to first-aid centers in ambulances provided by the Beijing Government.

THE GORBACHEV VISIT

On May 16, while Deng Xiaoping met with Gorbachev inside the Great Hall of the People, thereby bringing about the long-sought normalization of Sino-Soviet relations, tens of thousands of people from all corners of society demonstrated outside in support of the students.

On the evening of May 16, Zhao Ziyang called on Gorbachev at the elegant state guest house called Diaoyutai. It was here that Zhao made his fateful comment to Gorbachev that even though Deng Xiaoping had retired from his party posts in 1987, the party had recognized that his wisdom and experience were essential and that for the most important questions he would still be at the helm. Zhao's observation could be interpreted as a veiled way of saying that any mishandling of the student protests was ultimately Deng's responsibility, and it became one of the counts against him when he was later dismissed from the party leadership.

THE STANDING COMMITTEE MEETS IN EMERGENCY

On the evening of May 16 the members of the Politburo Standing Committee—Zhao Ziyang, Li Peng, Qiao Shi, Hu Qili, and Yao Yilin—held an emergency meeting. Party elders Yang Shangkun and Bo Yibo also attended. The hunger strike had evoked a strong, broad response in society, and the leaders were under pressure to find a solution.

Excerpts from Party Central Office Secretariat, "Minutes of the May 16 Politburo Standing Committee meeting":

Zhao Ziyang: . . . The students' hunger strike in the square has gone on for four days now. . . . We've had dialogues with their representatives and have promised we'll take them seriously and keep listening to their comments, asking only that they stop their fast, but it hasn't worked. The Square is so crowded—all kinds of excited people milling about with their slogans and banners—that the student representatives themselves say they have no real control of things.

Yang Shangkun: These last few days Beijing's been in something like anarchy. Students are striking at all the schools, workers from some offices are out on the streets, transportation and lots of other things are out of whack—it's what you could call anarchy. We are having a historic Sino-Soviet summit and should have had a welcoming ceremony in Tiananmen Square, but instead we had to make do at the airport. We're supposed to have had two sessions of summit talks today in the Great Hall of the People, but we had to meet at Diaoyutai instead. That's the kind of anarchy we're in.

Zhao Ziyang: . . . When I got back from North Korea I learned that the April 26 editorial had elicited a strong reaction in many parts of society and had become a major issue for the students. I thought it might be best simply to skirt the most sensitive issue of whether the student movement is turmoil, hoping it would fade away while we gradually turn things around using the methods of democracy and law. But then on May 13 a few hundred students began a hunger strike, and one of their main demands was to reverse the official view of the April 26 editorial. So now there's no way to avoid the problem. We have to revise the April 26 editorial, find ways to dispel the sense of confrontation between us and the students, and get things settled down as soon as possible.

Li Peng: It's just not true, Comrade Ziyang, that the official view in the April 26 editorial was aimed at the vast majority of students. It was aimed at the tiny minority who were using the student movement to exploit the young students' emotions and to exploit some of our mistakes and problems in order to begin a political struggle against the Communist Party and the socialist system and to expand this struggle from Beijing to the whole country and create national turmoil. These are indisputable facts. Even if a lot of the student demonstrators misunderstood the April 26 editorial, still it served an important purpose in exposing these truths.

Zhao Ziyang: As I see it, the reason why so many more students have joined the demonstrations is that they couldn't accept the editorial's label for the movement. The students kept insisting that the party and government express a different attitude and come up with a better way of characterizing the movement. I think we have to address this problem very seriously because there's no way around it. . . .

Li Peng: Comrade Ziyang, the key phrases of the April 26 editorial were drawn from Comrade Xiaoping's remarks on the 25th: "This is a well-planned plot," it is "turmoil," its "real aim is to reject the Chinese Communist Party and the socialist system," "the whole Party and nation are facing a most serious political struggle," and so on are all Comrade Xiaoping's original words. They cannot be changed.

Zhao Ziyang: We have to explain the true nature of this student movement to Comrade Xiaoping, and we need to change the official view of the movement.

ZHAO ZIYANG LOSES GROUND

On the morning of May 17 the Standing Committee of the Politburo met at Deng Xiaoping's home. Besides Zhao Ziyang, Li Peng, Qiao Shi, Hu Qili, and Yao Yilin, elders Yang Shangkun and Bo Yibo also attended.

Excerpts from Party Central Office Secretariat, "Minutes of the May 17 Politburo Standing Committee meeting," document supplied to Party Central Office Secretariat for its records by the Office of Deng Xiaoping:

Zhao Ziyang: The fasting students feel themselves under a spotlight that makes it hard for them to make concessions. This leaves us with a prickly situation. The most important thing right now is to get the students to de-link their fasting from their demands and then to get them out of the Square and back to their campuses. Otherwise, anything could happen, and in the blink of an eye. Things are tense.

Yang Shangkun: . . . Can we still say there's been no harm to the national interest or society's interest? This isn't turmoil? If anybody here takes the position that this isn't turmoil, I don't see any way to move ahead with reform and opening or to pursue socialist construction. . . .

Li Peng: I think Comrade Ziyang must bear the main responsibility for the escalation of the student movement, as well as for the fact that the situation has gotten so hard to control. When he was in North Korea and the Politburo asked Comrade Ziyang's opinion, he sent back a telegram clearly stating that he was "in complete agreement with Comrade Xiaoping's plan for dealing with the unrest."

After he came back on April 30 he again said at a Politburo meeting that he endorsed Comrade Xiaoping's remarks as well as the word "turmoil" that appeared in the April 26 editorial.

But then, just a few days later, on the afternoon of May 4 at the Asian Development Bank meetings—and without consulting anybody else on the Standing Committee—he gave a speech that flew in the face of the Standing Committee's decisions, Comrade Xiaoping's statement, and the spirit of the April 26 editorial.

First, in the midst of obvious turmoil, he felt able to say, "China will be spared any major turmoil."

Second, in the presence of a mountain of evidence that the aim of the turmoil was to end Communist Party rule and bring down the socialist system, he continued to insist the protesters "do not oppose our underlying system but demand that we eliminate the flaws in our work."

Third, even after many facts had clearly established that a tiny minority was exploiting the student movement to cause turmoil, he said only that there are "always going to be people ready to exploit" the situation. This explicitly contradicts Party Central's correct judgment that a tiny minority was already manufacturing turmoil. . . .

Yao Yilin: . . . I don't understand why Comrade Ziyang mentioned Comrade Xiaoping in his talk with Gorbachev yesterday. Given the way things are right now, this can only have been intended as a way to saddle Comrade Xiaoping with all the responsibility and to get the students to target Comrade Xiaoping for attack. This made the whole mess a lot worse.

Zhao Ziyang: Could I have a chance to explain these two things? The basic purposes of my remarks at the annual meeting of the directors of the [Asian Development Bank] were to pacify the student movement and to strengthen foreign investors' confidence in China's stability. The first reactions I heard to my speech were all positive, and I wasn't aware of any problems at the time. Comrades Shangkun, Qiao Shi, and Qili all thought the reaction to the speech was good; Comrade Li Peng said it was a good job and that he would echo it when he met with the ADB representatives. . . .

Now, about my comments to Gorbachev yesterday: Ever since the Thirteenth Party Congress, whenever I meet with Communist Party leaders from other countries I make it clear that the First Plenum of our Thirteenth Central Committee decided that Comrade Xiaoping's role as our Party's primary decision-maker would not change. I do this in order to make sure the world has a clearer understanding that Comrade Xiaoping's continuing power within our Party is legal in spite of his retirement. . . .

Deng Xiaoping: Comrade Ziyang, that talk of yours on May 4 to the ADB was a turning point. Since then the student movement has gotten steadily worse. Of course we want to build socialist democracy, but we can't possibly do it in a hurry, and still less do we want that Western-style stuff. If our one billion people jumped into multiparty elections, we'd get chaos like the "all-out civil war" we saw during the Cultural Revolution. . . .

I know there are some disputes among you, but the question before us isn't how to settle all our different views; it's whether we now should back off or not. . . . To back down would be to give in to their values; not backing down means we stick steadfastly to the April 26 editorial.

The elder comrades—Chen Yun, [Li] Xiannian, Peng Zhen, and of course me, too—are all burning with anxiety at what we see in Beijing these days. Beijing can't keep going like this. We first have to settle the instability in Beijing, because if we don't we'll never be able to settle it in the other provinces, regions, and cities. Lying down on railroad tracks; beating, smashing, and robbing; if these aren't turmoil then what are they? If things continue like this, we could even end up under house arrest.

After thinking long and hard about this, I've concluded that we should bring in the People's Liberation Army [PLA] and declare martial law in Beijing—more precisely, in Beijing's urban districts. The aim of martial law will be to suppress the turmoil once and for all and to return things quickly to normal. This is the unshirkable duty of the Party and the government. I am solemnly proposing this today to the Standing Committee of the Politburo and hope that you will consider it.

Zhao Ziyang: It's always better to have a decision than not to have one. But Comrade Xiaoping, it will be hard for me to carry out this plan. I have difficulties with it. Deng Xiaoping: The minority yields to the majority!

Zhao Ziyang: I will submit to Party discipline; the minority does yield to the majority. Standing Committee Stalemates

At 8 pm the meeting of the Politburo Standing Committee resumed at Zhongnanhai. Committee members Zhao Ziyang, Li Peng, Qiao Shi, Hu Qili, and Yao Yilin attended. Yang Shangkun and Bo Yibo participated in their role as party elders.

Excerpts from Party Central Office Secretariat, "Minutes of the May 17 Politburo Standing Committee meeting":

Zhao Ziyang: The question for this evening's meeting is martial law. First we need to consider whether the situation has reached a point where martial law is our only option. Will martial law help solve the problem or only enlarge it? Is it in fact necessary to impose martial law? I hope we can discuss these questions calmly.

Li Peng: The decision on martial law, Comrade Ziyang, was made by Comrade Xiaoping at this morning's meeting. I support Comrade Xiaoping's views on martial law. I believe that the topic for the present meeting is not whether martial law should or should not be imposed but, rather, what steps to use in carrying it out.

Yao Yilin: I strongly support Comrade Xiaoping's proposal to impose martial law in Beijing's urban districts. Taking this powerful measure will help restore the city to normalcy, end the state of anarchy, and quickly and effectively stop the turmoil.

Zhao Ziyang: I'm against imposing martial law in Beijing. My reason is that, given the extreme feelings of the students at this juncture, to impose martial law will not help calm things down or solve problems. It will only make things more complicated and more sharply confrontational. And after all, things are still under our control. Even among the demonstrators the vast majority is patriotic and supports the Communist Party. Martial law could give us total control of the situation, yes; but think of the terror it will strike in the minds of Beijing's citizens and students. Where will that lead?

In the forty years of the People's Republic, our Party has learned many lessons from its political and economic mistakes. Given the crisis we now face at home and abroad, I think that one more big political mistake might well cost us all our remaining legitimacy. So I see martial law as extremely dangerous. The Chinese people cannot take any more huge policy blunders.

Qiao Shi: I've wanted to express my view all along. We can't afford any more concessions to the student movement, but on the other hand we still haven't found a suitable means for resolving the situation. So on the question of martial law, I find it hard to express either support or opposition.

Bo Yibo: This is a Standing Committee meeting in which Comrade Shangkun and I are only observers. We don't have voting rights, but we both support Comrade Xiaoping's proposal to impose martial law.

Just now everyone on the committee had a chance to express his opinion. I think we should make the opinions even clearer by taking a vote. . . .

Following Bo Yibo's suggestion, the five members of the Standing Committee took a formal vote. Li Peng and Yao Yilin voted for martial law; Zhao Ziyang and Hu Qili voted against it; Qiao Shi abstained.

Yang Shangkun: The Party permits differing opinions. We can refer this evening's vote to Comrade Xiaoping and the other Party Elders and get a resolution as soon as possible.

THE ELDERS DECIDE ON MARTIAL LAW

On the morning of May 18, the eight elders—Deng Xiaoping, Chen Yun, Li Xiannian, Peng Zhen, Deng Yingchao, Yang Shangkun, Bo Yibo, and Wang Zhen—met with Politburo Standing Committee members Li Peng, Qiao Shi, Hu Qili, and Yao Yilin and with Military Affairs Commission members General Hong Xuezhi, Liu Huaqing, and General Qin Jiwei and formally agreed to declare martial law in Beijing. General Secretary Zhao Ziyang did not attend the meeting.

Li Peng opened by describing the split that had emerged within the Standing Committee on the evening of the 17th over the question of martial law. Bo Yibo provided additional detail. Then the elders began explaining why martial law was necessary.

Excerpts from Party Central Office Secretariat, "Minutes of an important meeting on May 18," document supplied to Party Central Office Secretariat for its records by the Office of Deng Xiaoping:

Deng Xiaoping: We old comrades are meeting with you today because we feel we have no choice. The Standing Committee should have come up with a plan long ago, but things kept dragging on, and even today there's no decision. Beijing has been chaotic for more than a month now, and we've been extremely restrained through the whole thing, and extremely tolerant. What other country in the world would watch more than a month of marches and demonstrations in its capital and do nothing about it?. . . .

Li Xiannian: I feel like the rest of you, and I think it's too bad that an accurate assessment of what's going on here has to depend on us old comrades. We have no choice but to show concern when things get as chaotic as they are now. General Secretary Zhao Ziyang has an undeniable responsibility here. What's the difference between what we're seeing all across the country and the Cultural Revolution? It's not just Beijing; all the cities are in chaos. . . .

Deng Xiaoping: The April 26 editorial defined the nature of the problem as turmoil. Some people object to the word, but it hits the nail on the head. The evidence shows that the judgment is correct.

Li Peng: . . . The reason Comrade Zhao Ziyang has not come today is that he opposes martial law. He encouraged the students right from the beginning. When he got back from North Korea, he came out with his May 4 speech at the Asian Development Bank without clearing it with anyone else on the Standing Committee.

The speech's . . . tone was completely different from the April 26 editorial's, but it got wide distribution and had a big propaganda impact. From then on we felt it was obvious that Comrade Zhao Ziyang's opinions were different from Comrade Xiaoping's and those of the majority of comrades on the Standing Committee. Anyone with political experience could see this, and certainly the ones causing the turmoil could also see it.

Yang Shangkun: . . . The problem we now face is that the two different voices within the party have been completely exposed; the students feel that someone at the Center supports them, so they've gotten more and more extreme. Their goals are to get the April 26 editorial repudiated and get official recognition for their autonomous federations [as opposed to the student organizations organized and controlled by the government].

The situation in Beijing and the rest of the country keeps getting grimmer. So we have to guarantee the stability of the whole country, and that means starting with Beijing. I resolutely support declaration of martial law in Beijing and resolutely support its implementation.

Wang Zhen: . . . These people are really asking for it! They should be nabbed as soon as they pop out again. Give 'em no mercy! The students are nuts if they think this handful of people can overthrow our Party and our government! These kids don't know how good they've got it! . . . If the students don't leave Tiananmen on their own, the PLA should go in and carry them out. This is ridiculous!

Bo Yibo: The whole imperialist Western world wants to make social-ist countries leave the socialist road and become satellites in the sys-tem of international monopoly capitalism. The people with ulterior motives who are behind this student movement have support from the United States and Europe and from the KMT [Kuomintang] re-actionaries in Taiwan. There is a lot of evidence that the U.S. Con-gress and other Western parliaments have been saying all kinds of things about this student movement and have even held hearings. . . . Members of the overseas Chinese Alliance for Democracy, which we have declared to be an illegal and reactionary organization, not only voice support for the student movement but openly admit that they advise the students and even plan how to reenter China and meddle directly. . . . So you see, it was no accident that the student movement turned into turmoil.

Hong Xuezhi: For a soldier, duty is paramount. I will resolutely carry out the order to put Beijing under martial law.

Qin Jiwei: . . . I resolutely support and will resolutely carry out the orders of Party Central and the Military Affairs Commission for mar-tial law in Beijing.

LI PENG MEETS WITH STUDENT LEADERS

Also on May 18, Li Peng and other government officials met at the Great Hall of the People with Wang Dan, Wuerkaixi, and other stu-dent representatives. Li said that no one had ever claimed the major-ity of students had been engaged in turmoil, but that too often people with no intention of creating turmoil had in fact brought it about.

He stood firm on the wording of the April 26 editorial and said the current moment was not an appropriate time to discuss the students' two demands. Wang Dan had said that the only way to get the students out of Tiananmen Square was to reclassify the student movement as patriotic and put the student-leader dialogue on live television.

ZHAO ZIYANG'S SORROWFUL SPEECH

At 4 am on May 19, following the close of the Politburo Standing Committee meeting, Zhao Ziyang and Li Peng visited Tiananmen

Square, accompanied respectively by Director of the Party Central Office Wen Jiabao and Secretary-General of the State Council Luo Gan. Knowing his political career was near an end, Zhao made remarks that brought tears to the eyes of those who heard him. "We have come too late," he said, and he begged the students to protect their health, to end the hunger strike, and to leave the Square before it was too late.

> "We demonstrated and lay across railroad tracks when we were young, too, and took no thought for the future," he told the students. "But I have to ask you to think carefully about the future. Many issues will be resolved eventually. I beg you to end the hunger strike."

Zhao was exhausted, and his doctor urged him to rest. On the morning of May 19 he requested three days' sick leave.

PROVINCIAL STUDENTS CONVERGE ON BEIJING

Many students had come from universities outside Beijing to camp. On the eve of martial law, the Railway Ministry reported to Zhongnanhai that a total of 56,888 students had entered the city on 165 trains between 6 pm on May 16 and 8 pm on May 19. The flood of students had stressed the already overstretched system. Most of the students had demanded to ride without tickets, took over the trains' public-address systems, asked passengers for contributions, hung posters in and on the cars, and even demanded free food.

Of some 50,000 students in Tiananmen Square on May 22, most were from outside Beijing, and many of the Beijing students had returned to their campuses or gone home. Official records showed that at least 319 different schools were represented in the square.

BACKLASH TO MARTIAL LAW

When martial law was declared, it applied to only five urban districts of Beijing. But it elicited fierce opposition throughout the capital, nationwide, and internationally. Troops from 22 divisions moved toward the city, but many were stopped in the suburbs or blocked in city streets and failed to reach their destinations. In the first of what would be many similar instructions, on May 20 Yang Shangkun ordered that the soldiers should never turn their weapons on innocent civilians, even if provoked.

Provincial authorities voiced the requisite support for Beijing while taking actions locally to try to assure that nothing spectacular happened in their own bailiwicks. On May 21, student leaders in the square voted to declare victory and withdraw but reversed their decision under pressure of widespread sentiment among new recruits in the square to continue the strike.

THE ELDERS DISCUSS A SUCCESSOR

The same day, Deng Xiaoping again convened the party elders, since the younger generation of leaders seemed unable to manage.

Excerpts from Party Central Office Secretariat, "Minutes of important meeting, May 21, 1989," document supplied to Party Central Office Secretariat for its records by the Office of Deng Xiaoping:

> **Deng Xiaoping:** We can all see what's happened. Martial law hasn't restored order. This isn't because we can't do it; it's because problems inside the Party drag on and keep us from solving things that should've been solved long ago. . . . Zhao Ziyang's intransigence has been obvious, and he bears undeniable responsibility. He wouldn't even attend the party-government-army meeting that the Standing Committee of the Politburo convened.
>
> When others saw that the Party general secretary didn't show up, they all knew something was wrong. He exposed the differences within the Standing Committee for all to see. He wanted to draw a strict line between himself and us in order to make his stand clear. So we've got to talk about the Zhao Ziyang problem.
>
> **Li Xiannian:** I've said all along that the problem's inside the party. The party now has two headquarters. Zhao Ziyang's got his own separate headquarters. We have to get to the bottom of this, have to dig out the roots. Otherwise there can never again be unity of thought inside the Party. . . . When he opposed martial law he had his own political agenda, which was to force us senior people to hand over power and step down, so that he could go ahead with his program of bourgeois liberalization. With us senior people in the way, his hands

were tied and he was stuck. Zhao Ziyang is no longer fit to be general secretary.

Wang Zhen: Zhao Ziyang's never paid a whit of attention to people like us. . . . What he really wants is to drive us old people from power. We didn't mistreat him; he's the one who's picked the fight. When he falls it'll be his own fault. . . .

Yang Shangkun: . . . We should look at the big picture and make solidarity our top priority. This isn't the right moment for replacing a general secretary. Instead we could ask Zhao Ziyang for a self-criticism and avoid making big changes on the Politburo Standing Committee. . . .

Deng Xiaoping: . . . In the recent turmoil Zhao Ziyang has exposed his position completely. He obviously stands on the side of the turmoil, and in practical terms he has been fomenting division, splitting the Party, and defending turmoil. It's lucky we're still here to keep a lid on things. Zhao Ziyang stimulated turmoil, and there's no reason to keep him. Hu Qili is no longer fit for the Standing Committee, either.

Chen Yun: . . . Comrade Xiannian has pointed out to me that Comrade Jiang Zemin from Shanghai is a suitable candidate. Every time I've gone down to Shanghai he always sees me, and he strikes me as a modest person with strong party discipline and broad knowledge. He gets along well in Shanghai, too.

Li Xiannian: . . . I noticed, after the April 26 editorial, that again it was Shanghai that took the lead in pushing the spirit of Party Central. Jiang Zemin called a meeting of more than ten thousand officials the very next day, and he yanked the World Economic Herald into shape. That was something! That move—given what was going on—put him under tremendous public pressure, but he stood firm, didn't budge, and stuck to principle. Then, when the Party, government, and army at the Center declared martial law, again it was Shanghai that took the lead in action. This kind of firm attitude's hard to come by. In political action and party loyalty, Jiang Zemin has been a constant. And of course, he's got a good knack for economic work. Shanghai's built a good economic foundation these last few years. . . . I like the idea of him as general secretary.

THE SELECTION OF JIANG ZEMIN

On the night of May 27, Deng Xiaoping and the other seven elders met for about five hours at Deng's residence to finalize a successor to Zhao Ziyang as Communist Party general secretary.

Excerpts from Party Central Office Secretariat, "Minutes of important meeting, May 27, 1989," document supplied to Party Central Office Secretariat for its records by the Office of Deng Xiaoping:

> **Deng Xiaoping:** I've checked with Comrades Chen Yun and Xiannian, and they completely agree with my view that the new leadership team must continue to carry out the political line, principles, and policies of the Third Plenum of the Eleventh Central Committee. Even the language should stay the same. The political report of the Thirteenth Party Congress was approved by all representatives at the time. Not a single word of it can be changed. The policies of reform and opening must not change, for several decades; we've got to press them through to the end. This should be what we expect and require from the new generation of [Party] Central leadership. Unless someone objects, I move that the new Standing Committee of the Politburo be made up of the following six comrades: Jiang Zemin, Li Peng, Qiao Shi, Yao Yilin, Song Ping, and Li Ruihuan, with Comrade Jiang Zemin as general secretary.

The motion to appoint Jiang as general secretary and to add Li and Song to the Standing Committee had been approved by the elders by a show of hands. But this violated the Chinese Communist Party Constitution, which stipulates that the Politburo Standing Committee should make such decisions.

THE ELDERS DECIDE TO CLEAR TIANANMEN SQUARE

On the morning of June 2, party elders Deng Xiaoping, Li Xiannian, Peng Zhen, Yang Shangkun, Bo Yibo, and Wang Zhen met with the Standing Committee of the Politburo, which at that juncture consisted only of Li Peng, Qiao Shi, and Yao Yilin.

Excerpts from Party Central Office Secretariat, "Minutes of important meeting, June 2, 1989," document supplied to Party Central Office Secretariat for its records by the Office of Deng Xiaoping:

> **Li Peng:** Yesterday the Beijing Party Committee and the State Security Ministry both submitted reports to the Politburo. These two reports give ample evidence that following the declaration of martial

law a major scheme of the organizers and plotters of the turmoil has been to occupy Tiananmen Square to serve as a command center for a final showdown with the Party and government. The square has become "a center of the student movement and eventually the entire nation."

Whatever decisions the government makes, strong reactions will emerge from the Square. It has been determined that, following the declaration of martial law, events such as putting together a dare-to-die corps to block the martial law troops, gathering thugs to storm the Beijing Public Security Bureau, holding press conferences, and recruiting the Flying Tiger Group to pass messages around were all plotted in and commanded from the Square. . . .

The reactionary elements have also continued to use the Square as a center for hatching counterrevolutionary opinion and manufacturing rumor. Illegal organizations such as the AFS [Autonomous Federation of Students] and AFW [Autonomous Federation of Workers] have installed loudspeakers on the Square and broadcast almost around the clock, attacking party and state leaders, inciting overthrow of the government, and repeating over and over distorted reports from [the Voice of America] and the Hong Kong and Taiwan press.

The reactionary elements believe the government will eventually crack down if they refuse to withdraw from the square. Their plot is to provoke conflict and create bloodshed incidents, clamoring that "blood will awaken the people and cause the government to split and collapse." A few days ago these reactionary elements openly erected a so-called goddess statue in front of the Monument to the People's Heroes. Today they are planning to launch another hunger strike in the Square.

. . . When the turmoil began employees of the U.S. embassy started to collect intelligence aggressively. Some of them are cia agents. Almost every day, and especially at night, they would go and loiter at Tiananmen or at schools such as Peking University and Beijing Normal. They have frequent contact with leaders of the AFS and give them advice. The Chinese Alliance for Democracy, which has directly meddled in this turmoil, is a tool the United States uses against China. This scum of our nation, based in New York, has collaborated with the pro-KMT Chinese Benevolent Association to set up a so-called Committee to Support the Chinese Democracy Movement. They also gave money to leaders of the AFS.

As soon as the turmoil started, KMT intelligence agencies in Taiwan and other hostile forces outside China rushed to send in agents disguised as visitors, tourists, businessmen, and so on. They have tried to intervene directly to expand the so-called democracy movement into an all-out "movement against communism and tyranny." They have also instructed underground agents to keep close track of things and to collect all kinds of information. There is evidence that KMT agents from Taiwan have participated in the turmoil in Beijing, Shanghai, Fujian, and elsewhere. . . . It is becoming increasingly clear that the turmoil has been generated by a coalition of foreign and domestic reactionary forces and that their goals are to overthrow the Communist Party and to subvert the socialist system.

Wang Zhen: Those goddamn bastards! Who do they think they are, trampling on sacred ground like Tiananmen so long?! They're really asking for it! We should send the troops right now to grab those counterrevolutionaries, Comrade Xiaoping! What's the People's Liberation Army for, anyway? What are martial law troops for? They're not supposed to just sit around and eat! They're supposed to grab counterrevolutionaries! We've got to do it or we'll never forgive ourselves! We've got to do it or the common people will rebel! Anybody who tries to overthrow the Communist Party deserves death and no burial!

Li Xiannian: The account that Comrade Li Peng just gave us shows quite clearly that Western capitalism really does want to see turmoil in China. And not only that; they'd also like to see turmoil in the Soviet Union and all the socialist countries of Eastern Europe. The United States, England, France, Japan, and some other Western countries are leaving no stone unturned in pushing peaceful evolution in the socialist countries. They've got a new saying about "fighting a smokeless world war." We had better watch out. Capitalism still wants to beat socialism in the end.

Deng Xiaoping: Comrade Xiannian is correct. The causes of this incident have to do with the global context. The Western world, especially the United States, has thrown its entire propaganda machine into agitation work and has given a lot of encouragement and assistance to the so-called democrats or opposition in China—people who in fact are the scum of the Chinese nation. This is the root of the chaotic situation we face today. . . . Some Western countries use things like "human rights," or like saying the socialist system is irrational or illegal, to criticize us, but what they're really after is our sovereignty. Those Western countries that play power politics have no right at all to talk about human rights!

Look how many people around the world they've robbed of human rights! And look how many Chinese people they've hurt the human rights of since they invaded China during the Opium war! . . .

Two conditions are indispensable for our developmental goals: a stable environment at home and a peaceful environment abroad. We don't care what others say about us. The only thing we really care about is a good environment for developing ourselves. So long as history eventually proves the superiority of the Chinese socialist system, that's enough. We can't bother about the social systems of other countries. Imagine for a moment what could happen if China falls into turmoil. If it happens now, it'd be far worse than the Cultural Revolution. . . . Once civil war got started, blood would flow like a river, and where would human rights be then? In a civil war, each power would dominate a locality, production would fall, communications would be cut off, and refugees would flow out of China not in millions or tens of millions but in hundreds of millions.

First hit by this flood of refugees would be Pacific Asia, which is currently the most promising region of the world. This would be disaster on a global scale. So China mustn't make a mess of itself. And this is not just to be responsible to ourselves, but to consider the whole world and all of humanity as well. . . .

Li Xiannian: . . . Tiananmen Square is now that root of our turmoil-disease. Just look at that thing—like neither human nor demon—that they've erected there in our beautiful Square! Are the people going to accept that? Absolutely not! We're never going to get a voluntary withdrawal from the Square. Tiananmen has been polluted for more than a month now, ravaged into a shadow of itself! We can't breathe free until the Square is returned to the hands of the people. We have to pull up the root of the disease immediately. I say we start tonight.

Yang Shangkun: The fact that we're going to clear the square, restore order, and stop the turmoil in no way means that we're giving up on reform or closing our country off from the world.

Deng Xiaoping: No one can keep China's reform and opening from going forward. Why is that? It's simple: Without reform and opening our development stops and our economy slides downhill. Living standards decline if we turn back. The momentum of reform cannot be stopped. We must insist on this point at all times.

Some people say we allow only economic reform and not political reform, but that's not true. We do allow political reform, but on one condition: that the Four Basic Principles are upheld. [The Four Basic Principles are Marxism-Leninism-Mao Zedong thought, socialism, the people's democratic dictatorship, and leadership by the Chinese Communist Party.] . . .

We can't handle chaos while we're busy with construction. If today we have a big demonstration and tomorrow a great airing of views and a bunch of wall posters, we won't have any energy left to get anything done. That's why we have to insist on clearing the Square.

Yang Shangkun: Troops have moved into the Great Hall of the People, Zhongshan Park, the People's Cultural Palace, and the Public Security Ministry compound. The thinking of all officers and soldiers has been thoroughly prepared for a clearing of Tiananmen Square. After nearly half a month of political thought work, all officers and soldiers have deepened their understanding of the severity and complexity of this struggle and have comprehended the necessity and the legality of martial law.

Li Peng: I strongly urge that we move immediately to clear Tiananmen Square and that we resolutely put an end to the turmoil and the ever expanding trouble.

Qiao Shi: The facts show that we can't expect the students on the Square to withdraw voluntarily. Clearing the square is our only option, and it's quite necessary. I hope our announcement about clearing will meet with approval and support from the majority of citizens and students. Clearing the Square is the beginning of a restoration of normal order in the capital.

Deng Xiaoping: I agree with all of you and suggest the martial law troops begin tonight to carry out the clearing plan and finish it within two days. As we proceed with the clearing, we must explain it clearly to all the citizens and students, asking them to leave and doing our very best to persuade them. But if they refuse to leave, they will be responsible for the consequences. . . .

THE ORDER TO CLEAR THE SQUARE

At 4 pm on June 3, Yang Shangkun, Li Peng, Qiao Shi, and Yao Yilin held an emergency meeting with responsible military officials.

Excerpts from Party Central Office Secretariat, "Minutes of the June 3 Politburo Standing Committee meeting":

Yang Shangkun: I really did not want to call this meeting. The situation has become extremely volatile—beyond what anybody's goodwill can handle. We have to settle on some resolute measures for clearing the square. Let's begin with you, Comrade Li Peng.

Li Peng: Late last night a counterrevolutionary riot broke out in Beijing. A small handful of counterrevolutionaries began spreading rumors and openly violating martial law. They were brazen and lawless, and their behavior has aroused extreme indignation among the masses. We must resolutely adopt decisive measures to put down this counterrevolutionary riot tonight. . . . The PLA martial law troops, the People's Armed Police, and Public Security are authorized to use any means necessary to deal with people who interfere with the mission. Whatever happens will be the responsibility of those who do not heed warnings and persist in testing the limits of the law.

Yang Shangkun: You all get the picture now. I've also just been in touch with Comrade Xiaoping, and he has asked me to relay two points to everyone. The first is: Solve the problem before dawn tomorrow. He means our martial law troops should completely finish their task of clearing the Square before sunup. The second is: Be reasonable with the students and make sure they see the logic in what we're doing; the troops should resort to "all means necessary" only if everything else fails. In other words, before we clear the Square, we should use TV and radio to advise students and citizens to avoid the streets at all costs, and we should ask the ones who are in the Square to leave of their own accord. In short, we've got to do an excellent job on propaganda work; it has to be clear to everyone that we stand with the people, and we must do everything we possibly can to avoid bloodshed. The Martial Law Command must make it quite clear to all units that they are to open fire only as a last resort. And let me repeat: No bloodshed within Tiananmen Square—period. What if thousands of students refuse to leave? Then the troops carry away thousands of students on their backs! No one must die in the Square. This is not just my personal view; it's Comrade Xiaoping's view, too. So long as everybody agrees, then it will be unanimous.

JUNE FOURTH

Tiananmen Square lies at the geographic center of the capital city and just southeast of Zhongnanhai, where the last dynasty's emperors had their hunting park and where top Communist Party leaders now work. Beginning with the May Fourth movement against imperialism and for democracy in 1919, Tiananmen has also become a traditional site for popular protests. These protests have often been led by university students, who are especially numerous here because Beijing is the country's preeminent center of higher education.

As soldiers entered the city in plainclothes and in uniform, instead of meeting with popular understanding they encountered anger and some violence. The party leaders' hopes of avoiding bloodshed foundered on this resistance and the troops' emotional reaction to it.

The government's internal reports claimed that Deng Xiaoping's goal of no deaths in Tiananmen Square was achieved. Most of the deaths occurred as troops moved in from the western suburbs toward Tiananmen along Fuxingmenwai Boulevard at a location called Muxidi, where anxious soldiers reacted violently to popular anger.

Excerpt from Martial Law Command, "Situation in the Muxidi district," Bulletin (Kuaibao), June 3:

Advance troops of the Thirty-Eighth Group Army, who were responsible for the western approaches, massed in the western suburbs at Wanshou Road, Fengtai, and Liangxiang. At 9:30 pm, these troops began advancing eastward toward the Square and encountered their first obstacle at Gongzhufen, where students and citizens had set up a blockade. An anti-riot squad fired tear gas canisters and rubber bullets into the crowd. At first the people retreated, but then they stopped. The anti-riot squad pressed forward, firing more tear gas and more rubber bullets. Again the crowd retreated but soon stopped.

The troops kept firing warning shots into the air, but the people displayed no signs of fear. The stretch from Gongzhufen to the military museum, Beifengwo Street, and Muxidi is less than two kilometers, but the troop advance was slow because of citizens' interference. The crowd threw rocks, soda bottles, and other things, but the troops maintained strict discipline and did not fire a single shot in return.

Believing the troops would not use live ammunition, the citizens grew increasingly bold. At 10:10 pm, tens of thousands formed a human wall at Beifengwo Street to block the troops, the two sides faced each other over a distance of twenty to thirty meters. Some of the citizens continued throwing rocks and other objects. Using an electric bullhorn, the commanding officer exhorted the citizens and students to disperse and let the troops pass. When the measure failed, he decided to use force to assure his soldiers could reach their positions on time.

Infantrymen led the way, firing into the air. The soldiers—with the first two rows in a kneeling position and those in the back standing—pointed their weapons at the crowd. Approximately 10:30 pm, under a barrage of rocks, the troops opened fire. Sparks flew from ricocheting bullets. When people in the crowd realized that live ammunition was in use, they surged in waves toward the Muxidi Bridge. Their retreat was hindered by the roadblocks they had set up, and for this reason some in the crowd were trampled and badly injured.

Excerpts from State Security Ministry, "Situation at Muxidi on the evening of the third," Important intelligence (Yaoqing), 2 am, June 4:

. . . At Muxidi Bridge the troops were stopped once again as citizens and students threw the broken bricks they had prepared in advance. A few dozen baton-wielding members of the troops' anti-riot brigade stormed onto the bridge, where they were met with a barrage of broken bricks as thick as rain. The brigade was driven back. Then regular troops, row by row, came rushing onto the bridge chanting, "If no one attacks me, I attack no one; but if people attack me, I must attack them," and turning their weapons on the crowd. People began crumpling to the ground. Each time shots rang out, the citizens hunkered down; but with each lull in the fire they stood up again. Slowly driven back by the troops, they stood their ground from time to time shouting "Fascists!" "Hooligan government!" and "Murderers!"

. . . Some soldiers who were hit by rocks lost their self-control and began firing wildly at anyone who shouted "Fascists!" or threw rocks or bricks. At least a hundred citizens and students fell to the ground in pools of blood; most were rushed to nearby Fuxing hospital by other students and citizens.

. . . After infantrymen had cleared the street of roadblocks, returning fire the whole time, armored cars and army trucks drove onto the Muxidi Bridge. From then on there were no more lulls in the shooting. Soldiers on the trucks fired into the air continuously until people hurled rocks or verbal insults, and then they fired into the crowd.

. . . Around 11 pm, armed foot soldiers, armored cars, and army trucks headed toward Tiananmen. After the troops had passed, citizens and students pushed electric buses back into the street, placing them across it, and set them on fire to block troops that were following. It was then approximately 11:40 pm.

At midnight some citizens set up new roadblocks on the eastern approach to Muxidi Bridge. To the east of the bridge, near the subway station, lay twelve lumps of flesh, blood, and debris. The bodies of dead and wounded were being delivered continually to the door of Fuxing hospital. Some arrived on three-wheeled flat-bed carts, others were carried on wooden doors, and some came on the backs of motorcycles. One bloody corpse whose face was unrecognizably mangled was carried on a door. Virtually everyone at Fuxing hospital was cursing "Fascists!," "Animals!," and "Bloody massacre!"

By 1:30 am, Fuxingmenwai Boulevard in the area of Muxidi Bridge was deserted and shrouded in deathly silence.

LIGHTS OUT IN THE SQUARE

By 1 am on June 4, all martial-law troops had entered Tiananmen Square and for three hours pressed students to voluntarily leave before the 4 am deadline for clearing the square.

Excerpt from State Security Ministry, "Trends in Tiananmen Square," fifth of six overnight faxes to Party Central and State Council duty offices, 6:08 am, June 4:

At four o'clock sharp all the lights in the square went out, sending its occupiers into a panic. At the same time, the Martial Law Command continued to broadcast its "Notice to Clear the Square," now adding: "We will now begin clearing the square, and we accept your appeal to evacuate."

The Beijing Government and the Martial Law Command then broadcast a "Notice Concerning the Immediate Restoration of Order in Tiananmen Square." It listed four demands:

- Anyone on the Square who hears this announcement must leave immediately.
- Martial law troops will use any means necessary to deal with those who resist this order or disobey by remaining on the Square.
- The Square will be under the strict control of martial law troops after it is cleared.

- All patriotic citizens and students who do not want to see turmoil in the country should cooperate with the martial law troops to clear the Square.

At this point students who were gathered on the steps of the Monument to the People's Heroes used blankets, sticks, canvas, and other things to light a bonfire on the western side of the monument. Then they began singing the "Internationale."

[Hunger strikers] Hou Dejian and Zhou Duo returned to the Square after meeting with martial law authorities. Over the student public-address system they called for an immediate evacuation. In the dark, people were saying school buses from Peking University had come to take students back to campus, but this news caused no notable reaction from the students. The area was shrouded in darkness, except for the distant flames and street lamps on Chang'an Boulevard.

Martial law troops advanced toward the monument from north to south in two columns. Soldiers of the shock brigade first smashed two AFS loudspeakers then advanced through the crowd on the western steps of the monument with their assault rifles pointed alternately into the air and at the students to frighten them off. About that time the students around the monument, who were under the direction of the General Headquarters for the Protection of Tiananmen Square, conducted a voice-vote. Those, including Hou Dejian's group, who shouted "Leave!" were louder than those who shouted "Stay!"

The leader of the command post then told the students in the Square to "prepare to leave the Square in an orderly manner under your school banners; students, citizens, workers, and citizen monitors should evacuate toward Haidian District and move toward Zhongguancun."

Around 4:30 am the lights in the Square came back on. Students found themselves facing a large number of armed soldiers, who pressed the students closer and closer together. Tension gripped the protesters, especially when they saw rows of tanks and armored cars moving slowly through the Square from its north edge. The Goddess of Democracy, in the northern part of the Square, fell with a resounding thud. The tanks and armored cars kept advancing, knocking down and crushing student tents along the way, until they flanked the students on the east and west, as close as twenty or thirty meters away. From the northwest corner of the Square rows of soldiers wearing helmets and carrying batons kept pressing toward the students at the

Square's center. Anti-riot police in protective headgear mingled with them.

About 5 am thousands of students, protected by the linked arms of monitors, retreated toward the southeast corner of the Square via the path between the grassy area and the monument. At first they moved slowly, but they soon began to bunch up as soldiers, some in fatigues, pressed toward them swinging batons. With their path to the monument blocked by troops and tanks, they threaded their way among tanks and armored cars toward the southern entrance at the east of the Square. They made an orderly retreat, carrying school flags and singing the "Internationale." Occasionally there were shouts of "Repressive Bloodbath!" "Down with Fascism!" "Bandits! Bandits!"—even "Fucking Animals!" and the like. Some spat on the soldiers as they passed.

Dawn broke about 5:20. The bulk of the students had left the Square, but about two hundred defiant students and citizens remained and were now completely hemmed in by tanks, which advanced on them slowly and patiently, gradually forcing them back. When this last group had finally been pushed from the Square and had rejoined its citizen supporters outside, some of its members mustered the courage to shout, "Fascists! Fascists!" and "Down with Fascism!" In reply, officers and soldiers who were gathered at the Chairman Mao Memorial Hall fired their weapons into the air and shouted in unison, "If no one attacks me, I attack no one!" By 5:40 am, the Square had been cleared.

Many investigations have established that in the entire process of clearing the Square, martial law troops did not shoot a single person to death and no person was run over by a tank.

Still, some killing of both citizens and soldiers continued during the morning hours. The populace was outraged, and rumors spread of casualties in the thousands.

In the following days the government confronted international and domestic reactions so vociferous that they threatened to fulfill Deng Xiaoping's worst fear: that a bloody denouement would make it impossible to continue reform at home and the open-door policy abroad.

NATIONWIDE PROTESTS CONTINUE

Between June 5 and 10, Zhongnanhai received nearly a hundred reports from the provinces on local reactions and on emergency meetings and police deployments undertaken in response. There were demonstrations in 181 cities, including all the provincial capitals, the major cities, and special economic zones. Many forms of protest, some of them violent, emerged. By June 8, the situation had begun to stabilize in some cities.

On the afternoon of June 9, Deng Xiaoping gave a talk to high-ranking officials of the martial law troops, and the State Council issued an "Announcement on Resolutely Preventing Disruption of Economic Order and Ensuring That Industrial Production Proceeds Normally." All province-level governments adopted procedures from the "Notice on Ensuring Urban Security and Stability" that the Party General Office and the State Council had issued. The Public Security Ministry's "Urgent Notice Demanding Close Surveillance and Control of Turmoil Elements" led municipal public security offices to launch an all-out campaign to arrest student leaders and citizen activists.

By June 10, this campaign effectively throttled protest activities everywhere, and an outward calm set over the country.

THE LEADERS TAKE STOCK

On June 6, two and a half days after what was now officially called "putting down the counterrevolutionary riots," the healthier elders (Deng Xiaoping, Li Xiannian, Peng Zhen, Yang Shangkun, Bo Yibo, and Wang Zhen) met with the currently serving members of the Politburo Standing Committee (Li Peng, Qiao Shi, and Yao Yilin), plus National People's Congress head Wan Li and the incoming Party general secretary, Jiang Zemin.

Excerpts from Party Central Office Secretariat, "Minutes of the CCP Central Politburo Standing Committee meeting," June 6, with a small number of supplements added from a tape recording of the meeting:

> **Deng Xiaoping:** If we hadn't been firm with these counterrevolutionary riots—if we hadn't come down hard—who knows what might have happened? The PLA has suffered a great deal; we owe them a lot, we really do. If the plots of the people who were pushing the riots had gotten

anywhere, we'd have had civil war. And if there had been civil war—of course our side would have won, but just think of all the deaths! . . .

Li Xiannian: If we hadn't put down those counterrevolutionary riots, could we be talking here now? The PLA soldiers really are the brothers of the Chinese people, as well as the sturdy pillars of the Party and the state. . . .

Yang Shangkun: We've paid a high price for putting down these counterrevolutionary riots. Restoring social order in Beijing should be our top priority now, and that means we've got a lot of political thought work to do.

Bo Yibo: I've got some material here—reports from all the big Western news services and TV networks about the so-called June 4 bloodbath at Tiananmen and the numbers of dead and wounded. Let me read it. Associated Press: "At least five hundred dead." NBC: "Fourteen hundred dead, ten thousand wounded." ABC: "Two thousand dead." American intelligence agencies: "Three thousand dead." BBC: "Two thousand dead, up to ten thousand injured." Reuters: "More than one thousand dead." L'Agence France-Presse: "At least fourteen hundred dead, ten thousand injured." UPI: "More than three hundred dead." Kyodo News Agency: "Three thousand dead, more than two thousand injured." Japan's Yomiuri Shimbun: "Three thousand dead."

The impact is huge when numbers like these get spread all over the world! We need to counterattack against these rumors right now.

Li Peng: Mr. Bo is right. Yuan Mu is holding a press conference this afternoon at Zhongnanhai to release the true facts. The General Office of the State Council reports that as of noon today the basic statistics—which have been double-and triple-checked with Martial Law Headquarters and the Chinese Red Cross—are these: Five thousand PLA soldiers and officers wounded, and more than two thousand local people (counting students, city people, and rioters together) also wounded.

The figures on the dead are these: twenty-three from the martial law troops, including ten from the PLA and thirteen from the People's Armed Police. About two hundred soldiers are also missing. The dead among city people, students, and rioters number about two hundred, of whom thirty-six are university students. No one was killed within Tiananmen Square itself.

Deng Xiaoping: . . . This incident has been a wake-up call for all of us. We'll never keep the lid on if we relax on the Four Basic Principles.

. . . Our use of martial law to deal with the turmoil was absolutely necessary. In the future, whenever it might be necessary, we will use severe measures to stamp out the first signs of turmoil as soon as they appear. This will show that we won't put up with foreign interference and will protect our national sovereignty.

Li Xiannian: The key to stabilizing things right now is to be super-tough in tracking down the counterrevolutionary rioters, especially the plotters who were organizing things behind the scenes. This conflict is a conflict with the enemy. . . .

Deng Xiaoping: We should mete out the necessary punishments, in varying degrees, to the ambitious handful who were trying to subvert the People's Republic. . . . But we should be forgiving toward the student demonstrators and petition signers, whether from Beijing, from elsewhere in China, or from overseas, and we shouldn't try to track down individual responsibility among them. We also need to watch our methods as we take control of the situation.

We should be extra careful about laws, especially the laws and regulations on assembly, association, marches, demonstrations, journalism, and publishing. Activities that break the law must be suppressed. We can't just allow people to demonstrate whenever they want to. If people demonstrate 365 days a year and don't want to do anything else, reform and opening will get nowhere. . . .

ROUNDING UP DEMOCRACY ACTIVISTS

The work of hunting down activists of the democracy movement in Beijing was shared by the martial law troops, the People's Armed Police, and the Municipal Public Security Bureau. Guidelines like the following help explain why most of those detained suffered physical abuse.

Excerpt from Martial Law Headquarters, "Unify thinking, distinguish right from wrong, complete the martial law task with practical actions," June 10:

> In order to dissipate the anger and antagonism that martial law troops feel toward the residents of Beijing, to clarify the muddled understanding that many people have, to isolate the tiny minority of rioters from the vast majority of Beijing residents, and to establish correct attitudes toward the people, we need to ask all the officers and soldiers to concentrate their hatred on the small handful of thugs and rioters,

to smash their evil nests, to punish the rioters, and to wrap up their martial law duties through concrete actions.

Issues number 26, 31, and 37 of the Beijing Public Security Bureau's *Public Order Situation* (Zhi'an qingkuang) show that 468 "counterrevolutionary rioters and creators of turmoil" had been arrested by June 10. On June 17, eight of these were sentenced to death for "beating, smashing, robbing, burning, and other serious criminal offenses during the counterrevolutionary riots in Beijing." By June 20, the number of "counterrevolutionary rioters" and "turmoil elements" who had been arrested was 831; by June 30, it was 1,103. Most of the arrestees were held in temporary detention centers or makeshift jails.

Once the situation in Beijing was under control and province-level authorities throughout the country had expressed their support, Party Central unfolded a series of measures against activists throughout the country.

MANY STUDENT LEADERS ESCAPE

Despite police efforts, people as well known as Yan Jiaqi, Chen Yizi, Wan Runnan, Su Xiaokang, Wuerkaixi, Chai Ling, Feng Congde, and Li Lu made their way out of China without a single person involved breaching confidence and collecting the rewards that such a breach would have brought.

Chai Ling, the Peking University graduate student who was general commander of the Tiananmen Square Command, evaded an arrest warrant and escaped from the country. Feng Congde, a Peking University graduate student and deputy commander of the Tiananmen student headquarters, also evaded an arrest warrant and fled the country.

Li Lu, a Nanjing University student and commander in chief of the non-Beijing students at Tiananmen, fled to the United States.

Wang Dan, a Peking University freshman and leader of the Autonomous Federation of Students, was arrested. In 1998, he was released for a medical parole and went to the United States.

Wuerkaixi, a Beijing Normal University freshman and a leader of the AFS, fled to the United States and eventually went to Taiwan.

THE MOOD ON CAMPUS

A national survey conducted by the Xinhua News Agency at the end of June found university students everywhere in a mood of terror and resistance blanketed in silence.

Excerpt from Xinhua News Agency, "The ideological condition of college students nationwide," Proofs on domestic situation (Guonei dongtai qingyang), June 29:

> Terror: A tense mood, under fear of punishment or arrest, pervades the universities. Leaders of the student movement have departed their campuses, and rumors are rampant about who is being picked up and when. The students who were most active in the movement are the most nervous. Some provinces have stipulated that even students who sat in to block traffic should be arrested, and many students have grown so insecure they cannot sleep well at night. A number of young lecturers at Wuhan University who had given speeches during the movement now are so terrified they sent their wives and children to their in-laws' homes and waited alone to be arrested at the university.
>
> It is noteworthy that even students who only marched in demonstrations and shouted some slogans are frightened as well. One university administrator said students "thought of the recent student movement as a patriotic movement; many took to the streets to protest against official profiteering and then were puzzled when the movement was labeled 'turmoil.' Now the common mood is worry; the students are all wondering, 'Am I going to get punished?'"
>
> A few nights ago about a hundred students were gathered at the gate of Heilongjiang University when a police car passed by. Someone yelled "Police!" and they all scattered like animals scurrying for cover. Some students have been thinking in terms of the arbitrary arrests during the Anti-Rightist Campaign and the Cultural Revolution, so when the slightest sign of something pops up, it has an exaggerated effect.
>
> Resistance: Nationwide about one in five university students remains defiant. These students scornfully resist government decrees and oppose efforts to put down the riots. Some have adopted a "four don'ts" policy toward the domestic media: don't listen, don't read, don't believe, don't ask. Some students make obscene comments while they watch television. Some write on the walls of their dormitories and classrooms things like "Shut up!" "Thunder from the silent zone!"

"China is dead!" "Where is justice?" "The government caused the turmoil!" "The truth will out some day!" "Yet another Tiananmen incident!" and so on. The students at many schools—especially the boys—sometimes seem crazed. When the lights go out at night they vent their rage with wild yelps and cries.

Silence: About one in three students maintains a purposeful silence. After June Fourth all the universities required students to reflect on their roles in the student movement. Many students kept going around in circles, willing to address only a limited number of concrete questions. On the matter of how to turn their own thinking around, they just kept silent. "I don't know" became the answer to every question, silence the shield against every arrow. When political study sessions were scheduled, some students just put up posters in their dorms and classrooms that read "silence is golden." The campuses had calmed down but had also turned as silent as graveyards. When the silence finally broke, students often avoided politics. They ignored the national news and turned to things like romance, mah-jongg, and other amusements.

The moods listed above affect not only students but quite a few university officials and teachers as well. It is reported that some Beijing officials and teachers, although they did not take part in the turmoil and are now actively working on the political thinking of students, cannot make their peace with phrases like "Riots took place in Beijing." They just cannot put their hearts into uttering such language. Some feel that it is understandable if the government makes some miscalculations and if the whole economy is not set right in a day but that embezzlement and corruption are unacceptable. To share ups and downs is fine, but for you to take the ups and leave me the downs is not.

An official from Peking University reports that things are tough for people from his university. When students check in at hotels, many get pushed out the door as soon as it is known where they are from. One Peking University student who was on business in Yanqing county actually got beaten up. The job assignments for seniors graduating in 1989 have been completed, but some employers, including the Central Party School, the Chinese Association of Handicapped People, and the Beijing Committee of the Youth League, have rejected certain students. This official is afraid that gifted students will not apply to Peking University this year, which in turn could lead to lower quality in the incoming class.

The report recommended that great care be taken in applying current policy to the students and that, at all costs, the numbers of those punished be strictly limited.

Chinese society fell into a deep anomie after June 4. Numbed, people everywhere turned away from politics. The sensitive intellectual class, and especially the young students with their exuberant idealism, entered the 1990s with nothing like the admirable social engagement they had shown in the 1980s. The campuses were tranquil, and China seemed shrouded in a dour mist that harbored a spiritual emptiness. Money ruled everything, morals died, corruption burgeoned, bribes were bartered, and when all this became known on the campuses it turned students thoroughly off politics. They had lost the idealism of the 1980s and now concentrated only on their own fates.

China: Erratic State, Frustrated Society

Lucian W. Pye

W hy does China thwart, frustrate and even embarrass those who are only trying to help? For all who befriend China, the story is the same: high hopes, then disappointment. The exhilaration of the Beijing Spring followed by the rage of the Tiananmen massacre was only the high-theater version of the countless commonplace ways China continually brings hope and then despair to its well-wishers. All governments, whether democratic or communist, have had their special problems in maintaining smooth relations with Chinese authorities. But it is of course the Chinese people themselves who are most hurt and frustrated.

China seems to evoke in others, particularly Americans, an irresistible desire to serve as China's teachers in the ways of the modern world, and thereby presumably help China improve itself. Yet, from the time of Lord Palmerston's efforts to get the Chinese to accept the conventions of Western diplomacy, to President Bush's humiliating attempts to alter the behavior of Beijing's current rulers, China seems impelled to reject the helping hand and to act in ways that seem perversely self-damaging in the eyes of those who believe they have that country's interests at heart.

Western frustrations with the conduct of Chinese officials began with the first efforts to "open" China. Even after 1842, when the Qing court agreed in the Treaty of Nanking to establish state-to-state

LUCIAN W. PYE is Ford Professor of Political Science at the Massachusetts Institute of Technology and immediate past President of the American Political Science Association.

relations, the British were driven again to using military muscle, in part to get the Chinese to establish a foreign office and conduct "normal" diplomatic relations. Faced with force majeure the Chinese reluctantly gave up their tradition of "managing barbarian affairs" through the offices of the Board of Rites, where specialists in protocol could teach uninformed foreigners the "usages of the empire," including how to get down on all fours when kowtowing to the August One. They did indeed set up a crude facsimile of a foreign office. The British, however, were driven to exasperation, for it seemed to them that in staffing the new office, the Tsung-li Yamen, the Chinese must have diabolically scoured the imperial bureaucracy to find the most dimwitted of officials. Additionally the Chinese had placed the foreign office on a back street in a rundown building, where passers-by could press their noses to the windows to watch Western diplomats attempt to lecture Chinese mandarins on why foreign affairs should not be treated as a mere nuisance.

It is of course understandable and hardly noteworthy that cultural differences should arise in relations among people with different traditions. The problem of disappointment with China, however, is of a more troublesome sort. Indeed the difficulties are particularly frustrating because outsiders often have an easy time establishing comfortable, even warm, relations with individual Chinese. Problems almost invariably arise out of the actions of the government and, specifically, from the ways in which power and authority operate in China. Chinese authority causes trouble not just for foreigners but for the vast majority of the Chinese people. Just when all appears to be going well, Chinese officials create problems for seemingly unaccountable reasons.

It is hard to pinpoint the intentions behind their disruptive acts because, in a world of grantedly irrational political systems, China's is possibly the most bizarre. Can it be that one year after Tiananmen more than one billion sullen people are left mute and passive victims, awaiting the outcome of power struggles among enfeebled strongmen, the one with top billing holding no posts at all, his presumed principal opponent's only claim to legitimacy being membership in an "advisory commission" of "retired" leaders? The problems with China are far more than just those associated with conventional communist oppression. China has a political system in which accountability seems to be absent altogether, in which no one appears to know where responsibility should lie anyway and, consequently, one in which awful things can happen to the ordinary citizen.

The accumulation of American frustrations with China can lead to feelings of betrayal. Americans may even come to believe that with the end of the Cold War China has lost its geopolitical relevance. But because a quarter of humanity cannot possibly be irrelevant, it is important to try understanding why the Chinese government, in contrast to the Chinese people, has been and remains such a disappointment. Unfortunately, the problems are not ephemeral; their roots extend deep into China's historical experience. Any true understanding of these problems, therefore, calls for an analysis of the complex and unique ways in which the Chinese state and society have evolved.

II

The starting point for understanding the problem is to recognize that China is not just another nation-state in the family of nations. China is a civilization pretending to be a state. The story of modern China could be described as the effort by both Chinese and foreigners to squeeze a civilization into the arbitrary, constraining framework of the modern state, an institutional invention that came out of the fragmentation of the

West's own civilization. Viewed from another perspective, the miracle of China has been its astonishing unity. In Western terms the China of today is as if the Europe of the Roman Empire and of Charlemagne had lasted until this day and were now trying to function as a single nation-state.

The fact that the Chinese state was founded on one of the world's great civilizations has given inordinate strength and durability to its political culture. The overpowering obligation felt by

Chinese rulers to preserve the unity of their civilization has meant that there could be no compromises in Chinese cultural attitudes about power and authority. Whereas pragmatic considerations have readily guided the Chinese in other spheres of life, this has not been possible with respect to the most fundamental values that determine the basis of the legitimacy of the state and govern the relationship between the state and society.

Chinese civilization has produced a distinctive and enduring pattern of relations between the state and society. Although the affairs of the state were always secret and tainted with the suspicion of scandal, the realm of government projected grandeur and thus gave all Chinese a right to pride and dignity. Chinese society, on the other hand, was peculiarly passive toward its government, made no claims on state policies and concentrated its energies on the private domain. It has always been a society composed of inward-looking groupings, and thus cellular in its structure. Society in China existed only at the local level; there were no national institutions of society, such as the church in Europe. Thus the state existed alone at the highest collective level.

One secret of the unity of China has been a conspiracy of make-believe, which masks the strengths and limitations of both the state and society. The Chinese state, both imperial and communist, has always pretended to omnipotence, but in reality its policy-implementing authority has been surprisingly limited. Chinese society for its part has gone along with the pretense of official omnipotence while following its own lead and making almost no demands on the government. Rulers and subjects have thus tended to keep their distance from each other while pretending to be harmoniously close.

This peculiar relationship sets the stage for the great Chinese political game of feigned compliance. Central authorities issue their "absolute" orders and local authorities proclaim their obedience, even as they quietly proceed to do what they think best. Higher authorities are hesitant to check too carefully about implementation of their orders for fear that it might reveal their impotence and shatter the pretentious of absolute power. Lower authorities are careful not to be too blatant in disregarding more troublesome orders, while overzealously carrying out those that are untroublesome. Should central authorities be embarrassed, however, they can act with mad fury.

In traditional China, as in present-day China, the clash of politics occurred among the uppermost rulers and their bureaucracies. The people as a whole had almost nothing to say or do about public affairs, even though the fiction might be that all policies were executed in their name. The struggles of factional politics among the elite operated to neutralize policy initiatives, and thus spared the population undue obtrusiveness. The Confucian mandarins understood that the purpose of bureaucratic government was to uphold the ideal of stability, which is best achieved when bureaucrats bend all their wits and energies toward blunting each other's initiatives.

Although government in the People's Republic involves more concerted policy efforts, it is one of the great illusions of the day that Chinese authorities are as omnipotent as they pretend to be. In a host of fields, from tax collecting to controlling economic activities in Guangdong, Fujian and other dynamic provinces, central authorities know that feigned compliance still reigns and that it is best not to attempt the impossible by demanding precise obedience. Sovereignty, after all, calls for theatrical representation.

In the meantime, the Chinese public ignores its aged leaders' buffoonery when they shrilly promise the imminent collapse of capitalism. The words of officialdom can hardly be taken seriously by an intelligent, pragmatic people when their leaders warn that "Western capitalist nations have never relinquished their goal of plundering China," while these same leaders simultaneously call for more foreign investment. The regime has now mounted a campaign warning that the West is plotting a "peaceful evolution" for China from socialism to democracy, a danger the people can only hope will come sooner rather than later. The political language of the elite at times loses all contact with reality. It speaks of the "bad old days" of Western domination, when only two percent of

China's national income was related to foreign trade and investment; it touts a proud new anti-capitalist, anti-imperialist era,
when nearly one third of China's national income currently depends on the world capitalist system. State and society in China
have quite different realities indeed.

This distinctively Chinese relationship between the state and
society was sustained by a shared belief in a moral order, the upholding of which gave the government legitimacy, and the existence of which gave the people security and peace. Although most
traditional societies had comparable moral orders, elsewhere the
process of modernization involved transitions to political orders
based on competing economic and social interests. With successful
modernization the balance of power shifts in favor of society and
the emerging interests of the people. The authority of government
comes to depend on the outcome of political processes. Instead of
legitimacy being derived from an orthodox moral order, it is in-
vigorated by the play of politics as codified in a system of laws.

In the case of China, however, significant competing interests
never emerged. Instead of a drive toward pluralism and a system of
legitimacy anchored in the realities of political processes, there was
a frantic search for a new moral order to replace the eroding Confucian order. Marxism-Leninism in its Maoist form became that
new moral order that reenergized rulers' pretentions of moral superiority and invincibility. The result is a distinctive system, which
can be called Confucian Leninism, in which rulers, especially under Mao Zedong, claim to have a monopoly on virtue, society is
guided by a moralistic ideology, and the hierarchy of officialdom is
supposedly composed of exemplary people skilled in doctrinal
matters. This continuing Chinese emphasis on a moral order explains the exaggerated importance of ideology in the Maoist years,
the current propensity to revert to orthodoxy at every sign of political difficulties, and the generally erratic behavior of the state.

Mao sought to do something that Chinese emperors and mandarins were far too prudent to try. He sought to use the legitimacy of
the moral order to mobilize the people for material advancement,

especially during the Great Leap Forward and the Cultural Revolution. When this effort failed, the legitimacy of the new moral order eroded and there was a crisis of faith. For a brief time Deng Xiaoping reestablished a sense of legitimacy by providing immediate materialistic pay-offs from his reforms. When economic problems began to emerge after 1985, however, the government had neither a moral order nor the benefit of a political process to provide it with legitimacy. The only immediate alternative was repression. Tiananmen has become the universally acknowledged code word for repression in the search for legitimacy.

For a time the horrors of the Cultural Revolution seemed great enough to extinguish any lingering legitimacy of Marxism-Leninism-Maoism. When Deng initiated his economic reforms, there existed a debate between party theorists advocating the "two whatevers"—whatever Mao said and whatever Mao did—and those advocating "seeking truth from fact." The debate confused the issue of what should be the criterion for evaluating policies with the larger question of what should be the basis of legitimacy now that Mao, the Superthinker, was dead. The pragmatists' argument that "practice is the sole criterion of truth" provided far too risky a basis for state legitimacy. No society has been so foolish as to make successful policies the basis of the legitimacy of its government, since the very essence of legitimacy is that it should sustain the government regardless of how partisan policies are working out. In practical terms, Deng used the debate long enough to eliminate his rival Hua Guofeng and his "whatever" faction, and then reasserted the authority of the Four Principles, which gave primacy to the party and to the moral order of Marxist-Leninist-Maoist thought. The debate helped party leaders to liberate their thinking from the silliness of Maoist rhetoric, but it failed to usher in a new basis of legitimacy for the state.

The inestimable importance of a moral order for political legitimacy has made Chinese leaders, both Confucian and communist, dogmatic believers that values can be vividly categorized into those that are at the core or essence of the moral order; those that are foreign but useful, such as Western science and technology; and those that are an abomination because they contaminate the purity of the core values. The third are to be vigilantly guarded against and denounced, for example, as they are today, as "spiritual pollution" and "bourgeois liberalism." All Chinese leaders, starting with the reformers at the end of the Qing Dynasty, have steadfastly followed this formula in trying to modernize China while still preserving its civilization. Serious troubles arise, however, when in practice it proves impossible to ensure that the three categories of values are being kept neatly separated. Panic grows at the thought that the purity of the core values is being contaminated by Chinese who are supposed to be learning only practical matters from alien cultures.

This hypersensitivity to what is precious in the Self and what may be useful in the Other makes the Chinese more extreme than other transitional peoples in having at the same time a superiority complex and an inferiority complex, a contradiction which does not particularly bother them. Enough has been said elsewhere about the "Middle Kingdom complex," but what needs to be noted here is that this complex is accompanied by a keen awareness of the need to learn from others, to send students abroad, to search for what is best and to replicate it in China—with little regard for patents or copyrights. In this process the Chinese have elevated science and technology to the ranks of their core values and have come to revere science in much the same spirit as the earlier mandarins did Confucianism. Thus, instead of science having the liberating effect it did in the West, in China it has become a new orthodoxy for a state-supported technocratic elite. The Chinese political approach to science and technology therefore has an absolutist character; it is assumed that there is always a single, best answer to all technical problems.

The Chinese tradition of orthodoxy suggests that technocrats should have a common solution to any problem, with disagreements fought out within the circle of the elite, in the style of defenders of a moral order. Chinese political leaders have refused to recognize that technical problems usually have multiple solutions, and that choosing among them calls for a clash of values and power inherent in competitive politics. Debates over alternative technocratic solutions in other countries have generally widened political participation and strengthened pluralistic tendencies. This is not so in China, precisely because "science" has been made a part of the Chinese core values that, ironically, must be protected from contamination from other aspects of Western culture that are not "science."

Expecting that science should provide absolute certainty, like answers to arithmetic problems, Chinese political leaders are easily angered by the fact that technology generally calls for probabilistic thinking. They thus imperiously demand the single "best" answer to a policy problem. Of course political leaders in other countries also have their frustrations with the contingent nature of applied scientific knowledge. Harry Truman, for example, once complained that he wished he could find a one-armed economist, one who would not always be talking about "on the one hand, and on the other hand." In China, however, the authoritarian traditions of the emperors and of Leninism-Maoism combine to produce hostility toward any suggestion of ambiguities and probabilities. Chinese rulers' reactions thus tend to be of the old imperial stripe: "Don't tolerate, exterminate."

This dogmatic approach to science, along with adherence to "scientific" Marxism-Leninism, has produced a troublesome psychological problem for communist leaders as they try to preserve the dichotomy between essential "Chinese" values and the "dangerous" values of foreign cultures. The core values now to be defended are, in fact, foreign imports: science and Marxism-Leninism. In an effort to get around this awkward reality, the leadership talks of "building socialism with Chinese characteristics." This does not solve the problem, however, because for forty years the party has been denouncing just about every feature of Chinese culture as a feudal abomination that should be obliterated. In the end it is not easy to articulate what exactly are the Chinese qualities that should now be defended. In practice all that is left of "Chineseness" is the belief that leaders have a claim to moral superiority as the defenders of the moral order, even if this means acting in erratic and arbitrary ways that set back the nation.

III

The stunted growth of interest groups in China is rooted in part in the nature of traditional Chinese society, which was essentially agrarian, and in which the only established channel for upward mobility was the government bureaucracy. China did not have the diversities that emerged in Europe with the rise of cities, the development of a merchant class, the growth of professions and occupations, and all of the other social changes that contributed to the pluralism basic to modern Western politics. In the West the rise of interest groups in society was also fueled by religious beliefs that valued the individual and gave legitimacy to individualism and the search for self-realization. In China the society was community oriented; individuals were expected to find their identities as a part of a group and to conform to the conventions of the collectivity.

This characteristic of Chinese culture had profound implications for the way Chinese political life developed, and explains why today the government can be so troublesome. The fact that all Chinese derived their identities from being members of a group, starting most importantly with the family and the clan, gave stability to China's unique structure of state-society relations, making it relatively easy for the government to rule. In the Ming Dynasty as few as 100,000 officials managed an empire of 100 million people, and a single magistrate was responsible for a county averaging 50,000 people. Collectivities governed themselves and the state could rely on the principle of collective responsibility. In policing it was not necessary to apprehend the particular person who committed a crime; Chinese justice could be administered by arresting, torturing and punishing the culprit's father, grandfather or the head of his or her clan. Since fathers had no desire to suffer for the bad acts of their sons, they could be counted on to go to great lengths to bring them up in the right way. Filial piety had practical as well as spiritual implications.

Society also benefited from this system in that individuals could derive a strong sense of security from being a part of solidarity groups that provided mutual support. Under the Chinese system of social connections, called guanxi, an individual might also have access to reciprocal ties with people beyond his or her primary group. An individual could thus become a part of a complex network of associations extending outward from the family to people from the same town, province, school or other institutions. People who shared any commonly recognized identity could count on each other.

For both the mandarins of the past and the cadres of today, these networks of personal relationships have provided the latent structures of factional Chinese politics. Guanxi ties, however, have not always provided security. In a forthcoming study, John K. Fairbank tells how the Hongwu emperor of the Ming Dynasty became so furious with his prime minister that he had him beheaded, along with all the members of his extended family. His fury still unappeased, the emperor then went after everyone who was known to have been in any way associated with any of them, to the extent that this early Stalinist-style purge exterminated over 40,000 people. Fairbank observes, "Guanxi has its dangers."

Since Tiananmen, state terror has been reimposed with ease, partly because the students and dissidents who need to use guanxi can never be certain that their networks have not been penetrated by informers. The environment became one in which people felt safe trusting each other only if they had some damaging information in reserve that could be used if necessary against another. The problem of trust has contributed to the factionalism that has splintered the opposition to the regime, even among those outside the country.

IV

The group-oriented character of Chinese society also makes governing easier because the collectivities are expected to look after their own members, while not making demands on the government. China has always had protective associations, but not pressure or interest groups. This was true of the family and clan in traditional China and is true of the work unit and the "iron rice bowl" in today's China. Just as individuals are not supposed to assert their own interests above those of the group that provides their identities, likewise all subordinate interests in China's hierarchical society are expected to defer to higher interests.

The taboo on the articulation of interests no doubt contributed to the unity of China, but it also set sharp limits on political development, even to the point of dictating the scope of discourse and determining who was a proper spokesman on public affairs. This prohibition meant that China never developed a real political economy in the sense of openly acknowledging that political power might be harnessed to advance economic interests. Those with interests that might be affected by governmental policies could not publicly call for allies or seek to mobilize opinion in favor of their interests. They could instead only try to operate quietly by seeking special favors in the implementation of policies, and thus risk being seen as a source of corruption. Consequently, although China has great regional differences, ranging from the rice economy of the south to the millet and wheat economies of the north, and from its cosmopolitan coast to its provincial interior, these differences have never been openly acknowledged. Everyone has simply gone along with the pretense that whatever the central authorities advocate is in the interest of all Chinese.

The rule against asserting one's own material interests has made selfishness China's ultimate political sin. Since openly advancing personal interests is seen as dishonorable, severe limits have been placed on even the vocabulary of Chinese politics. The language of Chinese politics has always been limited largely to supporting the values of the moral order. Political discourse thus becomes moralizing, not the analyzing of problems. No matter what scoundrels they may be as individuals, as self-conscious members of a supposed virtuocracy, Chinese officials are trained to praise all acts of the government as morally unassailable. Other Chinese are limited

Lucian W. Pye

to two acceptable levels of discussion: the ad hominem level of remonstrating against particular officials for their selfish wrongdoings, or the lofty plane of boasting of their own selfless patriotism. Thus Chinese political discourse is either thick with charges of corruption against selfish officials or, as people seek to demonstrate their selflessness, highly idealistic and patriotic.

The imperative of always needing to appear selfless also limits who participates in political discussions. Most people remain mute for fear of being viewed as selfish and concerned only with their own material interests. Intellectuals and students thus receive a near monopoly on speaking out, for they are thought to have no special interests beyond their prime responsibility of defending the moral order. This responsibility has made them prisoners of the status quo, unable to freely advocate genuinely alternative approaches. China never had the clash of church and state, of religion and science, that established the Western intellectual as a legitimate outside critic of authority. As a result the Chinese governmental process has rarely had the benefit of intellectual criticism. It is true that many noteworthy Confucian scholars bravely remonstrated against officials of the imperial government, or even the emperor, but it was almost always in orthodox terms.

The story of intellectual dissent in the People's Republic has been much the same. Intellectuals have criticized the personal failings of officials, and some have at great risk even questioned the correctness of Mao's and Deng's policies. The tyranny of patriotism, however, has imposed a form of self-censorship. The Chinese tendency to blur the distinctions between party, government and country has made it dangerous to challenge fundamental policies or the basic character of the political system for fear of appearing to be unpatriotic and subversive. Liu Binyan, China's famed investigative reporter, even after 22 years of exile in the countryside, until Tiananmen never questioned the values of the party and sought only to expose individual wrongdoing. In his essay "A Second Kind of Loyalty," which electrified the Chinese reading public, Liu suggested that, in addition to the simple-minded obedience to

the party of the good soldier Lei Feng, there was a second kind of loyalty, typified by two people who had chastised officials for their failings. As late as Tiananmen, few intellectuals questioned whether Liu was still too bonded to the party to recognize that there might be an even higher kind of loyalty, that of criticizing socialism out of love for China. What makes Fang Lizhi, China's Sakharov, stand out among Chinese intellectuals is his outspoken recognition that China has been cursed with what he calls "the problem of patriotism," which stops all reasoning because once you "criticize someone for being unpatriotic it will shut him right up."

V

A further problem in a society in which self-interest must be masked and people pretend to selflessness is that people never feel they know where others really stand. Everybody knows of course that people have hidden interests. There exists, therefore, considerable suspicion about hidden agendas and real motives. From ordinary social relations to international politics, inordinate attention is given to determining the real position of others. Are they potentially friends or foes? Stratagems abound, but they have to be followed with the greatest care because of the danger of causing the other party to "lose face," which is the grievous pain people experience when their masks are stripped away.

The social imperative not to offend, especially in face-to-face relations, contributes to an astonishing double paradox in contrasting Chinese and American political behavior. American politicians, operating in a democratic political culture, paradoxically discount what other politicians say publicly ("He had to say that for his constituents"; "it was only said for election purposes"), while believing that the hard currency of political communication is found in the privacy of meetings held behind closed doors, where they can talk "man to man."

Chinese leaders, operating in an authoritarian political culture, follow the opposite rule. They believe face-to-face meetings are where hypocrisy prevails. That is where it is obligatory to tell others what they want to hear, where ceremonial rituals must be carefully observed so that relations go smoothly; no one loses "face" and there is no hint of confrontation. In Chinese political culture one discerns where the other party stands only by reading between the lines of public statements and attaching importance to the code words employed.

This paradoxical difference between the Chinese and American evaluations of private communications makes even more puzzling the secret visit to Beijing after Tiananmen by President Bush's national security adviser, Brent Scowcroft. According to American logic, the trip's purpose might have been to reassure Beijing that the U.S. president was not as angry about Tiananmen as his public statements may have suggested and, further, that Bush's subsequent public statements about trying to keep China "open" should be discounted as conventional American hypocrisy employed to pacify his political constituents. Seen from a Chinese point of view, however, the trip was merely a ceremonial visit where flattering toasts are to be dismissed according to the conventional Chinese hypocrisy of face-to-face meetings.

The need in Chinese social and political life to probe where others stand as they uphold the ideal of selflessness makes the identification of friend and foe a constant concern. This produces layers of ritual about friendship that only further obscure whether or not the reality exists in any particular relationship. In Chinese culture people can become instant "old friends," but the obligations of friendship are vague; there is only the general notion that the more fortunate party ought to be helpful. Even a slight sign of coolness, however, can raise the suspicion that the relationship has become adversarial. This is not the place to analyze the complex sentiments associated with friendship in Chinese culture, but suffice to say that friendship is a highly valued ideal that is nonetheless hard to realize in practice. It is also an inappropriate ideal in institution-the institution relations for, ironically, just as cooperation seems to draw closer, the likelihood of trouble usually increases sharply.

China still actively plays the theme of friendship in the old tradition of treating well those who have come from afar to partake of its wonders. True, there is currently some embarrassment over the old Maoist slogans of "We have friends everywhere" and, in sports, "Friendship first, competition second." Yet when Chinese behavior is more soberly analyzed, it is striking how few allies China actually has and how easily its relations with others tend to sour. Usually trouble arises just when relations seem to be getting closer: as with the Soviet Union in the late 1950s, India in the early 1960s, Vietnam in the late 1970s and Japan and the United States in the late 1980s. Since the post-Mao era of "opening" to the world, China has of course been seeking "normal" international relations. It is significant, however, that China still has no particularly close allies. Over the last few years when Chinese officials have been systematically questioned as to the countries with whom they have the closest and easiest relations, they have generally been hard put to specify any country other than their formal ally, North Korea. Few knowledgeable people, meanwhile, believe that China and North Korea are really close friends.

The overriding duty to defend a great civilization by upholding a moral order seems to cause Chinese leaders to discount the risks of irritating other governments. At the same time they are themselves hypersensitive to perceived slights. Thus Chinese officials generally strive to claim the moral high ground in any diplomatic negotiations. Just as Chinese rulers traditionally believed they could shame their subjects into correct behavior, and much as Chinese parents use shaming to socialize their children, so Chinese leaders today seem to believe that it is to their advantage to tell other governments that their relations with China are either "bad" or not as "good" as they should be. They will speak of how there is "a cloud over the relationship," and claim that relations can be improved only if "he who tied the knot unties it." There is no hint of a quid pro quo, however, no concrete indication as to what it might be worth for the other party to improve its relationship with the Chinese. Other governments should simply do what is "right" and be thankful to China for providing moral instruction and guidance. It must be conceded that the Chinese tactic of blaming others for any setback in relations is remarkably effective when it comes to the United States. America's puritan instinct dictates that if something has gone wrong it is proper first to suspect that the fault is probably one's own; and even if it turns out to be the other's, one should remain as closemouthed as possible for fear of making things worse. This tendency in turn only compounds the problem, because Chinese culture takes for granted that an accused party who offers no defense must be guilty.

There is an additional twist to the differences in American and Chinese thinking about the role of morality in international affairs. As pointed out by George Kennan and Hans Morgenthau, among others, the United States tends toward a moralistic approach to foreign policy that inhibits the advancement of American interests and allows others undue advantage. Chinese leaders, as the practiced guardians of a moral order, turn the issue of morality the other way around. They use arguments of "right" and "wrong" as a way to inhibit the actions of other countries, thereby advancing China's own practical interests—interests that of course they pretend are of secondary concern. Chinese leaders' commitment to the advantages of being morally superior is so great that even after the horrors of Tiananmen they still thought they could benefit by blaming the United States and others for what had happened.

VI

The erratic behavior of the Chinese state in both domestic and international affairs is further exaggerated by the Chinese belief that benevolent government requires rule by men and not by law. (The Chinese tradition of rule by law was one of arbitrary and harsh authoritarianism.) New vigor was given to the Confucian ideal of rule by superior men when China adopted Leninist elitism, and the combination of Confucian Leninism has produced a system that gives successive top rulers extraordinary freedom. Consequently, and paradoxically, ultimate power in a society that is otherwise group oriented rests largely in the hands of individual personalities.

The peculiarly personal quality of sovereign authority has made leaders acutely sensitive to the need to take advantage of their every opportunity and to cling to power for as long as possible. Without a system of laws they cannot be sure their policies will survive their hold on power. No leader, not even a Mao or a Deng, can leave behind statutes that will bind the country to any particular policy course. New rulers bring new policies. This also means that questions of succession dominate Chinese politics. When things are going well, people wish "long life" to the paramount ruler; when they are going badly, people look forward to the arrival of the Grim Reaper. As long as leaders' influence ends at the grave, it is natural for them to try to hold on to power for as long as possible. Gerontocracy is the result. The "eight ancients" today rule over the entire political system and generational change is excruciatingly slow. Indeed, it is an oddity that aspiring Chinese leaders seem to get old faster than those ahead of them die.

The zigs and zags of Chinese policies made possible by the rule of men rather than law is also exaggerated by the Chinese spirit of pragmatism, which holds that changes in circumstances should prompt changes in action. In contrast to American politicians, who go into contortions to prove that through thick and thin they have always been consistent in their views, Chinese leaders find it painless to change their positions as circumstances change. For them it is a sign of wisdom to adapt to the logic of a situation, and it is an indication of power to be able to order policy changes. Proving that one has both wisdom and power is a combination hard to beat in any culture, and thus it is not surprising that Chinese leaders will confidently alter their policies. Americans are puzzled that Deng Xiaoping, who brought about such liberalizing reforms, could also be the butcher of Tiananmen. They forget that he is the same man (although his name was then spelled Teng Hsiao-p'ing) who in 1958 proposed the Anti-Rightist Campaign and who sold Mao on the idea of sending intellectuals down to the countryside to rusticate. Most Chinese leaders have likewise had several political incarnations.

The tradition of government by superior people, acting as the guardians of a moral order, has inhibited the institutionalization of government in China to the point that there is widespread speculation about how much of the communist system, built up over half a century of struggle, will outlast the octogenarians who are now the supreme rulers. Yet, paradoxically, in spite of the apparent fragility of a noninstitutionalized system of government, communism endures in its Confucian Leninist form, while being in crisis nearly everywhere else.

Optimists take heart from actuarial considerations and belief in the doctrine that "nothing succeeds like a successor." Pessimists recognize that the Chinese gerontocracy hangs on while American administrations come and go: an infirm Mao outlived Richard Nixon's presidency, and now an elderly but vigorous President Yang Shangkun is a good bet to outlast the current U.S. administration. Beijingologists scanning the ranks of the leadership to spot a possible future reformer place their hopes on Li Ruihuan, the former carpenter and now party propaganda czar, or Zhu Rongji, the mayor and cheerful booster of Shanghai. It is certainly wishful thinking, however, to believe that the Chinese political system is a well-integrated machine ready to respond to one man pushing a button labeled "reform," and thereby bring back the happy visions of the early 1980s. Prediction is made difficult precisely because the Chinese political system is capable of sudden zigs and zags according to the whims of a few men, while simultaneously carrying the burden of being true to a great and only slowly changing civilization. In a rhythmic way China's strengths turn into its weaknesses and its weaknesses become its strengths.

It is prudent to have guarded expectations about the immediate actions of Chinese leaders and the outcomes of their factional power struggles. It is nevertheless possible to be somewhat more certain about the evolution of modern China. It will probably continue to be the story of a society composed of people with remarkable talents for adapting to the modern world, but cursed with a political culture that constantly dashes any hope for smooth progress. The distinctive state-society relationship that has worked so successfully in preserving the unity of China also works to make progress erratic.

The failure of significant interests to emerge politically suggests that there is little prospect in the foreseeable future that the balance will shift from the state in favor of society, as has occurred in Eastern Europe and is occurring in Taiwan, South Korea and the other countries that are leading the worldwide transition away from authoritarianism. Dissidents trying to think through the future of China are mired in utopian debates that would at best call for heroic efforts to establish once more a new moral order. Some talk of a "third way" between capitalism and socialism; others dream of returning to the heady days of the early 1980s, before reforms ran into increasingly daunting problems and it became apparent that without solid political support there is no easy exit from a centrally planned economy. The prospects of such support are made dimmer by the Chinese tradition of believing that all successful leaders must be supermen, for today there are no charismatic figures among the dissidents.

Still others take hope from Chinese history. Out of the chaos of a disintegrating dynasty there have repeatedly emerged dynamic founders of new dynasties. Such a reliance on historical analogy is questionable, however, because in the past the Confucian moral order remained in place, ready to be reinvigorated by the new dynasty. It is harder today to identify what are the norms that could give vitality to a new political order, and therefore the drift of inertia becomes a guiding force. The strongest consideration uniting the opposition is a passion for revenge, for "settling scores," but there is no agreement even about which scores need settling first. Today there is widespread hope that "democracy" could become China's new moral order, but it is hard to imagine that a democracy could exist without a politics of competing interests.

China's distinctive state-society relationship has contributed to the peculiar rhythm of its politics. The factional struggles within the elite have produced not the Western pendulum swings between left and right, liberal and conservative, but an up-and-down motion of centralizing and decentralizing, of tightening and loosening the state's penetration of society. The vast majority of the population live as peasants in some five million hamlets and villages with their own largely self-contained social and political systems. They see the workings of government as much like the weather, to be thanked when favorable and cursed when bad. The urban population is not organized into interests, but rather is made up of strata or segments, such as the intellectuals and technocrats, industrial workers, managers, service people, entertainers, journalists, owners of small enterprises and the like. Their response to the politics of the state is largely one of mood: when things are favorable for them they are capable of enthusiasm, when things go wrong, of alienation. Most of the strata joyfully welcomed the early Deng reforms, but by 1985, and especially since 1988, they have one by one become disenchanted. Swings in mood between enthusiasm and alienation are humanly significant, but they are not a substitute for real politics.

Although it is hard to find a silver lining in the clouds, Chinese society, in spite of current repression, continues to have surprising dynamism. The coastal provinces have fought back the forces of political repression and economic recession and, consequently, economic progress at the local level continues. The modernizing elements in the society seek to expand their international contacts as best they can. Just as Soviet society made significant progress in urbanization, education and professionalization during the political stagnation of the Brezhnev era, so it is likely that Chinese society will advance in spite of its anachronistic government.

China's peculiar state-society relationship allows its leaders to rejoice in their presumed omnipotence, and its bureaucrats to engage in their factional struggles, while the Chinese people are left to seek comfort and security in the personal groupings that can protect them from more extreme political storms. Acts of make-believe smooth over the obvious contradictions and ensure that Chinese civilization will change only slowly in spite of all the zig-zags of an erratic state. The unshakable idea that China remains a great civilization fuels a comfortable superiority complex and makes the vast majority of Chinese optimists, for they must believe that it is only an anomaly that things are as bad as they currently are, and in the future greatness will inevitably return. In coping with the civilization as a state, the outside world has every reason to follow its own optimistic instincts and try to build ties with elements of China's distinctive society. At the same time, it should give careful heed to the pessimistic forebodings history provides of the erratic ways of China's political system. The fundamental goal in dealing with China should be to strengthen elements within Chinese society that can in time serve as more effective checks against the troublesomeness of the state. Even after Tiananmen, during a year when officially relations were "bad," this process has continued as, for example, trade with the United States has grown. Until a more substantial shift in power occurs in favor of society, however, the question of whether other governments have "good" or "bad" relations with the Chinese government will remain a trivial distinction.

Long Time Coming

The Prospects for Democracy in China

John L. Thornton

China's leaders have held out the promise of some form of democracy to the people of China for nearly a century. After China's last dynasty, the Qing, collapsed in 1911, Sun Yat-sen suggested a three-year period of temporary military rule, followed by a six-year phase of "political tutelage," to guide the country's transition into a full constitutional republic. In 1940, Mao Zedong offered followers something he called "new democracy," in which leadership by the Communist Party would ensure the "democratic dictatorship" of the revolutionary groups over class enemies. And Deng Xiaoping, leading the country out of the anarchy of the Cultural Revolution, declared that democracy was a "major condition for emancipating the mind."

When they used the term "democracy," Sun, Mao, and Deng each had something quite different in mind. Sun's definition—which envisioned a constitutional government with universal suffrage, free elections, and separation of powers—came closest to a definition recognizable in the West. Through their deeds, Mao and Deng showed that despite their words, such concepts held little importance for them. Still, the three agreed that democracy was not an end in itself but rather a mechanism for achieving China's

JOHN L. THORNTON is a Professor at Tsinghua University's School of Economics and Management and its School of Public Policy and Management, in Beijing, and Director of the university's Global Leadership Program. He is also Chair of the Board of the Brookings Institution.

real purpose of becoming a country that could no longer be bullied by outside powers.

Democracy ultimately foundered under all three leaders. When Sun died, in 1925, warlordism and disunity still engulfed many parts of China. In his time, Mao showed less interest in democracy than in class struggle, mass movements, continuous revolution, and keeping his opponents off balance. And Deng demonstrated on a number of occasions—most dramatically in suppressing the Tiananmen protests of 1989—that he would not let popular democratic movements overtake party rule or upset his plan for national development.

Today, of course, China is not a democracy. The Chinese Communist Party (CCP) has a monopoly on political power, and the country lacks freedom of speech, an independent judiciary, and other fundamental attributes of a pluralistic liberal system. Many inside and outside China remain skeptical about the prospects for political reform. Yet much is happening—in the government, in the CCP, in the economy, and in society at large—that could change how Chinese think about democracy and shape China's political future.

Both in public and in private, China's leaders are once again talking about democracy, this time with increasing frequency and detail. (This article is based on conversations held over the past 14 months with a broad range of Chinese, including members of the CCP's Central Committee—the group of China's top 370 leaders—senior government officials, scholars, judges, lawyers, journalists, and leaders of nongovernmental organizations.) President Hu Jintao has called democracy "the common pursuit of mankind." During his 2006 visit to the United States, Hu went out of his way to broach the subject at each stop. And Premier Wen Jiabao, in his address to the 2007 National People's Congress, devoted to democracy and the rule of law more than twice the attention he had in any previous such speech. "Developing democracy and improving the legal system," Wen declared, "are basic requirements of the socialist system."

As with earlier leaders, what the present generation has in mind differs from the definition used in the West. Top officials stress that the CCP's leadership must be preserved. Although they see a role for elections, particularly at the local level, they assert that a "deliberative" form of politics that allows individual citizens and groups to add their views to the decision-making process is more appropriate for China than open, multiparty competition for national power. They often mention meritocracy, including the use of examinations to test candidates' competence for office, reflecting an age-old Chinese belief that the government should be made up of the country's most talented. Chinese leaders do not welcome the latitude of freedom of speech, press, or assembly taken for granted in the West. They say they support the orderly expansion of these rights but focus more on the group and social harmony—what they consider the common good.

Below the top tier of leaders (who usually speak from a common script), Chinese officials differ on whether "guided democracy" is where China's current political evolution will end or is a way station en route to a more standard liberal democratic model. East Asia provides examples of several possibilities: the decades-long domination of politics by the Liberal Democratic Party in Japan, the prosperity with limited press freedom of Singapore, and the freewheeling multiparty system of South Korea. China might follow one of these paths, some speculate, or blaze its own.

In a meeting in late 2006 with a delegation from the Brookings Institution (of which I was a member), Premier Wen was asked what he and other Chinese leaders meant by the word "democracy," what form democracy was likely to take in China, and over what time frame. "When we talk about democracy," Wen replied, "we usually refer to three key components: elections, judicial independence, and supervision based on checks and balances." Regarding the first, he could foresee direct and indirect elections expanding gradually from villages to towns, counties, and even provinces. He did not mention developments beyond this, however. As for China's judicial system, which is riddled with corruption, Wen stressed the need for reform to assure the judiciary's "dignity, justice, and independence." And he explained that "supervision"—a Chinese term for ensuring effective oversight—was necessary to restrain abuses of official power. He called for checks and balances within the CCP and for greater official accountability to the public. The media and China's nearly 200 million Internet users should also participate "as appropriate" in the supervision of the government's work, he observed. Wen's bottom line: "We have to move toward democracy. We have many problems, but we know the direction in which we are going."

FREE TO CHOOSE

Given the gap between the democratic aspirations professed by leaders such as Hu and Wen and the skepticism that their words elicit in the West, a better understanding is needed of where exactly the process of democratization stands in China today. Chinese citizens do not have the right to choose their national leaders, but for more than a decade, peasants across the country have held ballots to elect village chiefs. What is happening in the vast space between the farm and Zhongnanhai, the CCP's leadership compound in Beijing? Some answers can be gleaned by examining the three pillars of Wen's definition: elections, judicial independence, and supervision.

The Chinese constitution calls for a combination of direct and indirect polls to choose government leaders. In practice, competitive popular elections occur widely only in the country's 700,000 villages. With over 700 million farmers living in these villages, this is not an insignificant phenomenon, but the details tell a complex and at times contradictory story.

The original impulse behind village elections, which began in the early 1980s, was to promote competent local leaders who would grow the rural economy and implement national priorities such as the one-child policy. With the abandonment of collectivization at the end of the Cultural Revolution, a power vacuum emerged in the countryside. By most accounts, at first elections enjoyed the central government's active support and were generally conducted fairly. But in the early 1990s, authorities were reportedly taken aback by figures showing that only 40 percent of elected village chiefs were CCP members. Beijing eventually instructed local officials to ensure that the "leading role" of the Communist Party was maintained. Today, the majority of village chiefs are again party members, although the size of that majority can vary widely by region. Over 90 percent of the village heads in the provinces of Guangdong, Hubei, and Shandong belong to the party, but the figure drops to 60–70 percent in Fujian and Zhejiang. And even these figures overstate the actual percentage of village chiefs who were elected as party members: when nonparty candidates are elected, the CCP nearly always recruits them so as to ensure that it remains in charge while giving farmers the leaders they want.

Village elections have serious problems, including nepotism, vote buying, and the selection of incompetent or corrupt leaders. Proponents nonetheless maintain that the polls serve as a grassroots training ground for democratic habits. In fact, the most fervent opponents of village elections in China tend to be the township officials whose own jobs would be in danger if the central government decided to expand direct voting to the next level up.

Some of the more intriguing electoral experiments in China over the past decade have in fact taken place in townships. Burdened with administering the numerous social programs and benefits on which many citizens depend, township governments are often the focus of antigovernment sentiment and social unrest. Effective leadership there is thus critical to preserving social stability, a top priority for Chinese leaders. A few competitive township polls took place as early as 1995–96; the boldest experiment occurred in 1998 in Buyun, in a remote corner of Sichuan. The local Buyun government conducted a competitive, direct election in which some 6,000 eligible adults cast votes. The process received wide media coverage inside China and was criticized in the official press for violating the constitution, which grants the local People's Congress authority to choose the township leader. But to the surprise of many, the central government neither approved the Buyun results nor nullified them, and the elected mayor, Tan Xiaoqiu, remained in office. In 2001, the CCP Central Committee reaffirmed that directly electing a township head was unconstitutional. Buyun responded by tweaking its election process to bring it in line with the letter of the law but not its spirit: in the next election, citizens elected a candidate for township head, who was then recommended by the local party committee and elected unopposed by the People's Congress.

Perhaps in part due to Buyun's legal troubles, most townships that have experimented with elections have chosen the less radical model called the "open recommendation and selection" system, under which any adult resident can run for township head, a council of community leaders then narrows the candidate pool to two finalists, and the local People's Congress makes the final selection. This is not a direct ballot but a way of introducing a measure of competition and transparency in the selection of local leaders. By 2001–2, there was some form of competitive ballot in almost 2,000 township elections, five percent of the national total.

The significance of township elections should not be overstated. Townships are at the lowest administrative rung in the Chinese government structure, and even election supporters acknowledge that the process is still in its infancy. Nonetheless, when conducted successfully, such electoral experiments can give township leaders a degree of popular legitimacy. They introduce competition among cadres and, to a lesser extent, between party and nonparty members where absolutely none existed before. The expectation is that competition, even if controlled, will raise the quality of governance. Some Chinese scholars also find it notable that some township heads are conducting themselves with greater confidence because they know they enjoy a popular mandate and are therefore more willing to challenge the local party secretaries. This can create headaches for the CCP, one central government researcher noted, but it may also be the first seed of a culture of checks and balances.

Authorities in Beijing, for their part, are closely watching the experiments. In an echo of the dynamic that initiated market reforms in the 1980s, the center now encourages governance experimentation at the local level, albeit within boundaries. A senior official at the Central Party School told me, for instance, that in the prosperous province of Jiangsu, a pilot program would soon have all of the townships conducting competitive polls. As different localities try different things, he said, the Central Party School will study the results.

Electoral experiments at the county level—one administrative rung up from a township—have also attracted attention. Since 2000, 11 counties in Hubei and Jiangsu have conducted "open recommendation and selection" polls for the position of county deputy chief. This represents less than half a percent of the counties and county-level cities nationwide, but any reform of leadership selection in counties, which have an average population of about 450,000 each, would be significant news.

Limited experimentation has also occurred in urban areas. In 2003, 12 private citizens stood as independent candidates for district People's Congresses in the city of Shenzhen, with two of them winning seats. A handful of independent candidates have also run for the People's Congress of the Haidian district in Beijing, home to China's top universities. Almost all independent candidates for people's congresses fail in their bids, yet the number of such candidates is exploding: from fewer than 100 nationwide in 2003 to more than 40,000 in 2006–7, according to Li Fan, a former government official who is now a leading election-reform advocate. Li predicts that the number of independent candidates will reach the hundreds of thousands in 2011–12 and thinks popular demand for political participation will continue to grow as Chinese society diversifies and opens up.

In recent years, China's leaders have also made an effort to expand competitive selection within the CCP. Some experts believe that the development of "intraparty democracy" is even more significant for China's long-term political reform than the experiments in local governance. They consider a CCP that accepts open debate, internal leadership elections, and decision-making by ballot to be a prerequisite for democracy in the country as a whole. President Hu and Premier Wen routinely call for more discussion, consultation, and group decision-making within the CCP. Intraparty democracy was a centerpiece of Hu's keynote address to the CCP's 17th Party Congress last fall. Not long after the meeting, Li Yuanchao, the newly appointed head of the Party Organization Department, published a 7,000-character essay in the People's Daily elaborating on Hu's call for further reform in the party. The fact that Hu himself does not wield the personal authority of Mao, Deng, or his predecessor, Jiang Zemin, and relies on consensus within the nine-member Politburo Standing Committee, is itself noted as progress in unwinding the overcentralization of power at the national level.

One of the ways the CCP has begun to introduce intraparty democracy is by putting forward multiple candidates for positions. Fifteen percent of the nominees for the 17th Party Congress were rejected in party ballots. In the 2006–7 national election cycle, the official media reported, 296 townships in 16 provinces chose local party leaders through direct voting by party members as part of a pilot project. In a handful of localities, one government scholar told me, county party secretaries were also being elected through a direct vote.

If intraparty democracy takes hold, some scholars predict a trend in which like-minded cadres will coalesce to form more distinct interest groups within the CCP. A senior official of the Central Party School told our Brookings delegation that "interest groups" were no longer taboo within the party, although organized "factions" were not permitted. Still, some analysts predict that the CCP may one day resemble Japan's ruling Liberal Democratic Party, within which formal, organized factions compete for senior political slots and advocate different policy positions.

In a major speech at the Central Party School in June last year, Hu exhorted the CCP's top leadership to "perfect the intraparty democratic system and bring into full play the party's creative vigor." Then, seemingly in a demonstration of the very intraparty democracy Hu was advocating, a nonbinding straw poll was conducted among the several hundred senior leaders present to gauge their preferences for candidates to the next Politburo and its Standing Committee—in other words, for who should rule China over the next five years.

Some Chinese analysts believe that Hu, in his remarks at the Central Party School, may have been foreshadowing a new policy approach. "Emancipating the mind, an essential requirement of the party's ideological line and a magic weapon of ours in dealing with all kind[s] of new situation[s] and problems lying on the road ahead of us and in our continuous efforts to create a new phase in our cause, must be upheld firmly," Hu told his audience. In asking his colleagues to unshackle themselves from rigid thinking, he was understood to be encouraging them to be more pragmatic in their thinking as China evolves politically. More specifically, Hu was thought to be both indicating to orthodox party thinkers that Mao's was not the only way to define "democracy" and signaling to more reform-minded members of the Central Committee that simply copying Western models was not necessarily the answer either.

THE RULE OF LAW

Of Wen's three pillars of democracy—elections, judicial independence, and supervision—judicial independence is in some ways the most striking. The question of whether the CCP serves the law or vice versa has always made judicial independence a delicate subject in China.

The Chinese judicial system has made great strides over the past three decades, but it still has far to go. In 1980, when the judicial system was just starting to rebuild itself after the devastation of the Cultural Revolution, Chinese courts nationwide accepted a total of 800,000 cases. By 2006, that number had jumped tenfold, reflecting the transformation of the place of law in society. China has passed over 250 new laws in the past 30 years and is in the midst of creating an entire national code from nothing.

Until the mid-1980s, the majority of Chinese judges and prosecutors were former military personnel with little formal education of any sort, let alone legal training. Judicial independence was not the goal of such a system; if anything, it was something to be guarded against. Unsurprisingly, given that the purpose of the courts was to carry out the party line, judges and prosecutors were highly ideological. But starting in the mid-1980s, university graduates were assigned by the state to become judges and prosecutors. By the late 1990s, a master's degree in law was considered an unwritten prerequisite to becoming a senior judge.

Paralleling the rise in the quality of judges and prosecutors has been the change in the status of China's lawyers. Before the late 1980s, all lawyers were employees of the state; private practice did not exist. The first "cooperative law firms" appeared in 1988–89, and today China has 118,000 licensed lawyers practicing in 12,000 firms. (To compare, the United States has more than eight times as many lawyers for a population one-fourth the size of China's.) The growth of private practice has propelled the further professionalization of the system as a whole, partly because lawyers need to win cases (or at least lighter sentences) for their clients in order to prosper. Prosecutors still win over 90 percent of their cases, but as the quality of lawyers has improved and arguments have grown more intricate, prosecutors—and judges—have had to improve their own competence. Party bosses still interfere in the judicial process, and the central government still decides politically sensitive cases, but most observers agree that with disputes becoming more complex, the frequency and degree of such interference are declining.

China has adopted a number of major statutes intended to protect citizens from government wrongdoing. The Public Servants Law of 2005 sets a high standard for conduct by officials. The State Compensation Law of 1994 is meant to make amends for government failures. Perhaps most significant, the Administrative Litigation Law, adopted in 1989, enables citizens to sue the state; some 13,000 suits were filed in the law's first year. Today, more than 150,000 cases are filed annually against the government, and several successful ones have been hailed in the media.

Still, Chinese officials acknowledge that the judicial process remains rife with problems. One of the most serious obstacles to impartial verdicts is the web of personal relationships known as guanxi—bonds forged over years by the exchange of favors and assistance—on which so many decisions in China are based. These ties can have an especially constraining effect on prosecutorial and court decisions. Judges in China routinely talk to the parties in a case privately, creating situations in which guanxi and corruption can readily contaminate the process. Some experts have suggested raising judges' salaries and taking other steps to create a judicial elite distinct from other government officials in order to address this endemic weakness.

China's main challenge is no longer the lack of a comprehensive legal code but the chasm between what is on the books and its implementation, especially at the local level and in politically sensitive cases. Rights guaranteed by the landmark Criminal Procedure Law of 1996, such as timely access to counsel and exculpatory evidence, are often denied or simply ignored. A small but growing group of private lawyers—sometimes referred to as "rights defenders"—take on sensitive cases and unjust prosecutions, in part to highlight instances in which the judicial system itself violates the law. Although they rarely win and are sometimes themselves harassed or even jailed, these activist lawyers believe that insistently pointing out the discrepancy between the official goal of a fair judicial system and the reality on the ground can over time narrow the gap.

Another major obstacle is the sway that local officials continue to hold over the courts. Local CCP committees are integrally involved in the appointment of judges and prosecutors, and local governments have discretion over salaries and budgets throughout the judicial system. The situation shares some similarities with the Chinese banking system a decade ago, when the influence of local officials over bank branches resulted in a vast pool of so-called policy loans. The explosion in nonperforming debt eventually forced Beijing to spend $60 billion from central government coffers to bail out the banks, after which then Premier Zhu Rongji pushed through a reorganization that transferred final authority over personnel and loan decisions to the banks' headquarters. Banking reform may offer a promising model for the restructuring that the judicial system needs.

According to the 1999 amendment to the constitution, China is now officially a "country governed according to law." But the CCP, not the government, holds ultimate power. An increasing number of scholars argue that what the country needs, therefore, is a party and party members who unambiguously understand that they are not above the law.

One proponent of this view, Professor Zhuo Zeyuan, of the Central Party School, last year gave a two-hour talk on his ideas to all 24 members of the Politburo. A Central Party School leader told me later that the proper relationship between the ruling party and the constitution was unambiguous: the CCP should be governed by the law. As with so many things in China today, the rub is the gap between theory and practice.

The CCP firmly maintains the levers that control the courts and manipulates them when necessary. In addition, it operates a separate, parallel system for dealing with errant party members that includes the use of detention and interrogation and in some cases is more draconian than the regular legal system. Recently, there have been signs that the party may be starting to see the need for more due process in its practices. Professor Jerome Cohen, of New York University Law School, one of the West's foremost experts on the Chinese legal system, has noted that local party organizations in at least 20 provinces have established a disciplinary system for CCP members that includes guarantees such as a notice of alleged wrongdoing, the opportunity to defend oneself against charges (including the right to call supporting witnesses), a statement of reasons for a final decision, and an opportunity to appeal. Some of these rights have long been in the CCP charter but were never implemented seriously.

Chinese leaders appear to realize that the China of 2008 is far too complex to be ruled entirely by fiat from Beijing and has to be governed by laws through a competent legal system enjoying the public's confidence. Lack of faith in the courts is one reason people take to the streets, and official figures show that tens of thousands of public protests occur in China each year. It is not surprising then that leaders such as Premier Wen want the party and the state to stop interfering in routine judicial matters. But the leadership still insists on controlling sensitive cases and the judicial system at the macro level. The question is whether the CCP can succeed in building a fair and independent judicial system while maintaining control at the very top.

OVERSIGHT

The Chinese system does not lack for institutions meant to keep officials honest. The oldest of these is the traditional petition system, dating to the imperial era, which allows people to take their grievances directly to higher authorities. Each ministry in Beijing has an office that handles such complaints. But the petition is seen as a last resort, and few cases are satisfactorily resolved: the process is opaque and depends on the goodwill of the anonymous officials evaluating the appeals.

Another oversight institution, the CCP's Central Commission for Discipline Inspection, staffed by eight deputies and 120 senior members and headed by a Politburo Standing Committee member, is charged with fighting corruption and other misconduct by party members. Its counterparts on the government side are the Ministry of Supervision and the Anti-Corruption Bureau of the Supreme People's Procuratorate, responsible for prosecuting errant government officials. One of the functions of the official Xinhua News Agency, finally, is to gather information on corruption nationwide and produce internal reports for the central leadership.

Yet despite these multiple mechanisms, the problem of official corruption remains serious, and leaders routinely cite moral turpitude as one of the party's main challenges. As the economy has surged for more than two decades, so have opportunities for graft. High-profile cases such as that of Zheng Xiaoyu, the former head of the State Food and Drug Administration executed this past July for taking bribes from pharmaceutical companies, feed the perception of endemic rot. According to the CCP, over 97,000 officials were disciplined in 2006, of whom 80 percent were guilty of dereliction of duty, taking bribes, or violating financial regulations. "The formal [supervision] system on the whole has failed," one government researcher told me. At lower levels, a basic structural flaw in the supervision system mirrors that of the courts: the heads of the discipline inspection commissions are appointed by local leaders, who predictably tend to select relatives, friends, protégés, or colleagues. It was only in 2006 that a rule was implemented requiring that commission heads at the provincial level be appointed by the central government.

President Hu and Premier Wen face a basic dilemma. They know that rooting out corruption, which makes citizens cynical about one-party rule, must be their top governance priority. But they must act while maintaining the loyalty of local officials, through whom the CCP governs the country. To augment the formal mechanisms of supervision, the government is increasingly turning to alternative channels. In Beijing, some districts are using public opinion polling to gauge satisfaction with individual government offices, and Beijing's Urban Planning Commission has retained a consulting firm to help it take better account of public opinion in assessing redevelopment projects.

Another promising trend is the rapid commercialization of the Chinese press. The government still exercises extensive control over the media through government ownership of outlets and censorship. The redlines that journalists cannot cross still exist. But changes are taking place. As independent Chinese publications seek readers and advertisers, they pursue stories that people want to read; like their counterparts in the West, they have discovered that investigative journalism sells. In one widely discussed case, a veteran reporter for the China Economic Times wrote an in-depth account in 2002 of the Beijing taxi-licensing system. Due to alleged collusion between company owners and the government supervisory body, drivers were being forced to work shockingly long hours for low wages. The newspaper sold out almost immediately. The Central Propaganda Bureau responded by banning other publications from reporting on the story. The city's Transportation Bureau ordered drivers not to read the article. Some of the taxi drivers quoted in the article received death threats, and the author had to be protected by bodyguards for three months. The public uproar mounted, however, as the news spread to the Internet. Eight days after the story was printed, then Vice Premier Wen Jiabao issued an official statement supporting the taxi drivers and directing that a report on the situation be prepared for then Premier Zhu Rongji.

One experiment that has caught the attention of many Chinese is the government's decision to allow foreign journalists to travel and report freely throughout China (with the exception of Tibet) from January 2007 through the 2008 Beijing Olympics. "It's clearly a test," a Chinese newspaper editor said, "to see how the foreign press uses its new freedom. Unless something goes terribly wrong, it's hard to see how the government can reimpose the old system when the Olympics are over." Not surprisingly, there have been numerous teething problems: in July, several foreign journalists covering an antigovernment demonstration held by an international human rights group were detained for several hours. Still, foreign correspondents in Beijing report that, in general, restrictions on their movements and activities have been relaxed noticeably since the new policy was announced.

In the past several years, the Internet and cell phones have started to challenge traditional media by becoming channels for the expression of citizen outrage, at times forcing the government to take action. One celebrated instance was the "nail house" incident in the sprawling metropolis of Chongqing, in central China. For three years, a middle-class couple stubbornly refused to sell their house to property developers who, with the municipal government's permission, planned to raze the entire area and turn it into a commercial district. The neighbors had long ago moved away. The developer tried to intimidate the couple by digging a three-story canyon around their lone house, but the tactic backfired spectacularly. Photos of their home's precarious situation were posted on the Internet, sparking outrage among Chinese across the country. Within weeks, tens of thousands of messages had been posted lambasting the Chongqing government for letting such a thing happen. Reporters camped out at the site; even official newspapers took up the couple's cause. In the end, the couple settled for a new house and over $110,000 in compensation. The widely read daily Beijing News ran a commentary that would have been inconceivable in a Chinese newspaper a decade ago: "This is an inspiration for the Chinese public in the emerging age of civil rights. . . . Media coverage of this event has been rational and constructive. This is encouraging for the future of citizens defending their rights according to the law."

In another example of the marriage of new technology and citizen action, last May angry residents in the southern coastal city of Xiamen launched a campaign to force the city government to stop the construction of a large chemical plant on the outskirts of the city. Their weapon was the cell phone. In a matter of days, hundreds of thousands of text messages opposing the plant were forwarded, spreading like a virus throughout the country. Xiamen authorities, who had ignored popular opposition to the plant before, suddenly announced that construction would be suspended until an environmental impact study could be completed. Dissatisfied with this half measure, citizens again used message networking to organize a march of some 7,000 people to demand a permanent halt to the construction. Although local party newspapers blasted the protest as illegal, it was allowed to proceed without incident, marking one of the largest peaceful demonstrations in China in recent years.

DEMOCRACY IN CHINA

Recent progress in elections, judicial independence, and oversight is part of the transformation of Chinese society and the expansion of personal freedoms that have accompanied three decades of breakneck economic reform and development. The government remains intrusive in many areas but much less so than before.

In the past 20 years, several hundred million Chinese have migrated from the countryside to the cities—the largest wave of rapid urbanization in history. Until a decade ago, the government enforced stringent controls on internal migration. Today, officials cite the additional 300 million farmers expected to move to cities over the next two decades as a positive force that will help alleviate China's urban-rural income gap. The state once assigned jobs and housing to every urban resident. Now, urban Chinese enjoy overseas travel to study, work, or play. Ten years ago, a Chinese citizen needed to get permission from his supervisor, his work unit's party secretary, and the local police just to apply for a passport, a process that could take six months, assuming the passport was approved at all. The entire procedure takes less than a week today, and approval is nearly as automatic as it is in the United States. Less than two decades ago, all foreigners in Beijing were forced to live in designated locations, such as hotels or compounds guarded by military police. Today, foreigners and Chinese live side by side. When Chinese are asked about the democratization of their society, they are as likely to mention these sorts of changes as they are elections or judicial reform. They may be confusing the concept of liberty with that of democracy, but it would be a mistake to dismiss the expansion of their personal freedom as insignificant. A senior Communist Party official I know marveled privately that ten years ago it would have been unimaginable for someone in his position to even be having an open discussion about democracy with an American. Now, the debate in China is no longer about whether to have democracy, he said, but about when and how. One thing the party should do immediately, he felt, was reform the National People's Congress so that it does not become a "retirement home" for former officials; the National People's Congress should be populated by competent professionals and eventually become a true legislative body. The government should also implement direct elections up to the provincial level, he argued, not Western-style multiparty elections but at least a contest involving a real choice of candidates.

The chair of one of China's largest corporations, who is also an alternate member of the CCP Central Committee, told me that better corporate governance in companies listed on overseas stock exchanges (and thus held to international norms), such as his, was another example of the expansion of "democratic habits" in China. Although corporate governance in China remains a work in progress, this chair said, the general trend among state-owned enterprises, especially those listed abroad, is toward greater transparency, stronger and more independent boards of directors, and management by mutually agreed rules. Over time, working in such an environment is likely to inculcate more democratic patterns of thinking in China's business elite, as well as in senior government officials who sit on the boards of state-owned enterprises.

Over the last century, no one has thought more about the promise of democracy in their country or been more dismayed by its elusiveness than the Chinese themselves. Again and again, they have witnessed a native democratic impulse surge and crash or be crushed prematurely. The empress dowager Cixi quashed the 1898 "hundred days of reform" initiated by advisers to the emperor Guangxu. The optimism that surrounded Sun's inauguration as provisional president of the Chinese Republic on January 1, 1912, was soon extinguished by the military ruler Yuan Shikai, who tried to crown himself as the first emperor of a new dynasty in 1915. Progressives within both the Nationalist and the Communist Parties espoused democratic forms of government in the 1930s before the onslaught of wars with Japan and then with each other. The establishment of the People's Republic in 1949 augured an era of self-determination, prosperity, and democracy. But that hope was crushed under the foot of Mao's relentless political campaigns, culminating in the Cultural Revolution. Before the tragedy of Tiananmen in 1989, the 1980s were a period of intense political ferment, when democracy was debated inside the government, think tanks, universities, and intellectual salons.

Compared to in those periods, the way in which China's leaders talk about democracy today may seem cautious. Critics argue that this reflects the government's lack of real commitment to political reform. Optimists believe that gradualism will make the current liberalization last longer than the euphoric, but ultimately failed, experiences of the past. One of China's elder statesman—who has known personally all of the country's top leaders since Mao—insisted to me that democracy has always been the "common aspiration" of the Chinese people. They are determined to get it right, he argued, but they require patience from the West. "Please let the Chinese experiment," he said. "Let us explore."

Where that exploration will lead is an open question. There is a range of views among Chinese about how long will be required for democracy to take root, but there is also some agreement. One official put it this way: "No one predicts five years. Some think ten to 15. Some say 30 to 35. And no one says 60." Others predict that the process will take at least two more generational changes in the CCP's leadership—a scenario that would place its advent around the year 2022.

In 2004, a survey was conducted among nearly 700 local officials who had attended a provincial training program. More than 60 percent of the officials polled said that they were dissatisfied with the state of democracy in the country then, and 63 percent said that political reform in China was too slow. On the other hand, 59 percent of them said that economic development should take precedence over democracy. And tellingly, 67 percent of the cadres supported popular elections for village leaders and 41 percent supported elections for county heads, compared with only 13 percent for elections for provincial governors and just 9 percent for elections for China's president.

Some Chinese like to point out that it took the United States almost two centuries to achieve universal suffrage. In the first several American presidential elections, most states restricted voting to white male landowners—no more than ten percent of the adult U.S. population at the time. Women had to wait until the twentieth century, and blacks in effect until the 1960s. "This is one issue," a Beijing newspaper editor joked, "about which we Chinese may be less patient than you Americans."

Last spring, an article provocatively titled "Democracy Is a Good Thing" caused a small sensation in China. Published in a journal closely linked to the CCP, the article was authored by Yu Keping, the head of a think tank that reports directly to the CCP Central Committee. Although hardly blind to democracy's drawbacks (it "affords opportunities for certain sweet-talking political fraudsters to mislead the people"), Yu was forthright and specific in his approval of it: "Among all the political systems that have been invented and implemented, democracy is the one with the least number of flaws. That is to say, relatively speaking, democracy is the best political system for humankind."

Yu did not predict an easy road to democracy in China. "Under conditions of democratic rule," he observed, "officials must be elected by the citizens and they must gain the endorsement and support of the majority of the people; their powers will be curtailed by the citizens, they cannot do whatever they want, they have to sit down across from the people and negotiate. Just these two points alone already make many people dislike it. Therefore, democratic politics will not operate on its own; it requires the people themselves and the government officials who represent the interests of the people to promote and implement [it]."

Clearly, some people at the center of the Chinese system are thinking actively about these fundamental questions. The issue is whether and how these ideas will be translated into practice. China must now complete the transition begun in recent years, from a system that relies on the authority and judgment of one or a few dominating figures to a government run by commonly accepted and binding rules. The institutionalization of power is shared by all countries that have successfully made the transition to democracy. China's ongoing experiments with local elections, reform of the judicial system, and the strengthening of oversight are all part of the shift to a more rule-based system. So are the ways in which Chinese society continues to open and diversify, incrementally creating a civil society.

Institutionalization may progress the most over the next few years in an area that could be decisive in determining China's political evolution: leadership succession. How a country manages the transfer of power at the very top sends an unmistakable signal to all levels below. On this point, China has already come some way. To be chosen as Mao's successor was the most perilous position one could be put in. Deng had his own problems anointing a durable successor; he remained the most powerful man in China for nearly a decade after relinquishing all his official posts in 1989. It was his successor, Jiang, who saw the first peaceful transfer of power in modern Chinese history, when he gave up his positions to Hu. Jiang has remained a power behind the scenes, but no one would suggest that he holds the influence that Deng did.

One senior leader told me that the issue of succession can no longer be managed effectively in the ad hoc manner of the past. Both China and the world have changed too much; the process of selecting the country's leaders needs to be institutionalized. The problem, he explained, was that an acceptable new process has yet to be put in place, and until one is, it would be impractical to jettison the old system. China finds itself in an ambiguous transition at the moment. For his part, this leader believed that progress might be seen by the time of the Third Plenum of the 17th Party Congress, in 2009. Some party members have even suggested that Hu's heir as general secretary of the CCP could be chosen through a vote of the entire Central Committee when Hu retires in 2012. The method by which Hu's successor is selected will be an unmistakable indicator of the political future China's current generation of leaders envisions—signaling whether they believe, as Sun did a century ago, that democracy can best deliver the prosperity, independence, and liberty for which the Chinese people have struggled and sacrificed for so many years.

The Life of the Party

The Post-Democratic Future Begins in China

Eric X. Li

In November 2012, the Chinese Communist Party (CCP) held its 18th National Congress, setting in motion a once-in-a-decade transfer of power to a new generation of leaders. As expected, Xi Jinping took over as general secretary and will become the president of the People's Republic this March. The turnover was a smooth and well-orchestrated demonstration by a confidently rising superpower. That didn't stop international media and even some Chinese intellectuals, however, from portraying it as a moment of crisis. In an issue that was published before the beginning of the congress, for example, *The Economist* quoted unnamed scholars at a recent conference as saying that China is "unstable at the grass roots, dejected at the middle strata and out of control at the top." To be sure, months before the handover, the scandal surrounding Bo Xilai, the former party boss of the Chongqing municipality, had shattered the CCP's long-held facade of unity, which had underwritten domestic political stability since the Tiananmen Square upheavals in 1989. To make matters worse, the Chinese economy, which had sustained double-digit GDP growth for two decades, slowed, decelerating for seven straight quarters. China's economic model of rapid industrialization, labor-intensive manufacturing, large-scale government investments in infrastructure, and export growth seemed to have nearly run its course. Some in

ERIC X. LI is a venture capitalist and political scientist in Shanghai.

Eric X. Li

China and the West have gone so far as to predict the demise of the one-party state, which they allege cannot survive if leading politicians stop delivering economic miracles.

Such pessimism, however, is misplaced. There is no doubt that daunting challenges await Xi. But those who suggest that the CCP will not be able to deal with them fundamentally misread China's politics and the resilience of its governing institutions. Beijing will be able to meet the country's ills with dynamism and resilience, thanks to the CCP's adaptability, system of meritocracy, and legitimacy with the Chinese people. In the next decade, China will continue to rise, not fade. The country's leaders will consolidate the one party model and, in the process, challenge the West's conventional wisdom about political development and the inevitable march toward electoral democracy. In the capital of the Middle Kingdom, the world might witness the birth of a post-democratic future.

ON-THE-JOB LEARNING

The assertion that one-party rule is inherently incapable of self-correction does not reflect the historical record. During its 63 years in power, the CCP has shown extraordinary adaptability. Since its founding in 1949, the People's Republic has pursued a broad range of economic policies. First, the CCP initiated radical land collectivization in the early 1950s. This was followed by the policies of the Great Leap Forward in the late 1950s and the Cultural Revolution in the late 1960s to mid-1970s. After them came the quasi-privatization of farmland in the early 1960s, Deng Xiaoping's market reforms in the late 1970s, and Jiang Zemin's opening up of the CCP's membership to private businesspeople in the 1990s. The underlying goal has always been economic health, and when a policy did not work-for example, the disastrous Great Leap Forward and Cultural Revolution-China was able to find something that did: for example, Deng's reforms, which catapulted the Chinese economy into the position of second largest in the world.

On the institutional front as well, the CCP has not shied away from reform. One example is the introduction in the 1980s and 1990s of term limits for most political positions (and even of age limits, of 68–70, for the party's most senior leadership). Before this, political leaders had been able to use their positions to accumulate power and perpetuate their rules. Mao Zedong was a case in point. He had ended the civil wars that had plagued China and repelled foreign invasions to become the father of modern China. Yet his prolonged rule led to disastrous mistakes, such as the Cultural Revolution. Now, it is nearly impossible for the few at the top to consolidate long-term power. Upward mobility within the party has also increased.

In terms of foreign policy, China has also changed course many times to achieve national greatness. It moved from a close alliance with Moscow in the 1950s to a virtual alliance with the United States in the 1970s and 1980s as it sought to contain the Soviet Union. Today, its pursuit of a more independent foreign policy has once more put it at odds with the United States. But in its ongoing quest for greatness, China is seeking to defy recent historical precedents and rise peacefully, avoiding the militarism that plagued Germany and Japan in the first half of the last century.

As China undergoes its ten-year transition, calls at home and abroad for another round of political reform have increased. One radical camp in China and abroad is urging the party to allow multiparty elections or at least accept formal intraparty factions. In this view, only full-scale adversarial politics can ensure that China gets the leadership it needs. However sincere, these demands all miss a basic fact: the CCP has arguably been one of the most self-reforming political organizations in recent world history. There is no doubt that China's new leaders face a different world than Hu Jintao did when he took over in 2002, but chances are good that Xi's CCP will be able to adapt to and meet whatever new challenges the rapidly changing domestic and international environments pose. In part, that is because the CCP is heavily meritocratic and promotes those with proven experience and capabilities.

MAKING THE GRADE

China watchers in the West have used reports of corruption—compounded by sensational political scandals such as the Bo Xilai affair—to portray the ruling party as incurably diseased. The disease exists, to be sure, but the most important treatment is the party itself. As counterintuitive as it might seem to Westerners, the CCP, whose political preeminence is enshrined in the Chinese constitution, is one of the most meritocratic political institutions in the world.

Of the 25 members that made up the pre-18th-Congress Politburo, the highest ruling body of the CCP, only five (the so-called princelings) came from privileged backgrounds. The other 20, including the president, Hu, and the premier, Wen Jiabao, came from middle-or lower-class backgrounds. In the CCP's larger Central Committee, which was made up of more than 300 people, the percentage of people born into wealth and power was even smaller. The vast majority of those in government worked and competed their way through the ranks to the top. Admittedly, the new general secretary, Xi, is the son of a previous party leader. However, an overwhelming number of those who moved up the ranks this past fall had humbler beginnings.

So how does China ensure meritocracy? At the heart of the story is a powerful institution that is seldom studied in the West, the Organization Department of the CCP. This department carries out an elaborate process of bureaucratic selection, evaluation, and promotion that would be the envy of any corporation. Patronage continues to play a role, but by and large, merit determines who will rise through the ranks.

Every year, the government and its affiliated organizations recruit university graduates into entry-level positions in one of the three state-controlled systems: the civil service, state-owned enterprises, and government-affiliated social organizations such as universities or community programs. Most new recruits enter at the lowest level, or *ke yuan*. After a few years, the Organization Department reviews their performance and can promote them up through four increasingly elite managerial ranks: *fu ke, ke, fu chu*, and *chu*. The range of positions at these levels is wide, covering anything from running the health-care system in a poor village to attracting commercial investment in a city district. Once a year, the Organization Department reviews quantitative performance records for each official in each of these grades; carries out interviews with superiors, peers, and subordinates; and vets personal conduct. Extensive and frequent public opinion surveys are also conducted on questions ranging from satisfaction with the country's general direction to opinions about more mundane and specific local policies. Once the department has gathered a complete dossier on all the candidates, and has confirmed the public's general satisfaction or dissatisfaction with their performances, committees discuss the data and promote winners.

After this stage, public employees' paths diverge, and individuals can be rotated through and out of all three tracks (the civil service, state-owned enterprises, and social organizations). An official might start out working on economic policy and then move to a job dealing with political or social issues. He or she could go from a traditional government position to a managerial role in a state-owned enterprise or a university. In many cases, the Organization Department will also send a large number of promising officials abroad to learn best practices around the world. The likes of Harvard University's Kennedy School of Government and the National University of Singapore regularly host Chinese officials in their training programs.

Over time, the most successful workers are promoted again, to what are known as the *fu ju* and *ju* levels, at which point a typical assignment is to manage districts with populations in the millions or companies with hundreds of millions of dollars in revenues. To get a sense of how rigorous the selection process is, in 2012, there were 900,000 officials at the *fu ke* and *ke* levels and 600,000 at the *fu chu* and *chu* levels. There were only 40,000 at the *fu ju* and *ju* levels.

After the *ju* level, a very talented few move up several more ranks and eventually make it to the party's Central Committee.

The entire process could take two to three decades, and most of those who make it to the top have had managerial experience in just about every sector of Chinese society. Indeed, of the 25 Politburo members before the 18th Party Congress, 19 had run provinces larger than most countries in the world and ministries with budgets higher than that of the average nation's government. A person with Barack Obama's pre-presidential professional experience would not even be the manager of a small county in China's system.

Xi's career path is illustrative. Over the course of 30 years, Xi rose from being a *fu ke* level deputy county chief in a poor village to party secretary of Shanghai and a member of the Politburo. By the time he made it to the top, Xi had already managed areas with total populations of over 150 million and combined GDPs of more than $1.5 trillion. His career demonstrates that meritocracy drives Chinese politics and that those who end up leading the country have proven records.

INNOVATE OR STAGNATE

China's centralized meritocracy also fosters government entrepreneurship. The practice of conducting top-down policy experiments in select locales and expanding the successful ones nationwide is well documented. The best-known example is Deng's creation of "special economic zones" in the 1980s. The first such zone was in Shenzhen. The district was encouraged to operate under market principles rather than the dictates of central planners. Shenzhen's economy grew rapidly, which prompted the central government to replicate the program in the cities of Zhuhai and Shantou, in Guangdong Province; Xiamen, in Fujian Province; and throughout Hainan Province.

There are also thousands of policy experiments that rise up from the local level. The competitive government job market gives capable local officials incentives to take risks and differentiate themselves from the pack. Among the 2,326 party representatives who attended the 18th Party Congress, one such standout was Qiu

He, who is vice party secretary of Yunnan Province. At the congress, Qiu was selected as an alternate member of the Central Committee, putting the 55-year-old maverick near the top of the nation's political establishment. Qiu is the ultimate political entrepreneur. Born into poverty in rural China, Qiu watched two of his eight siblings die of childhood illness and malnutrition. After taking the national college entrance exam, China's great equalizer, he was able to attend university. When he entered the work force, he held several low-level civil service jobs before being appointed party secretary of Shuyang County, in northern Jiangsu Province, in the 1990s. With a peasant population of 1.7 million and an annual per capita GDP of only $250 (less than one-fifth the national average), Shuyang was one of the poorest rural areas in the country. The county also suffered from the worst crime rate in the region and endemic government corruption.

Qiu carried out a broad range of risky and controversial policy experiments that, if they failed, would have sunk his political career. His first focus was Shuyang's floundering economy. In 1997, Qiu initiated a mandatory municipal bond purchase program. The policy required every county resident to purchase bonds to fund much-needed infrastructure development. The genius of the plan was twofold. First, he could not have raised the funds through taxes because, at his level, he had no taxation authority. Second, the mandatory bond program offered the citizens of Shuyang something taxes would not have: yes, they were required to buy the bonds, but they eventually got their money back, with interest. Qiu also assigned quotas to almost every county government official for attracting commercial investments. To support their efforts, in addition to building up the area's infrastructure, Qiu offered favorable tax rates and cheap land concessions to businesses. In just a few years, thousands of private enterprises sprang up and transformed a dormant, centrally planned rural community into a vibrant market economy.

Qiu's second focus was combating corruption and mistrust between the population and the government. In the late 1990s, he instituted two unprecedented measures to make the selection of officials more open and competitive. One was to post upcoming official appointments in advance of the final decisions to allow for a public comment period.

The other was the introduction of a two-tier voting system that enabled villagers to vote among party members for their preferred candidates for certain positions. The local party committee then picked between the top two vote getters.

Qiu initially met tremendous resistance from the local bureaucracy and population. But today, he is credited with turning one of the country's most backward regions into a vibrant urban center of commerce and manufacturing. Other poor regions have adopted many of his economic policy experiments. Moreover, the public commenting period has been widely adopted across China. Competitive voting is finding its way into ever-higher levels of the party hierarchy. Qiu has been personally rewarded, too, moving rapidly up the ladder: to vice governor of Jiangsu Province, mayor of Kunmin, vice party secretary of Yunnan Province, and now an alternate member of the Central Committee.

BY POPULAR DEMAND

Even if critics accept that the Chinese government is adaptable and meritocratic, they still question its legitimacy. Westerners assume that multiparty elections are the only source of political legitimacy. Because China does not hold such elections, they argue, the CCP's rule rests on inherently shaky ground. Following this logic, critics have predicted the party's collapse for decades, but no collapse has come. The most recent version of the argument is that the CCP has maintained its hold on power only because it has delivered economic growth—so-called performance legitimacy.

No doubt, performance is a major source of the party's popularity. In a poll of Chinese attitudes published by the Pew Research Center in 2011, 87 percent of respondents noted satisfaction with the general direction of the country, 66 percent reported significant progress in their lives in the past five years, and a whopping

74 percent said they expected the future to be even better. Performance legitimacy, however, is only one source of the party's popular support. Much more significant is the role of Chinese nationalism and moral legitimacy.

When the CCP built the Monument to the People's Heroes at the center of Tiananmen Square in 1949, it included a frieze depicting the struggles of the Chinese to establish the People's Republic. One would expect the CCP, a Marxist-Leninist party, to have its most symbolic political narrative begin with communism—the writing of *The Communist Manifesto*, for example, or perhaps the birth of the CCP in 1921. Instead, the first carving of the frieze depicts an event from 1839: the public burning of imported opium by the Qing dynasty's imperial minister, Lin Zexu, which triggered the first Opium War. China's subsequent loss to the British inaugurated the so-called century of humiliation. In the following hundred years, China suffered countless invasions, wars, and famines—all, in the popular telling, to reach 1949. And today, the Monument to the People's Heroes remains a sacred public site and the most significant symbol of the CCP's national moral authority.

The CCP's role in saving and modernizing China is a far more durable source of its legitimacy than the country's economic performance. It explains why, even at the worst times of the party's rule in the past 63 years, including the disastrous Great Leap Forward and Cultural Revolution, the CCP was able to keep the support of mainstream Chinese long enough for it to correct its mistakes. China's recent achievements, from economic growth to space exploration, are only strengthening nationalist sentiments in the country, especially among the youth. The party can count on their support for decades to come.

A final type of staying power comes from repression, which China watchers in the West claim is the real force behind the CCP. They point to censorship and the regime's harsh treatment of dissidents, which undoubtedly exist. Still, the party knows very well that general repression is not sustainable. Instead, it seeks to employ smart containment. The strategy is to give the vast majority of people the widest range possible of personal liberties. And today, Chinese people are freer than at any other period in recent memory; most of them can live where they want and work as they choose, go into business without hindrance, travel within and out of the country, and openly criticize the government online without retaliation. Meanwhile, state power focuses on containing a small number of individuals who have political agendas and want to topple the one-party system. As any casual observer would know, over the last ten years, the quantity of criticism against the government online and in print has increased exponentially—without any reprisals. Every year, there are tens of thousands of local protests against specific policies. Most of the disputes are resolved peacefully. But the government deals forcefully with the very few who aim to subvert China's political system, such as Liu Xiaobo, an activist who calls for the end of single-party rule and who is currently in jail.

That is not to say that there aren't problems. Corruption, for one, could seriously harm the CCP's reputation. But it will not derail party rule anytime soon. Far from being a problem inherent to the Chinese political system, corruption is largely a byproduct of the country's rapid transformation. When the United States was going through its industrialization 150 years ago, violence, the wealth gap, and corruption in the country were just as bad as, if not worse than, in China today. According to Transparency International, China ranks 75th in global corruption and is gradually getting better. It is less corrupt than Greece (80th), India (95th), Indonesia and Argentina (tied at 100th), and the Philippines (129th)—all of which are electoral democracies. Understood in such a context, the Chinese government's corruption is by no means insurmountable. And the party's deeply rooted popular support will allow it the breathing room to grapple with even the toughest problems.

ENTER THE DRAGON

China's new leaders will govern the country for the next ten years, during which they will rely on the CCP's adaptability, meritocracy, and legitimacy to tackle major challenges. The current economic slowdown is worrying, but it is largely cyclical, not structural. Two forces will reinvigorate the economy for at least another generation: urbanization and entrepreneurship. In 1990, only about 25 percent of Chinese lived in cities. Today, 51 percent do. Before 2040, a full 75 percent—nearly one billion people—are expected to be urban. The amount of new roads, housing, utilities, and communications infrastructure needed to accommodate this expansion is astounding. Therefore, any apparent infrastructure or housing bubbles will be momentary. In fact, China's new leadership will need to continue or even increase investment in these sectors in the years to come. That investment and the vast new urban work force, with all its production and consumption, will drive high economic growth rates. The party's extraordinary ability to develop and execute policy and its political authority will help it manage these processes.

Meanwhile, entrepreneurship will help China overcome threats to its export-fueled economic model. Externally, the global economic downturn and a rising currency value have dampened Chinese trade. Internally, labor costs have risen in the country's coastal manufacturing regions. But the market will sort out these problems. After all, China's economic miracle was not just a centrally planned phenomenon. Beijing facilitated the development of a powerful market economy, but private entrepreneurs are the lifeblood of the system. And these entrepreneurs are highly adaptive. Already, some low-end manufacturing has moved inland to contain labor costs. This is coinciding with local governments' aggressive infrastructure investments and innovative efforts to attract new business. In the costal regions, many companies are producing increasingly-high-value goods.

Of course, the government will need to make some economic adjustments. For one, many state-owned enterprises have grown too big, crowding out the private-sector growth that is critical to economic vitality. Plans to require companies to pay out dividends to shareholders and other limits on expansion are already in the works. These will likely be implemented early on in the new administration. And some stalled measures encouraging financial liberalization, such as allowing the market to determine interest rates and the development of private small and medium-sized lending institutions, which would break the large state-owned banks' near monopoly in commercial lending, are likely to get picked up. These reforms would facilitate more efficient flows of capital to businesses.

Economic liberalization will likely be matched by a two-track reform of social policy. First, the process of making the party more inclusive, which began with Jiang's inclusion of businesspeople in the CCP, will be accelerated. Second, the CCP will begin experimenting with outsourcing certain social welfare functions to approved nongovernmental organizations. Rapid urbanization is facilitating the growth of a large middle-income society. Instead of demanding abstract political rights, as many in the West expected, urban Chinese are focused on what are called *min sheng* (livelihood) issues. The party may not be able to manage these concerns alone. And so private businesses or nongovernmental organizations might be called in to provide health care and education in the cities, which has already started to happen in Guangdong Province.

Corruption remains the hardest nut to crack. In recent years, family members of some party leaders have used their political influence to build up large networks of commercial interests. Cronyism is spreading from the top down, which could eventually threaten the party's rule. The CCP has articulated a three-pronged strategy to attack the problem, which the new leadership will carry out. The most important institution for containing corruption is the CCP's Central Commission for Discipline Inspection. Its leader usually sits on the Standing Committee of the Politburo and has more power than the state judiciary. This person can detain and interrogate party members suspected of corruption without legal limits. In recent years, the commission has been very aggressive. In 2011, it conducted formal investigations into 137,859 cases that resulted in disciplinary actions or legal convictions against party officials. This number represents a nearly fourfold increase since the years before 1989, when corruption was one of the main issues that drove the Tiananmen protests. One sign to watch in the next administration is whether the commission is authorized to investigate wrongdoing within the inner sanctum of the party leadership, where corruption can be the most detrimental to the party's credibility.

Complementing the party's own antigraft efforts is the increasing independence of media outlets, both state- and privately owned. News organizations have already exposed cases of official corruption and disseminated their findings on the Internet. The CCP has responded by pursuing some of the cases that the media have brought to light. Of course, this system is not perfect, and some media outlets are themselves corrupt. Illicit payments to journalists and fabricated stories are commonplace. If these problems are not corrected quickly, Chinese media will lose what little credibility they have gained.

Accordingly, the next administration might develop more sophisticated political regulations and legal constraints on journalists to provide space for the sector to mature. Officials have already discussed instituting a press law that would protect legitimate, factual reporting and penalize acts of libel and misrepresentation. Some might view the initiative as the government reining in journalists, but the larger impact would be to make the media more credible in the eyes of the Chinese public. Journalists who take bribes or invent rumors to attract readers can hardly check government corruption.

Also to tackle corruption, the party plans to increase open competition within its own ranks, inspired by the efforts of officials such as Qiu. The hope is that such competition will air dirty laundry and discourage unseemly behavior. The Hu administration initiated an "intraparty democracy" program to facilitate direct competition for seats on party committees, an idea that received high praise at the 18th Congress.

Eric X. Li

HISTORY'S RESTART

Should the 18th Party Congress' initiatives succeed, 2012 might one day be seen as marking the end of the idea that electoral democracy is the only legitimate and effective system of political governance. While China's might grows, the West's ills multiply: since winning the Cold War, the United States has, in one generation, allowed its middle class to disintegrate. Its infrastructure languishes in disrepair, and its politics, both electoral and legislative, have fallen captive to money and special interests. Its future generations will be so heavily indebted that a sustained decline in average living standards is all but certain. In Europe, too, monumental political, economic, and social distress has caused the European project to run aground. Meanwhile, during the same period, China has lifted hundreds of millions of people out of poverty and is now a leading industrial powerhouse.

The West's woes are self-inflicted. Claims that Western electoral systems are infallible have hampered self-correction. Elections are seen as ends in themselves, not merely means to good governance. Instead of producing capable leaders, electoral politics have made it very difficult for good leaders to gain power. And in the few cases when they do, they are paralyzed by their own political and legal systems. As U.S. Secretary of State Hillary Clinton travels around the world extolling electoral democracy, the legitimacy of nearly all U.S. political institutions is crumbling. The approval rating of the U.S. Congress among the American people stood at 18 percent in November. The president was performing somewhat better, with ratings in the 50s. And even support for the politically independent Supreme Court had fallen below 50 percent.

Many developing countries have already come to learn that democracy doesn't solve all their problems. For them, China's example is important. Its recent success and the failures of the West offer a stark contrast. To be sure, China's political model will never supplant electoral democracy because, unlike the latter, it does not pretend to be universal. It cannot be exported. But its success does show that many systems of political governance can work when they are congruent with a country's culture and history. The significance of China's success, then, is not that China provides the world with an alternative but that it demonstrates that successful alternatives exist. Twenty-four years ago, the political scientist Francis Fukuyama predicted that all countries would eventually adopt liberal democracy and lamented that the world would become a boring place because of that. Relief is on the way. A more interesting age may be upon us.

Democratize or Die

Why China's Communists Face Reform or Revolution

Yasheng Huang

In 2011, standing in front of the Royal Society (the British academy of sciences), Chinese Premier Wen Jiabao declared, "Tomorrow's China will be a country that fully achieves democracy, the rule of law, fairness, and justice. Without freedom, there is no real democracy. Without guarantee of economic and political rights, there is no real freedom." Eric Li's article in these pages, "The Life of the Party," pays no such lip service to democracy. Instead, Li, a Shanghai-based venture capitalist, declares that the debate over Chinese democratization is dead: the Chinese Communist Party (CCP) will not only stay in power; its success in the coming years will "consolidate the one-party model and, in the process, challenge the West's conventional wisdom about political development." Li might have called the race too soon.

Li cites high public approval of China's general direction as evidence that the Chinese prefer the political status quo. In a country without free speech, however, asking people to directly evaluate their leaders' performance is a bit like giving a single-choice exam.

More rigorous surveys that frame questions in less politically sensitive ways directly contradict his conclusion. According to 2003 surveys cited in *How East Asians View Democracy*, edited by

YASHENG HUANG is Professor of Political Economy and International Management at the MIT Sloan School of Management and the author of *Capitalism With Chinese Characteristics: Entrepreneurship and the State*.

the researchers Yun-han Chu, Larry Diamond, Andrew Nathan, and Doh Chull Shin, 72.3 percent of the Chinese public polled said they believed that democracy is "desirable for our country now," and 67 percent said that democracy is "suitable for our country now." These two numbers track with those recorded for well-established East Asian democracies, including Japan, South Korea, and Taiwan.

There are calls for more democracy in China. It is true that the party's antireform bloc has had the upper hand since the 1989 Tiananmen Square crackdown. But recently, voices for reform within the CCP have been gaining strength, aided in large part by calls for honesty, transparency, and accountability from hundreds of millions of Internet-using Chinese citizens. China's new leaders seem at least somewhat willing to adopt a more moderate tone than their predecessors, who issued strident warnings against "westernization" of the Chinese political system. So far, what has held China back from democracy is not a lack of demand for it but a lack of supply. It is possible that the gap will start to close over the next ten years.

THE NOT-SO-GREAT WALL

Li acknowledges that China has problems, namely, slowing economic growth, the inadequate provision of social services, and corruption, but he claims that the CCP is more capable than any democratic government of fixing them. The CCP, Li argues, will be able to make tough decisions and follow through on them thanks to the party's ability to self-correct, its meritocratic structure, and its vast reserves of popular legitimacy.

In its six-decade rule, the CCP has tried everything from land collectivization to the Great Leap Forward and the Cultural Revolution to privatization. According to Li, that makes the CCP "one of the most self-reforming political organizations in recent world history." Unfortunately, China's prime minister does not have Li's confidence that Beijing has learned from the disasters of its past and can correct its mistakes. Last March, in response to myriad corruption and political scandals, Wen warned that without political reforms, "such historical tragedies as the Cultural Revolution may happen again."

China does seem light years beyond both the Great Leap Forward and the Cultural Revolution, which were disastrous for the country. But the party has never explicitly repudiated or accepted culpability for either, nor has it dealt with the question of how to prevent similar catastrophes in the future. In a system with no true accountability or checks and balances, Wen's worries—and those of hundreds of millions of Chinese who suffered through the horrors of those events—are sincere and justified.

After extolling the CCP's adaptability, Li moves on to praising its meritocracy. Here, he relates the story of Qiu He, who, thanks to his innovative public policies, rose from small-time apparatchik in a backward county to vice party secretary of Yunnan Province. The fact that the Chinese political system is sufficiently flexible to have allowed someone like Qiu to experiment with reforms is one reason it has not crumbled sooner. Nevertheless, it is odd that Li uses Qiu's story in his case against democracy. The features of the Chinese political system that allowed Qiu to experiment with policy innovations, subsidiarity (the organizational principle that matters should be handled by the lowest authority capable of addressing them) and federalism, are actually the foundation of any well-functioning democracy. Unlike in China, where the central government decrees subsidiarity and federalism, most democracies constitutionally enshrine the decentralization of political power.

There is another problem with the story: for each Qiu, there are countless Chinese politicians who were promoted up through the CCP for less positive reasons. Systematic data simply do not bear out Li's assertion that the Chinese political system as a whole is meritocratic. In a rigorous analysis of economic and political data, the political scientists Victor Shih, Christopher Adolph, and Mingxing Liu found no evidence that Chinese officials with good economic track records were more likely to be promoted than those who performed poorly. What matters most is patronage—what Wu

Si, a prominent historian and editor in China, calls the "hidden rule" of the promotion system.

Li contends that a person with the credentials of Barack Obama before he was elected U.S. president would not have gone far in Chinese politics. He is right, but so is the flip side. Consider Bo Xilai, the former member of the Politburo whose wife confessed to murder, who could mysteriously afford an expensive overseas education for his son on a public servant's salary, and who oversaw a red terror campaign against journalists and lawyers, torturing and throwing in jail an untold number of citizens without a modicum of due process. No one with Bo's record would go very far in the United States. In China, however, he excelled. And before his downfall, he possessed the same unchecked power as Qiu, which he used to resurrect the very elements of the Cultural Revolution that Wen spoke out against.

Another of Li's claims is about the popular legitimacy of the CCP. But corruption and abuse of power undermine that legitimacy. This is one of the lessons party leaders have drawn from the Bo Xilai affair. Remarkably, both Hu Jintao, the outgoing president, and Xi Jinping, the incoming one, have recently issued dire warnings that corruption could lead to the collapse of the party and the state. They are right, especially in light of China's ongoing economic slowdown. That is not to say that some individual CCP leaders are not still widely respected by the Chinese population. But these officials tend to have been the reformers of the party, such as Deng Xiaoping, who initiated China's market reforms beginning in the late 1970s, and Hu Yaobang, who was general secretary of the CCP during Deng's leadership. The fact that such reformers remain popular today provides the CCP with an opportunity: it could pursue a proactive reform agenda to achieve a gradual and peaceful transition to democracy, avoiding the chaos and upheavals that are engulfing the Middle East. But the key would be to start those reforms now.

THE TRUTH IS OUT THERE

After walking through the positives of China's political system, Li moves on to the problems with the West's. He sees all of the West's

Yasheng Huang

problems—a disintegrating middle class, broken infrastructure, indebtedness, politicians captured by special interests—as resulting from liberal democracy. But such problems are not limited to liberal democratic governments. Authoritarian regimes experience them, too. Think of the economic turmoil that struck the juntas of Latin America in the 1970s and 1980s and Indonesia in 1997. The only authoritarian governments that have historically managed to avoid financial crises were those with centrally planned economies that lacked financial systems to begin with. Instead of sharp cyclical ups and downs, those types of economies produce long-term economic stagnation.

Li cites Transparency International data to argue that many democracies are more corrupt than China. Putting aside the irony of using data from an organization committed to transparency to defend an opaque authoritarian system, Li's argument reveals a deeper analytic point. Uncovering corruption requires information. In a one-party system, real information is suppressed and scarce. The Indian Web site I Paid a Bribe was set up in 2010 as a way for Indians to post anonymously to report incidents of having needed to pay someone off to get a government service. As of November 2012, the Web site had recorded more than 21,000 reports of corruption. Yet when Chinese netizens tried to set up similar sites, such as I Made a Bribe and www.522phone.com, the government shut them down. It would therefore be useless to compare India's 21,000 reported incidents with China's zero and conclude that India is more corrupt. Yet that is essentially what Li did.

To be sure, there are many corrupt democracies. As Li points out, Argentina, Indonesia, and the Philippines have terrible track records on that score. But ruthless military dictators governed each of those countries for decades before they opened up. Those autocracies created the corrupt systems with which the new democracies must contend. Democracies should be taken to task for their failure to root out corruption, but no one should confuse the symptom with the cause. Worldwide, there is no question that autocracies as a whole are far more corrupt than democracies. As a 2004

Transparency International report revealed, the top three looting officials of the preceding two decades were Suharto, the ruler of Indonesia until 1998; Ferdinand Marcos, who led the Philippines until 1986; and Mobutu Sese Seko, president of the Democratic Republic of the Congo until 1997. These three dictators pillaged a combined $50 billion from their impoverished people.

Since 1990, according to a report briefly posted a few months ago on the Web site of China's central bank, corrupt Chinese officials—about 18,000 of them—have collectively funneled some $120 billion out of the country. That figure is equivalent to China's entire education budget between 1978 and 1998. Beyond the sheer financial loss, corruption has also led to extremely poor food-safety records, since officials are paid to not enforce regulations. A 2007 Asian Development Bank report estimated that 300 million people in China suffer from food-borne diseases every year. Food safety is not the only woe. Corruption leads to bridge and building collapses that kill and chemical factory spills that poison China's environment—and their cover-ups.

The problem is not that China is lenient on corruption. The government routinely executes complicit officials. And some are high ranking, such as Cheng Kejie, who was vice chair of the National People's Congress before he was executed in 2000, and Zheng Xiaoyu, director of the State Food and Drug Administration, who was executed in 2007. The problem is the absence of any checks and balances on their power and the lack of the best breaks on corruption of all, transparency and a free press.

DEMOCRACY IS COMING

Even as Li argues that the CCP's one-party system is the best China can get, he also lays out some sensible reforms for improving it. He proposes stronger nongovernmental organizations, which would help the government deliver better services; more independent media, which would help check corruption; and elements of so-called intraparty democracy, which would help air the party's "dirty laundry and discourage unseemly behavior." He is right. Ironically, these are all core components of a well-functioning democracy.

No country can adopt such foundational elements of democracy without eventually adopting the whole thing. It would be impossible to sustain vibrant primary elections or caucuses, such as that in Iowa, but have a central government that ruled like Stalin. Consider Taiwan, where democracy evolved over time. In the early 1970s, Chiang Ching-kuo, who was to become president in 1978, began to reform the ruling party, the Kuomintang, in order to allow local competitive elections, indigenous Taiwanese participation (before, only those living in mainland China had been allowed to stand for important positions), and public scrutiny of the party's budget process. He also released political prisoners and became more tolerant of the press and nongovernmental organizations. When an opposition party, the Democratic Progressive Party, sprang up in 1986, it was a natural outgrowth of Chiang's earlier reforms. For Taiwan, it was eventually impossible to draw a line between some democracy and full democracy. The same will be true for China.

And that is a good thing. Li is right that China has made huge economic and social gains in the past few decades. But it has also proved ineffective at creating inclusive growth, reducing income inequality, culling graft, and containing environmental damage. It is now time to give democracy a try. As the scholars David Lake and Matthew Baum have shown, democracies simply do a better job than authoritarian governments at providing public services. And countries that make the transition to democracy experience an immediate improvement. Already, China is seeing some of these effects: Nancy Qian, an economist at Yale University, has shown that the introduction of village elections in China has improved accountability and increased expenditures on public services.

It is unlikely that a democratic China would beat today's China in GDP growth, but at least the growth would be more inclusive. The benefits would flow not just to the government and to a small number of connected capitalists but to the majority of the Chinese population, because a well-functioning democracy advances the greatest good for the most possible.

Two aspects of the Chinese economy presage a path to democratization. One is the level of per capita GDP. China has already crossed what some social scientists believe to be the threshold beyond which most societies inevitably begin to democratize— between $4,000 and $6,000. As the China scholar Minxin Pei has pointed out, of the 25 countries with higher per capita GDPs than China that are not free or partially free, 21 of them are sustained by natural resources. Other than this exceptional category, countries become democratic as they get richer.

The second structural condition presaging democratization is that China's torrid growth will almost certainly slow down, heightening conflicts and making corruption a heavier burden to bear. When the economy is growing, people are willing to put up with some graft. When it isn't, the same level of corruption is intolerable. If China continues with its political status quo, conflicts are likely to escalate sharply, and the pace of capital flight from the country, already on the rise due to declining confidence in China's economic and political future, will accelerate. If not stemmed, the loss of confidence among economic elites will be extremely dangerous for the Chinese economy and could trigger substantial financial instabilities.

To be sure, democratization is in the CCP's hands. But on that score, too, things are getting better. Even some of China's establishment figures have come to believe that stability comes not from repression but from greater political and economic openness. On the eve of the 18th Party Congress, which was held in November, an open letter calling for more transparency and more intraparty democracy swirled around the Internet. One of the letter's authors was Chen Xiaolu, the youngest son of one of the most decorated marshals of the Chinese army, who was also a former vice premier and foreign minister and a trusted aid to former Premier Zhou Enlai. Chen and many other Chinese elites no longer believe the status quo is viable.

Yasheng Huang

Since 1989, the CCP has not adopted any genuine political re-forms, relying on high growth rates to maintain its rule. This strategy can work only when the economy is booming—something Beijing cannot take for granted. It matters tremendously whether the CCP proactively adopts political reforms or is forced to do so in reaction to a catastrophic crisis. It would be far better for the political system to change gradually and in a controlled manner, rather than through a violent revolution. The CCP could regain its prestige by reclaiming the mandate of reform, and it could improve China's political system without having to surrender its power. Not many autocratic regimes get this kind of an opportunity; the CCP should not squander it.

How China Is Ruled

Why It's Getting Harder for Beijing to Govern

David M. Lampton

C hina had three revolutions in the twentieth century. The first was the 1911 collapse of the Qing dynasty, and with it, the country's traditional system of governance. After a protracted period of strife came the second revolution, in 1949, when Mao Zedong and his Communist Party won the Chinese Civil War and inaugurated the People's Republic of China; Mao's violent and erratic exercise of power ended only with his death, in 1976.

The third revolution is ongoing, and so far, its results have been much more positive. It began in mid-1977 with the ascension of Deng Xiaoping, who kicked off a decades-long era of unprecedented reform that transformed China's hived-off economy into a global pacesetter, lifting hundreds of millions of Chinese out of poverty and unleashing a massive migration to cities. This revolution has continued through the tenures of Deng's successors, Jiang Zemin, Hu Jintao, and Xi Jinping.

Of course, the revolution that began with Deng has not been revolutionary in one important sense: the Chinese Communist

DAVID M. LAMPTON is George and Sadie Hyman Professor of China Studies and Director of SAIS-China at the Johns Hopkins School of Advanced International Studies. This essay is adapted from his book *Following the Leader: Ruling China, From Deng Xiaoping to Xi Jinping*, published by the University of California Press. © 2014 by the Regents of the University of California.

Party (CCP) has maintained its monopoly on political power. Yet the cliché that China has experienced economic reform but not political reform in the years since 1977 obscures an important truth: that political reform, as one Chinese politician told me confidentially in 2002, has "taken place quietly and out of view."

The fact is that China's central government operates today in an environment fundamentally different, in three key ways, from the one that existed at the beginning of Deng's tenure. First, individual Chinese leaders have become progressively weaker in relation to both one another and the rest of society. Second, Chinese society, as well as the economy and the bureaucracy, has fractured, multiplying the number of constituencies China's leaders must respond to, or at least manage. Third, China's leadership must now confront a population with more resources, in terms of money, talent, and information, than ever before.

For all these reasons, governing China has become even more difficult than it was for Deng. Beijing has reacted to these shifts by incorporating public opinion into its policymaking, while still keeping the basic political structures in place. Chinese leaders are mistaken, however, if they think that they can maintain political and social stability indefinitely without dramatically reforming the country's system of governance. A China characterized by a weaker state and a stronger civil society requires a considerably different political structure. It demands a far stronger commitment to the rule of law, with more reliable mechanisms—such as courts and legislatures—for resolving conflicts, accommodating various interests, and distributing resources. It also needs better government regulation, transparency, and accountability. Absent such developments, China will be in for more political turmoil in the future than it has experienced in the last four-plus decades. The aftershocks would no doubt be felt by China's neighbors and the wider world, given China's growing global reach. China's past reforms have created new circumstances to which its leaders must quickly adapt. Reform is like riding a bicycle: either you keep moving forward or you fall off.

NOT ALL LEADERS ARE THE SAME

According to the German sociologist Max Weber, governments can derive their authority from three sources: tradition, the qualities and charisma of an individual leader, and constitutional and legal norms. China, over the reform period, has shifted away from the first two types of legitimacy and toward something like the third.

Like Mao, Deng enjoyed a mix of traditional and charismatic authority. But the leaders who followed him earned their legitimacy in different ways. Jiang (who ruled from 1989 to 2002) and Hu (ruling from 2002 to 2012) to various extents were both designated as leaders by Deng himself, and Xi's elevation to the top position, in 2012, was the product of a collective political process within the CCP. Over time, a set of norms that regulate leadership selection has developed, including term and age limits, performance measures, and opinion polling within the party. Although important, these norms should not be mistaken for law—they are incomplete, informal, and reversible—but they do mark a dramatic departure from Mao's capricious system.

As the foundations of legitimacy have shifted, Deng's successors have seen their capacity to single-handedly initiate policies diminish. Although Deng did not enjoy the unbridled power that Mao did, when it came to strategic decisions, he could act authoritatively and decisively once he had consulted influential colleagues. Moreover, the scale and scope of his decisions were often enormous. Besides embarking on economic reform, Deng made other pivotal choices, such as rolling out the one-child policy in 1979, suppressing the Democracy Wall protest movement that same year, and, in 1989, declaring martial law and deploying troops in Beijing. And when it came to Taiwan, Deng felt secure enough to adopt a relaxed attitude toward the island, leaving the resolution of cross-strait relations to the next generation.

Jiang, Hu, and Xi, by contrast, have been more constrained. The difference was on full display in late 2012 and into 2013, as Xi took over from Hu. In the 1970s, in order to build ties with Japan, Deng was able to sidestep the explosive nationalist politics surrounding questions of sovereignty over the disputed Diaoyu Islands (known in Japan as the Senkaku Islands). But Xi, having just risen to the top post and eager to consolidate his power in the wake of Japan's September 2012 nationalization of the islands, felt obliged to act muscularly in response to Tokyo's move.

China, in other words, has gone from being ruled by strongmen with personal credibility to leaders who are constrained by collective decision-making, term limits and other norms, public opinion, and their own technocratic characters. As one senior Chinese diplomat put it to me in 2002, "Mao and Deng could decide; Jiang and the current leaders must consult."

China's rulers have strayed from Mao and Deng in another important respect: they have come to see their purpose less as generating enormous change and more as maintaining the system and enhancing its performance. Deng's goals were transformational. Deng sought to move China up the economic ladder and the global power hierarchy, and he did. He opened China up to foreign knowledge, encouraged China's young people to go abroad (an attitude influenced by his own formative years in France and the Soviet Union), and let comparative advantage, trade, and education work their magic.

Deng's successor, Jiang, came to power precisely because he represented a change in leadership style: in the wake of the 1989 Tiananmen Square protests, both the forces in favor of reform and those wary of it viewed him as capable and nonthreatening. But he eventually jumped off the fence on the side of rapid reform. Jiang got China into the World Trade Organization, set the stage for its first manned space mission, and articulated, for the first time, that the CCP needed to bring large numbers of creative and skilled people into its ranks. During his 13-year rule, China's economy grew at an average annual rate of 9.7 percent.

Yet Jiang, by virtue of both his character and his circumstances, was far from the transformational strongman Deng was. An engineer by training, Jiang was practical and focused on making things work. In 1992, for example, he told a group of Americans that a decade earlier, when he was a lower-ranking official, he had visited Chicago and paid special attention to the city's garbage collection because he hoped to find a solution to the problem of littered watermelon rinds back home. He then boasted to the Americans that as mayor of Shanghai, he had saved land by building corkscrew-shaped bridge on-ramps that reduced the need to displace city residents. Precipitous social change this was not, but Jiang's preoccupations materially improved the lives of ordinary Chinese.

Hu and his premier, Wen Jiabao, proved less transformational still. The evolution was foreseeable even in 2002, on the eve of Hu's assumption of power. "Another trend will be toward collective leadership, rather than supreme leaders," a senior Chinese diplomat told me at the time. "Future leaderships will be collective, more democratic; they will seek consensus rather than make arbitrary decisions. But the downside is that they will enjoy lesser amounts of authority. It will be more difficult for them to make bold decisions when bold decisions are needed." Hu enacted virtually no political or economic reforms; his most notable achievement was enhancing relations with Taiwan. The charitable interpretation of Hu's years in office is that he digested the sweeping changes Deng and Jiang had initiated.

Following his promotion to top party leader in November 2012, Xi impressively consolidated his authority in 2013, allowing a vigorous debate on reform to emerge, even as he has tightened restrictions on freedom of expression. The core of the debate concerns how to reinvigorate economic growth and the degree to which political change is a precondition for further economic progress.

After the Central Committee meeting of November 2013 (the Third Plenum), the Xi administration stated its intention to "comprehensively deepen reform" and has created a group to do so. The need for such a body signals that many policy disputes remain and that the central government intends to stay focused on change until at least 2020. But there simply is no clear-cut path forward, because in some areas, China needs marketization; in others, it needs decentralization; and in still others, it needs centralization.

Although many ambiguities remain, the thrust of emerging policy is to have the market play a decisive role in allocating resources, with Beijing leveling the domestic playing field between state enterprises and nonstate firms and simplifying bureaucratic approval processes. Foreigners can find things to like in the government's promise to "relax investment access, accelerate the construction of free-trade zones, and expand inland and coastal openness." Such policies would have political consequences, too, and the meeting's communiqué mentioned the need for changes in the judiciary and in local governments, while vaguely suggesting more rights for peasants. That said, in calling for the creation of a national security committee, it identified both internal and external security as major concerns. A long march lies ahead.

THE FRACTURED SOCIETY

These changes in individual leadership style have coincided with another tectonic shift: the pluralization of China's society, economy, and bureaucracy. During the Mao era, leaders asserted that they served only one interest—that of the Chinese masses. The job of the government was to repress recalcitrant forces and educate the people about their true interests. Governance was not about reconciling differences. It was about eliminating them.

Since Mao, however, China's society and bureaucracy have fragmented, making it harder for Beijing to make decisions and implement policies. To deal with the challenge, the Chinese government, particularly since Deng, has developed an authoritarian yet responsive system that explicitly balances major geographic, functional, factional, and policy interests through representation at the highest levels of the CCP. Although the pathways for political self-expression remain limited, and elite decision-making opaque, China's rulers now try to resolve, rather than crush, conflicts among competing interests, suppressing such conflicts only when they perceive them to be especially big threats. They have attempted to co-opt the rank and file of various constituencies while cracking down on the ringleaders of antigovernment movements.

Many of China's powerful new interest groups are economic in nature. Labor and management now clash over working conditions and pay. Likewise, as Chinese businesses come to look more like Western corporations, they are only partially submissive to party directives. For example, as the scholar Tabitha Mallory has pointed out, the fishing industry has become increasingly privatized—in 2012, 70 percent of China's "distant-water" fishing companies were privately owned—making it far harder for the central government to prevent overfishing.

Meanwhile, in the state-owned sector, the China National Offshore Oil Corporation, or CNOOC, is supporting policies that favor more assertiveness in the South China Sea, where significant hydrocarbon deposits are thought to lie, and it has found common ground with the Chinese navy, which wants a bigger budget and a modernized fleet. On issues both foreign and domestic, interest groups have become increasingly vocal participants in the policy process.

China's bureaucracy has adapted to the proliferation of interests by becoming more pluralized itself. Officials use forums called "leading small groups" (*lingdao xiaozu*) to resolve fights among squabbling organizations and localities, and vice premiers and state councilors spend much of their time settling such disputes. Meanwhile, provinces, big cities such as Shanghai, and industrial and commercial associations increasingly rely on representatives in Beijing to promote their interests by lobbying national decision-makers—a model that has been replicated at the provincial level as well.

PEOPLE POWER

Mao almost never allowed public opinion to restrain his policies; the popular will was something he himself defined. Deng, in turn, did adopt reforms, because he feared that the CCP was close to losing its legitimacy, yet he only followed public opinion when it comported with his own analysis.

Today, in contrast, almost all Chinese leaders openly speak about the importance of public opinion, with the goal being to preempt problems. In August 2013, for instance, the state-run newspaper *China Daily* reminded readers that the National Development and Reform Commission had issued regulations requiring local officials to conduct risk assessments to determine the likelihood of popular disturbances in reaction to major construction projects and stated that such undertakings should be shut down temporarily if they generated "medium-level" opposition among citizens.

China has built a large apparatus aimed at measuring people's views—in 2008, the most recent year for which data are available, some 51,000 firms, many with government contracts, conducted polling—and Beijing has even begun using survey data to help assess whether CCP officials deserve promotion. "After Deng, there has been no strongman, so public opinion has become a kind of civil society," one pollster, who has seen more and more of his business come from the central government, told me in 2012. "In the United States, polling is used for elections, but in China, a major use is to monitor government performance."

Such developments suggest that China's leaders now recognize that government must be more responsive, or at least appear that way. Indeed, since 2000, they have increasingly invoked public opinion in explaining their policies on exchange rates, taxes, and infrastructure. Public opinion may even lie behind the uptick in Beijing's regional assertiveness in 2009 and 2010. Niu Xinchun, a Chinese scholar, has argued that Beijing adopted a tougher posture in maritime disputes and other foreign issues during this period as a direct response to public anger over Western criticism of China's human rights record, especially in the run-up to the 2008 Olympic Games, when some Western leaders suggested that they might not attend. The Chinese were so fed up with France's behavior, in particular, that *China Daily* reported that the "Chinese people do not want the French president, Nicolas Sarkozy, to attend the opening ceremonies of the Beijing Olympics."

Beijing's greater responsiveness stems in large part from its recognition that as local governments, nonstate organizations, and individuals all grow more powerful, the central government is progressively losing its monopoly on money, human talent, and information. Take the question of capital. Ever since the Deng era, more and more of it has accumulated in coffers outside the central government. From 1980 to 2010, the portion of total state revenues spent at the local level rose from 46 percent to 82 percent. Meanwhile, the share of total industrial output produced by the state-owned sector dropped from 78 percent in 1978 to 11 percent in 2009. Of course, the state still holds firm control over strategic sectors such as those relating to defense, energy, finance, and large-scale public infrastructure, and ordinary Chinese still do not enjoy anything close to unlimited economic freedom. The change has also benefited corrupt local officials, military leaders, crime syndicates, and rogue entrepreneurs, all of whom can work against citizens' interests. But when people gain control over economic resources, they have far more choice in terms of where they live, what property they acquire, how they educate their children, and what opportunities they will pursue. This is not unfettered liberty, but it is certainly a beginning.

As for human capital, in the 1977–78 academic year, the first after the Cultural Revolution, some 400,000 students matriculated at Chinese universities; by 2010, that number had risen to 6.6 million. Moreover, many Chinese students now go abroad for education—in the 2012–13 academic year, more than 230,000 studied in the United States alone—and many are returning home after graduation. The result is that China now possesses a massive pool of talented individuals who can empower organizations and businesses outside of the state's control. Every day, these entities grow in number and power, and in some instances, they have begun performing duties that were traditionally handled by the state—or not handled at all. For example, the Institute of Public and Environmental Affairs, a nongovernmental organization that collects and publicizes data on factories' waste-disposal practices, has managed to pressure some companies that pollute into reforming their ways.

Ordinary Chinese are also gaining unprecedented access to information. More than half a billion Chinese now use the Internet. In addition to stanching the flow of information with the so-called Great Firewall, the government now has to fight information with information. In reaction to online rumors about the fallen CCP official Bo Xilai, for example, the government released limited portions of court testimony to Chinese social media. The central government has undertaken gargantuan efforts to both harness the benefits of the Internet and insulate itself from its most destabilizing effects.

At the same time, more and more Chinese citizens are flocking to cities. Urbanization tends to be associated with higher educational and income levels and elevated popular expectations. As one senior Chinese economist put it to me in 2010, "In the city, people breathe the fresh air of freedom."

The combination of more densely packed urban populations, rapidly rising aspirations, the spread of knowledge, and the greater ease of coordinating social action means that China's leaders will find it progressively more challenging to govern. They already are. In December 2011, for example, *The Guardian* reported that Zheng Yanxiong, a local party secretary in Guangdong Province who had been confronted by peasants angry about the seizure of their land, said in exasperation, "There's only one group of people who really experience added hardships year after year. Who are they? Cadres, that's who. Me included."

CITIZENS OR SUBJECTS?

China's reformist revolution has reached a point that Deng and his compatriots could never have anticipated. China's top leaders are struggling to govern collectively, let alone manage an increasingly complex bureaucracy and diffuse society. Their job is made all the more difficult by the lack of institutions that would articulate various interests, impartially adjudicate conflicts among them, and ensure the responsible and just implementation of policy. In other words, although China may possess a vigorous economy and a powerful military, its system of governance has turned brittle.

These pressures could lead China down one of several possible paths. One option is that China's leaders will try to reestablish a more centralized and authoritarian system, but that would ultimately fail to meet the needs of the country's rapidly transforming society. A second possibility is that in the face of disorder and decay, a charismatic, more transformational leader will come to the fore and establish a new order—perhaps more democratic but just as likely more authoritarian. A third scenario is much more dangerous: China continues to pluralize but fails to build the institutions and norms required for responsible and just governance at home and constructive behavior abroad. That path could lead to chaos.

But there is also a fourth scenario, in which China's leaders propel the country forward, establishing the rule of law and regulatory structures that better reflect the country's diverse interests. Beijing would also have to expand its sources of legitimacy beyond growth, materialism, and global status, by building institutions anchored in genuine popular support. This would not necessarily mean transitioning to a full democracy, but it would mean adopting its features: local political participation, official transparency, more independent judicial and anticorruption bodies, an engaged civil society, institutional checks on executive power, and legislative and civil institutions to channel the country's diverse interests. Only after all these steps have been taken might the Chinese government begin to experiment with giving the people a say in selecting its top leaders.

The key questions today are whether Xi favors such a course, even in the abstract, and whether he is up to the task of seeing it through. Preliminary indications suggest that proponents of economic reform have gained strength under his rule, and the important policies adopted by the Third Plenum will intensify the pressure for political reform. But Xi's era has only just begun, and it is still too early to say whether his time in the military and experience serving in China's most modernized, cosmopolitan, and globally interdependent areas—Fujian, Zhejiang, and Shanghai—have endowed the leader with the necessary authority and vision to push the country in the direction of history. Xi and the six other current members of the Politburo Standing Committee, China's most powerful decision-making body, come from a wider range of educational backgrounds than have the members of previous Standing Committees. This diversity could presage a period of creativity, but it could also produce paralysis.

There is also the danger that those who climb to the top of a political system cannot see beyond it. But history offers hope: in China, Deng saw beyond Mao and the system he had fashioned, and in Taiwan, Chiang Ching-kuo ushered in liberalizing reforms in the 1980s that his father, Chiang Kai-shek, had prevented. The dangers of standing still outweigh those of forging ahead, and China can only hope that its leaders recognize this truth and push forward, even without knowing where exactly they are headed. Should Xi and his cohort fail to do so, the consequences will be severe: the government will have forgone economic growth, squandered human potential, and perhaps even undermined social stability. If, however, China's new leaders manage to chart a path to a more humane, participatory, and rules-based system of governance—while maintaining vigorous economic growth and stability—then they will have revitalized the nation, the goal of patriots and reformers for over a century and a half.

Chinese Dissidence From Tiananmen to Today

How the People's Grievances Have Grown

Sharon K. Hom

On June 5, 1989, the day after the bloody crackdown on protesters in Tiananmen Square, Fang Lizhi, a prominent astrophysicist, and his wife, Li Shuxian, sought refuge in the U.S. embassy in Beijing. Fang, an intellectual and a strong proponent of democracy and human rights, and his wife were at the top of the Chinese government's wanted list. Fang was accused of being one of the "black hands" behind the student demonstrations. For more than a year, he and Li lived in the basement of the U.S. embassy while, outside, the Chinese authorities tracked down, detained, and imprisoned others suspected of so-called "counterrevolutionary crimes." In June 1990, they were allowed to leave China for the United States, where they lived in exile for the next 22 years.

The negotiation over Fang's future was complicated by international response to the Tiananmen crackdown. In the United States, Congress was engaged in debates over annual renewal of China's most-favored-nation (MFN) status. On June 5, 1989, it also

---

SHARON K. HOM is Executive Director of Human Rights in China.

imposed an arms embargo on China, and seven governments, including the United States, levied economic sanctions on China. Ultimately, one of Deng Xiaoping's conditions for releasing Fang was the lifting of those sanctions. Much as they are today, human rights issues were clearly tied up with trade and domestic U.S. politics.

On April 6 of this year, Fang died in Tucson, Arizona. A few weeks later, the blind activist and dissident Chen Guangcheng surfaced at the U.S. embassy in China, creating yet another diplomatic crisis for officials in both Beijing and Washington (coming less than two months after regional police chief Wang Lijun sought refuge in the U.S. consulate in Chengdu). On April 22, Chen had made a dramatic escape from 19 months of house arrest in his home village in Linyi, Shandong province. Helped by supporters, he traveled more than 250 miles to Beijing to find refuge with the Americans.

For the better part of two decades, Chen had been a vocal advocate for the disabled and other disadvantaged Chinese groups. In 2006, he helped expose coercive population control practices in Linyi, and was subsequently tried and convicted for "intentional damage of property and organizing people to block traffic." He was sentenced to four years and three months of imprisonment. During Chen's imprisonment, his family was subjected to threats, detention, surveillance, and verbal and physical abuse.

After six days inside the embassy compound, during which he told supporters and U.S. officials that he did not want to apply for asylum or go into exile, Chen left it. Washington and Beijing had reached an agreement to allow Chen to remain in China and study law there. He was escorted to a hospital for medical exams and for treatment of his foot, which he had injured during his escape.

Western media began to report contradictory and shifting stories about whether Chen had been pressured to leave the embassy. The Congressional-Executive Commission on China convened an emergency session, and even presidential hopeful Mitt Romney weighed in. "If these reports were true . . . it's a dark day for freedom," he said. He accused the Obama administration of rushing into an agreement that did not give Chen and his family adequate protection.

Considering the Fang and Chen cases side by side reveals how remarkably different the political landscape is for dissidents and activists in China today. The 1989 demonstrations began with calls to end corruption. They later expanded to an appeal for democratic reforms, something that had not been heard since 1978, when the human rights activist Wei Jingsheng declared that democracy was the "fifth modernization." He was sentenced to 15 years in prison.

After Tiananmen, the only options for intellectuals like Fang and student leaders like Wang Dan were exile or prison. During most of the 1990s, China used imprisoned dissidents as bargaining chips: it parlayed permission to leave China for independent trade union leader Han Dongfang (1993) and political dissident Liu Qing (1992) to keep U.S. most-favored-nation status; it used the 1998 release of student leader Wang Dan to pressure the United States to withdraw its sponsorship of a UN resolution condemning China's human rights policies.

Today, China is a major global power. It is a member of the World Trade Organization, and a significant creditor of world governments, including that of the United States. The United States also gave China permanent normal trade relations (PNTR) status in 2000, eliminating the annual MFN renewal debates. With the exception of the International Covenant on Civil and Political Rights (signed in 1998, but not yet ratified), China has also ratified all the major international human rights treaties, including treaties that protect the rights of women, children, and ethnic minority groups. Instead of playing by the rules, however, China has remained hostile to any voice perceived as critical, fearful of the open free flow of information, and distrustful of its own people.

Without a functioning rule of law and independent courts, Chinese lawyers and activists continue to face severe constraints and risks, including physical violence, harassment, forced disappearances, illegal detentions, and prosecutions for trumped-up criminal charges. On April 12, two hundred new Chinese lawyers had to swear a revised oath of loyalty that prioritizes loyalty to the party leadership.

At the same time, the nature, scope, and impact of activism in China have changed, in large part due to the Internet. By March of 2012, the number of netizens in China was over 500 million (up from 16.9 million in 2000); the country boasts more than one billion mobile phone users, 190 million of whom have smartphones. Weibo (the Chinese version of Twitter) has more than 300 million users and is growing. Weibo users actively comment and report on corruption scandals, major transportation accidents, pollution, housing, and land disputes, and even illegality in the legislative processes.

As popular discontent and citizen activism have spread online, they have also spread in scope to include demands not only for political reforms but also for official accountability on environmental crises, rampant corruption, tainted consumer products, massive theft of community land, dangerous workplaces, and increasing social and economic equalities.

Beijing may have constructed a state-of-the-art Great Firewall, but there will always be cracks. Even as the Linyi thugs were threatening and beating people who attempted to visit and support Chen and his family, the authorities were unable to prevent a video of Chen and his wife detailing their abuses from getting on the Internet. Neither could Beijing completely shut down earlier online campaigns such as the "Dark Glasses Portrait" campaign, which compiled photos of citizens wearing dark glasses in solidarity with Chen. Yet in the party propaganda chief's report to the National People's Congress in 2010, it was clear that China's comprehensive Internet management strategy insists on countering and controlling the very nature of the Internet: "As long as our country's Internet is linked to the global Internet, there will be channels and means for all sorts of harmful foreign information to appear."

As the handling of the negotiations and the public messaging of the Chen incident demonstrate, however, party authorities have also developed nuanced and sophisticated strategies to censor the media. Earlier, when the story broke that Chen had escaped, the Chinese authorities censored Chen's name, Linyi, embassy, and even the names of the nine members of the CPC Standing Committee. During Chen's initial hospitalization, it was clear that access to Chen and the flow of information to the outside world were also being controlled.

Yet, as Chen's story continues to develop, the challenges for China's activists and lawyers remain. In the early 2000s, lawyers were professionalizing and developing an identity distinct from legal cadres of the state. Those concerned about social justice wanted to work within the system, to help build China's legal framework. They tended to carefully distance themselves publicly from human rights and reform advocates. But over the past decade the Chinese authorities have demonstrated the limits of working within the system, and thus have contributed to radicalizing many of China's lawyers and activists.

Ironically, instead of building the vibrant informed citizenry critical to tackling the massive environmental, social, and economic challenges facing the country, China continues to heighten its political and social control, even as it loses its ability to shore up the millions of cracks in its Great Firewall. The anticorruption protests in Wukan in late 2011 are a prime example of citizens demanding their rights and winning, as demonstrated through the images of 13,000 villagers peacefully demonstrating circulated on YouTube, the subsequent removal of the local officials, and new village elections. Another example should be the investigation of the massive corruption and abuses in Chen Guangcheng's village as requested of Premier Wen.

The increasing number of mass protests, independent lawyers, and online citizen activists urgently demonstrates that the only way forward for China's future is one shaped through respect for the rights of the citizens. The question now is: Are the authorities reading the writing on the wall, or are they too blinded by their own self-interest for party survival at all costs?

The Geography of Chinese Power

How Far Can Beijing Reach on Land and at Sea?

Robert D. Kaplan

The English geographer Sir Halford Mackinder ended his famous 1904 article, "The Geographical Pivot of History," with a disturbing reference to China. After explaining why Eurasia was the geostrategic fulcrum of world power, he posited that the Chinese, should they expand their power well beyond their borders, "might constitute the yellow peril to the world's freedom just because they would add an oceanic frontage to the resources of the great continent, an advantage as yet denied to the Russian tenant of the pivot region." Leaving aside the sentiment's racism, which was common for the era, as well as the hysterics sparked by the rise of a non-Western power at any time, Mackinder had a point: whereas Russia, that other Eurasian giant, basically was, and is still, a land power with an oceanic front blocked by ice, China, owing to a 9,000-mile temperate coastline with many good natural harbors, is both a land power and a sea power. (Mackinder actually feared that China might one day conquer Russia.) China's virtual reach extends from Central Asia, with all its mineral and hydrocarbon wealth, to the main shipping lanes of the Pacific Ocean. Later,

ROBERT D. KAPLAN is a Senior Fellow at the Center for a New American Security and a correspondent for *The Atlantic*. His book *Monsoon: The Indian Ocean and the Future of American Power* will be published in the fall.

in *Democratic Ideals and Reality*, Mackinder predicted that along with the United States and the United Kingdom, China would eventually guide the world by "building for a quarter of humanity a new civilization, neither quite Eastern nor quite Western."

China's blessed geography is so obvious a point that it tends to get overlooked in discussions of the country's economic dynamism and national assertiveness. Yet it is essential: it means that China will stand at the hub of geopolitics even if the country's path toward global power is not necessarily linear. (China has routinely had GDP growth rates of more than ten percent annually over the past 30 years, but they almost certainly cannot last another 30.) China combines an extreme, Western-style modernity with a "hydraulic civilization" (a term coined by the historian Karl Wittfogel to describe societies that exercise centralized control over irrigation) that is reminiscent of the ancient Orient: thanks to central control, the regime can, for example, enlist the labor of millions to build major infrastructure. This makes China relentlessly dynamic in ways that democracies, with all of their temporizing, cannot be. As China's nominally Communist rulers—the scions of some 25 dynasties going back 4,000 years—are absorbing Western technology and Western practices, they are integrating them into a disciplined and elaborate cultural system with a unique experience in, among other things, forming tributary relationships with other states. "The Chinese," a Singaporean official told me early this year, "charm you when they want to charm you, and squeeze you when they want to squeeze you, and they do it quite systematically."

China's internal dynamism creates external ambitions. Empires rarely come about by design; they grow organically. As states become stronger, they cultivate new needs and—this may seem counterintuitive—apprehensions that force them to expand in various forms. Even under the stewardship of some of the most forgettable presidents—Rutherford Hayes, James Garfield, Chester Arthur, Benjamin Harrison—the United States' economy grew steadily and quietly in the late nineteenth century. As the country traded more with the outside world, it developed complex

Robert D. Kaplan

economic and strategic interests in far-flung places. Sometimes, as in South America and the Pacific region, for example, these interests justified military action. The United States was also able to start focusing outward during that period because it had consolidated the interior of the continent; the last major battle of the Indian Wars was fought in 1890.

China today is consolidating its land borders and beginning to turn outward. China's foreign policy ambitions are as aggressive as those of the United States a century ago, but for completely different reasons. China does not take a missionary approach to world affairs, seeking to spread an ideology or a system of government. Moral progress in international affairs is an American goal, not a Chinese one; China's actions abroad are propelled by its need to secure energy, metals, and strategic minerals in order to support the rising living standards of its immense population, which amounts to about one-fifth of the world's total.

To accomplish this task, China has built advantageous power relationships both in contiguous territories and in far-flung locales rich in the resources it requires to fuel its growth. Because what drives China abroad has to do with a core national interest— economic survival—China can be defined as an über-realist power. It seeks to develop a sturdy presence throughout the parts of Africa that are well endowed with oil and minerals and wants to secure port access throughout the Indian Ocean and the South China Sea, which connect the hydrocarbon-rich Arab-Persian world to the Chinese seaboard. Having no choice in the matter, Beijing cares little about the type of regime with which it is engaged; it requires stability, not virtue as the West conceives of it. And because some of these regimes—such as those in Iran, Myanmar (also known as Burma), and Sudan—are benighted and authoritarian, China's worldwide scouring for resources brings it into conflict with the missionary-oriented United States, as well as with countries such as India and Russia, against whose own spheres of influence China is bumping up.

To be sure, China is not an existential problem for these states. The chance of a war between China and the United States is remote; the Chinese military threat to the United States is only indirect. The challenge China poses is primarily geographic—notwithstanding critical issues about debt, trade, and global warming. China's emerging area of influence in Eurasia and Africa is growing, not in a nineteenth-century imperialistic sense but in a more subtle manner better suited to the era of globalization. Simply by securing its economic needs, China is shifting the balance of power in the Eastern Hemisphere, and that must mightily concern the United States. On land and at sea, abetted by China's favorable location on the map, Beijing's influence is emanating and expanding from Central Asia to the South China Sea, from the Russian Far East to the Indian Ocean. China is a rising continental power, and, as Napoleon famously said, the policies of such states are inherent in their geography.

IRRITABLE BORDER SYNDROME

Xinjiang and Tibet are the two principal areas within the Chinese state whose inhabitants have resisted the pull of Chinese civilization. This makes them imperial properties of Beijing, in a way. In addition, ethnic nationalist tensions in these areas are complicating Beijing's relationships with adjacent states.

"Xinjiang," the name of China's westernmost province, means "new dominion," and it refers to Chinese Turkestan, an area twice the size of Texas that lies far from China's heartland, across the Gobi Desert. China has been a state in some form for thousands of years, but Xinjiang formally became part of it only in the late nineteenth century. Since then, as the twentieth-century British diplomat Sir Fitzroy Maclean once put it, the history of the province "has been one of sustained turbulence," punctuated by revolts and various periods of independent rule well into the 1940s. In 1949, Mao Zedong's Communists marched into Xinjiang and forcibly integrated the province into the rest of China. But as recently as 1990 and again last year, ethnic Turkic Uighurs—descendants of the

Turks who ruled Mongolia in the seventh and eighth centuries—rioted against Beijing's rule.

The Uighurs in China number about eight million and make up less than one percent of China's population, but they account for 45 percent of Xinjiang's. China's majority Han population is heavily concentrated in the lowlands in the center of the country and by the Pacific, whereas the drier plateaus in the country's west and southwest are the historical homes of the Uighur and Tibetan minorities. This distribution is a continuing source of tension, because in Beijing's eyes, the modern Chinese state should exert total control over these tablelands. In order to secure these areas—and the oil, natural gas, copper, and iron ore in their soil—Beijing has for decades been populating them with Han Chinese from the country's heartland. It has also been aggressively courting the independent ethnic Turkic republics of Central Asia, partly to deprive the Uighurs of Xinjiang of any possible rear base.

Beijing has also been courting Central Asian governments in order to expand its sphere of influence; China already stretches far into Eurasia, but not far enough given its demand for natural resources. Beijing's sway in Central Asia takes the form of two soon-to-be-completed major pipelines to Xinjiang: one to carry oil from the Caspian Sea across Kazakhstan, the other to carry natural gas from Turkmenistan across Uzbekistan and Kazakhstan. China's hunger for natural resources also means that Beijing will take substantial risks to secure them. It is mining for copper south of Kabul, in war-torn Afghanistan, and has its eye on the region's iron, gold, uranium, and precious gems (the region has some of the world's last untapped deposits). Beijing hopes to build roads and energy pipelines through Afghanistan and Pakistan as well, linking up its budding Central Asian dominion to ports on the Indian Ocean. China's strategic geography would be enhanced if the United States stabilized Afghanistan.

Like Xinjiang, Tibet is essential to China's territorial self-conception, and like Xinjiang, it affects China's external relations. The mountainous Tibetan Plateau, rich in copper and iron ore, accounts for much of China's territory. This is why Beijing views with horror the prospect of Tibetan autonomy, let alone independence, and why it is frantically building roads and railroads across the area. Without Tibet, China would be but a rump—and India would add a northern zone to its subcontinental power base.

With its one-billion-plus population, India already is a blunt geographic wedge in China's zone of influence in Asia. A map of "Greater China" in Zbigniew Brzezinski's 1997 book *The Grand Chessboard* makes this point vividly. To some degree, China and India are indeed destined by geography to be rivals: neighbors with immense populations, rich and venerable cultures, and competing claims over territory (for example, the Indian state of Arunachal Pradesh). The issue of Tibet only exacerbates these problems. India has been hosting the Dalai Lama's government in exile since 1957, and according to Daniel Twining, a senior fellow at the German Marshall Fund, recent Chinese-Indian border tensions "may be related to worries in Beijing over the Dalai Lama's succession": the next Dalai Lama might come from the Tibetan cultural belt that stretches across northern India, Nepal, and Bhutan, presumably making him even more pro-Indian and anti-Chinese. China and India will play a "great game" not only in those areas but also in Bangladesh and Sri Lanka. Xinjiang and Tibet fall within China's legal borders, but the Chinese government's tense relations with the peoples of both provinces suggest that as Beijing expands its influence beyond its ethnic Han core, it is bound to encounter resistance.

CREEPING CONTROL

Even where China's borders are secure, the country's very shape makes it appear as though it is dangerously incomplete—as if parts of an original Greater China had been removed. China's northern border wraps around Mongolia, a giant territory that looks like it was once bitten out of China's back. Mongolia has one of the world's lowest population densities and is now being threatened demographically by an urban Chinese civilization next door.

Having once conquered Outer Mongolia to gain access to more cultivable land, Beijing is poised to conquer Mongolia again, after a fashion, in order to satisfy its hunger for the country's oil, coal, uranium, and rich, empty grasslands. Chinese mining companies have been seeking large stakes in Mongolia's underground assets because unchecked industrialization and urbanization have turned China into the world's leading consumer of aluminum, copper, lead, nickel, zinc, tin, and iron ore; China's share of the world's metal consumption has jumped from ten percent to 25 percent since the late 1990s. With Tibet, Macao, and Hong Kong already under Beijing's control, China's dealings with Mongolia will be a model for judging the degree to which China harbors imperialist intentions.

North of Mongolia and of China's three northeastern provinces lies Russia's Far East region, a numbing vastness twice the size of Europe with a meager and shrinking population. The Russian state expanded its reach into this area during the nineteenth century and the early twentieth century, while China was weak. Now, China is strong, and the Russian government's authority is nowhere as feeble as it is in the eastern third of the country. Just across the border from the roughly seven million Russians who live in the Russian Far East—a figure that could fall as low as 4.5 million by 2015—in the three abutting Chinese provinces, live some 100 million Chinese: the population density is 62 times as great on the Chinese side as on the Russian side. Chinese migrants have been filtering into Russia, settling in large numbers in the city of Chita, north of Mongolia, and elsewhere in the region. Resource acquisition is the principal goal of China's foreign policy everywhere, and Russia's sparsely populated Far East has large reserves of natural gas, oil, timber, diamonds, and gold. "Moscow is wary of large numbers of Chinese settlers moving into this region, bringing timber and mining companies in their wake," David Blair, a correspondent for London's *Daily Telegraph*, wrote last summer.

As with Mongolia, the fear is not that the Chinese army will one day invade or formally annex the Russian Far East. It is that

Beijing's creeping demographic and corporate control over the region—parts of which China held briefly during the Qing dynasty—is steadily increasing. During the Cold War, border disputes between China and the Soviet Union brought hundreds of thousands of troops to this Siberian back of beyond and sometimes ignited into clashes. In the late 1960s, these tensions led to the Sino-Soviet split. Geography could drive China and Russia apart, since their current alliance is purely tactical. This could benefit the United States. In the 1970s, the Nixon administration was able to take advantage of the rift between Beijing and Moscow to make an opening toward China. In the future, with China the greater power, the United States might conceivably partner with Russia in a strategic alliance to balance against the Middle Kingdom.

SOUTHERN PROMISES

China's influence is also spreading southeast. In fact, it is with the relatively weak states of Southeast Asia that the emergence of a Greater China is meeting the least resistance. There are relatively few geographic impediments separating China from Vietnam, Laos, Thailand, and Myanmar. The natural capital of a sphere of influence centering on the Mekong River and linking all the countries of Indochina by road and river would be Kunming, in China's Yunnan Province.

The largest country of mainland Southeast Asia is Myanmar. If Pakistan is the Balkans of Asia, at risk of being dismembered, Myanmar is like early-twentieth-century Belgium, at risk of being overrun by its great neighbors. Like Mongolia, the Russian Far East, and other territories on China's land borders, Myanmar is a feeble state abundant in the natural resources that China desperately needs. China and India are competing to develop the deepwater port of Sittwe, on Myanmar's Indian Ocean seaboard, with both harboring the hope of eventually building gas pipelines running from offshore fields in the Bay of Bengal.

As for the region as a whole, Beijing has in some respects adopted a divide-and-conquer strategy. In the past, it negotiated with each country in ASEAN (the Association of Southeast Asian Nations) separately, not with all of them as a unit. Even its newly inaugurated agreement on a free-trade area with ASEAN demonstrates how China continues to develop profitable relationships with its southern neighbors. It uses ASEAN as a market for selling high-value Chinese manufactured goods while buying from it low-value agricultural produce. This has led to Chinese trade surpluses, even as ASEAN countries are becoming a dumping ground for industrial goods produced by China's cheap urban labor.

This is occurring as the once strong state of Thailand, which has been shaken by domestic political problems lately, plays less and less of a role as a regional anchor and inherent counterweight to China. The Thai royal family, with its ailing king, cannot be as much of a stabilizing force as it once was, and factionalism is roiling the Thai military. (China is developing a bilateral military relationship with Thailand, as well as building such relationships with other Southeast Asian countries, even as the United States is focusing less on military exercises in the region in order to concentrate on its wars in Afghanistan and Iraq.) To Thailand's south, both Malaysia and Singapore are heading into challenging democratic transitions as their nation-building strongmen, Mahathir bin Mohamad and Lee Kuan Yew, respectively, pass from the scene. Malaysia is further coming under the shadow of China economically, even as its ethnic Chinese population feels threatened by the majority Muslim Malays. And the government of Singapore, even though Singapore is a state whose population is mostly ethnic Chinese, fears becoming a vassal of China; for years now, it has nurtured a military training relationship with Taiwan. Lee has publicly urged the United States to stay engaged in the region, militarily and diplomatically. Indonesia, for its part, is caught between needing the United States' naval presence to hedge against China and fearing that if it looks too much like a U.S. ally it will anger the rest of the Islamic world. As the United States' power in Southeast Asia passes its prime and China's rises, states in the region are increasingly cooperating with one another to mitigate Beijing's divide-and-conquer strategy. Indonesia, Malaysia, and Singapore have banded together against piracy, for example. The more self-reliant these states can become, the less threatened they will be by China's rise.

IN THE ARMY

Central Asia, Mongolia, the Russian Far East, and Southeast Asia are natural zones of Chinese influence. But they are also zones whose political borders are unlikely to change. The situation on the Korean Peninsula is different: the map of China is particularly truncated there, and there political borders could well shift.

The hermetic North Korean regime is fundamentally unstable, and its unraveling could affect the whole region. Jutting out from Manchuria, the Korean Peninsula commands all maritime traffic to and from northeastern China. No one really expects China to annex any part of the Korean Peninsula, of course, yet China remains inconvenienced by the sovereignty of other states there, particularly in the north. And although it supports Kim Jong Il's Stalinist regime, it has plans for the peninsula beyond his reign.

Beijing would like to eventually send back the thousands of North Korean defectors who now are in China so that they could build a favorable political base for Beijing's gradual economic takeover of the Tumen River region, where China, North Korea, and Russia meet and which has good port facilities across from Japan on the Pacific Ocean.

This is one reason why Beijing would prefer to see a far more modern, authoritarian state develop in North Korea—such a state would create a buffer between China and the vibrant, middle-class democracy of South Korea. But reunification on the Korean Peninsula would also eventually benefit Beijing. A reunified Korea would be nationalist and harbor some hostility toward China and Japan, both of which have sought to occupy it in the past. But Korea's enmity toward Japan is significantly greater than its enmity toward China. (Japan occupied the peninsula from 1910 to 1945, and Seoul and Tokyo continue to argue over the status of the Tokdo/Takeshima islets.) Economic relations would be stronger with China than with Japan: a unified Korea would be more or less under Seoul's control, and China already is South Korea's biggest trading partner. Finally, a reunified Korea that tilted slightly toward Beijing and away from Japan would have little reason to continue hosting U.S. troops. In other words, it is easy to conceive of a Korean future within a Greater China and a time when the United States' ground presence in Northeast Asia will diminish.

As the example of the Korean Peninsula shows, China's land borders beckon with more opportunities than hazards. As Mackinder suggested, China seems to be developing as a great land and sea power that will at the very least overshadow Russia in Eurasia. The political scientist John Mearsheimer wrote in *The Tragedy of Great Power Politics* that "the most dangerous states in the international system are continental powers with large armies." This might be reason to fear China's influence as the country becomes more of a continental power. But China only partially fits Mearsheimer's description: its army, 1.6 million strong, is the largest in the world, but it will not have an expeditionary capability for years to come. The People's Liberation Army did respond to the earthquake emergency in Sichuan in 2008, to recent ethnic unrest in Tibet and Xinjiang, and to the security challenge posed by the 2008 Olympics in Beijing. However, according to Abraham Denmark of the Center for a New American Security, this shows only that the PLA can move troops from one end of continental China to another, not that it can yet move supplies and heavy equipment at the rate required for military deployments. Perhaps gaining such a capability does not much matter anyway, since the PLA is unlikely to cross China's borders other than by miscalculation (if there is another war with India) or to fill a void (if the North Korean regime collapses). China can fill power vacuums on its vast frontiers through demographic and corporate means, without needing the backup of an expeditionary ground force.

China's unprecedented strength on land is partly thanks to Chinese diplomats, who in recent years have busily settled many border disputes with Central Asian republics, Russia, and other neighbors (India is the striking exception). The significance of this change cannot be overstated. There no longer is an army bearing down on Manchuria; during the Cold War, that ominous presence had forced Mao to concentrate China's defense budget on its army and neglect its navy. As the Great Wall attests, China had been preoccupied with land invasions of one sort or another since antiquity. No longer.

GETTING SEA LEGS

Thanks to this favorable situation on land, China is now free to work at building a great navy. Whereas coastal city-states and island nations pursue sea power as a matter of course, doing so is a luxury for historically insular continental powers such as China. In China's case, this might be a luxury that is fairly easy to acquire since the country is as blessed by its seaboard as by its continental interior. China dominates the East Asian coastline in the temperate and tropical zones of the Pacific, and its southern border is close enough to the Indian Ocean that it might one day be linked to it by roads and energy pipelines. In the twenty-first century, China will project hard power abroad primarily through its navy.

That said, it faces a far more hostile environment at sea than it does on land. The Chinese navy sees little but trouble in what it calls the "first island chain": the Korean Peninsula, the Kuril Islands, Japan (including the Ryukyu Islands), Taiwan, the Philippines, Indonesia, and Australia. All except for Australia are potential flashpoints. China is already embroiled in various disputes over parts of the energy-rich ocean beds of the East China Sea and the South China Sea: with Japan over the Diaoyu/Senkaku Islands and with the Philippines and Vietnam over the Spratly Islands. Such disputes allow Beijing to stoke nationalism at home, but for Chinese naval strategists, this seascape is mostly grim. This first island chain is, in the words James Holmes and Toshi

Yoshihara of the U.S. Naval War College, a kind of "Great Wall in reverse": a well-organized line of U.S. allies that serve as a sort of guard tower to monitor and possibly block China's access to the Pacific Ocean.

China's answer to feeling so boxed in has been aggressive at times. Naval power is usually more benign than land power: navies cannot by themselves occupy vast areas and must do far more than fight—namely, protect commerce. Thus, one might have expected China to be as benevolent as other maritime nations before it— Venice, Great Britain, the United States—and to concern itself primarily, as those powers did, with preserving a peaceful maritime system, including the free movement of trade. But China is not so self-confident. Still an insecure sea power, it thinks about the ocean territorially: the very terms "first island chain" and "second island chain" (the second island chain includes the U.S. territories of Guam and the Northern Mariana Islands) suggest that the Chinese see all these islands as archipelagic extensions of the Chinese landmass. In thinking in such a zero-sum fashion about their country's adjoining seas, China's naval leaders are displaying the aggressive philosophy of the turn-of-the-twentieth-century U.S. naval strategist Alfred Thayer Mahan, who argued for sea control and the decisive battle. But they do not yet have the blue-water force to apply it, and this discrepancy between aspirations and means has led to some awkward incidents over the past few years. In October 2006, a Chinese submarine stalked the USS *Kitty Hawk* and then surfaced within a torpedo's firing range of it. In November 2007, the Chinese denied the USS *Kitty Hawk* carrier strike group entry into Victoria Harbor when it was seeking a respite from building seas and deteriorating weather. (But another carrier, the USS *George Washington*, did make the visit to Hong Kong in 2010.) In March 2009, a handful of PLA navy ships harassed the U.S. surveillance ship the USNS *Impeccable* while it was openly conducting operations outside China's 12-mile territorial limit in the South China Sea, blocking its way and pretending to ram it. These are the actions not of a great power but of a still immature one.

China's assertiveness at sea is also demonstrated by its capital purchases. Beijing is developing asymmetric niche capabilities designed to block the U.S. Navy from entering the East China Sea and other Chinese coastal waters. China has modernized its destroyer fleet and has plans to acquire one or two aircraft carriers but is not acquiring warships across the board. Instead, it has focused on building new classes of conventional, nuclear attack, and ballistic missile submarines. According to Seth Cropsey, a former deputy undersecretary of the U.S. Navy, and Ronald O'Rourke of the Congressional Research Service, China could field a submarine force larger than the U.S. Navy's, which has 75 submarines in commission, within 15 years. Moreover, the Chinese navy, says Cropsey, plans to use over-the-horizon radars, satellites, seabed sonar networks, and cyberwarfare in the service of antiship ballistic missiles. This, along with China's burgeoning submarine fleet, is designed to eventually deny the U.S. Navy easy access to significant portions of the western Pacific.

As part of its effort to control its offshore waters in the Taiwan Strait and the East China Sea, China is also improving its minewarfare capability, buying fourth-generation jet fighters from Russia, and deploying some 1,500 Russian surface-to-air missiles along its coast. Furthermore, even as they are putting fiber-optic systems underground and moving their defense capabilities deep into western China, out of potential enemies' naval missile range, the Chinese are developing an offensive strategy to strike that icon of U.S. power, the aircraft carrier.

China is not going to attack a U.S. carrier anytime soon, of course, and it is still a long way from directly challenging the United States militarily. But its aim is to develop such capabilities along its seaboard to dissuade the U.S. Navy from getting between the first island chain and the Chinese coast whenever and wherever it wants. Since the ability to shape one's adversary's behavior is the essence of power, this is evidence that a Greater China is being realized at sea as on land.

Robert D. Kaplan

STRAIGHT TO TAIWAN

Most important to the advent of a Greater China is the future of Taiwan. The issue of Taiwan is often discussed in moral terms: Beijing talks about the need to consolidate the national patrimony and unify China for the good of all ethnic Chinese; Washington talks about preserving this model democracy. But the real issue is something else. As U.S. General Douglas MacArthur put it, Taiwan is an "unsinkable aircraft carrier" midway up China's seaboard. From there, say the naval strategists Holmes and Yoshihara, an outside power such as the United States can "radiate" power along China's coastal periphery. If Taiwan returned to the bosom of mainland China, the Chinese navy not only would suddenly be in an advantageous strategic position vis-à-vis the first island chain but also would be freed up to project power beyond it to an unprecedented degree. The adjective "multipolar" is thrown around liberally to describe the next world order; only the fusing of Taiwan with the Chinese mainland would mark the real emergence of a multipolar military order in East Asia.

According to a 2009 RAND study, by the year 2020, the United States will no longer be able to defend Taiwan from a Chinese attack. The Chinese, argues the report, will by that time be able to defeat the United States in a war in the Taiwan Strait even if the United States has F-22s, two carrier strike groups, and continued access to the Kadena Air Base, in Okinawa, Japan. The report emphasizes the air battle. The Chinese would still have to land tens of thousands of troops by sea and would be susceptible to U.S. submarines. Yet the report, with all its caveats, does highlight a disturbing trend. China is just 100 miles away from Taiwan, whereas the United States must project military power from half a world away and with more limited access to foreign bases than it had during the Cold War. China's strategy to deny the U.S. Navy entry into certain waters is designed not only to keep U.S. forces away generally but also, specifically, to foster its dominance over Taiwan.

Beijing is preparing to envelop Taiwan not just militarily but economically and socially, too. Some 30 percent of Taiwan's exports go to China. There are 270 commercial flights per week between Taiwan and the mainland. Two-thirds of Taiwanese companies have made investments in China in the last five years. Half a million tourists go from the mainland to the island annually, and 750,000 Taiwanese reside in China for about half of every year. Increasing integration appears likely; how it comes about, however, is uncertain and will be pivotal for the future of great-power politics in the region. If the United States simply abandons Taiwan to Beijing, then Japan, South Korea, the Philippines, Australia, and other U.S. allies in the Pacific Ocean, as well as India and even some African states, will begin to doubt the strength of Washington's commitments. That could encourage those states to move closer to China and thus allow the emergence of a Greater China of truly hemispheric proportions.

This is one reason why Washington and Taipei must consider asymmetric ways to counter China militarily. The aim should be not to defeat China in a war in the Taiwan Strait but to make the prospect of war seem prohibitively costly to Beijing. The United States could then maintain its credibility with its allies by keeping Taiwan functionally independent until China became a more liberal society. The Obama administration's announcement, in early 2010, that it would sell $6.4 billion worth of weapons to Taiwan is thus vital to the United States' position vis-à-vis China, and in Eurasia overall. And the goal of transforming China domestically is not a pipe dream: the millions of Chinese tourists who travel to Taiwan see its spirited political talk shows and the subversive titles in its bookstores. And yet, somewhat counterintuitively, a more democratic China could be an even more dynamic great power than a repressive China would be, in an economic sense and hence in a military sense, too.

In addition to concentrating its forces on Taiwan, the Chinese navy is projecting more power in the South China Sea, China's gateway to the Indian Ocean and to the world's hydrocarbon transport route. The challenges of piracy, radical Islam, and the rise of India's navy reside all along the way, including near the bottle-necks through which a large proportion of China's oil tankers and merchant ships must pass. In terms of overall strategic significance, the South China Sea could become, as some have said, a "second Persian Gulf." Nicholas Spykman, the twentieth-century scholar of geopolitics, noted that throughout history, states have engaged in "circumferential and transmarine expansion" to gain control of ad-jacent seas. Greece sought control over the Aegean, Rome over the Mediterranean, the United States over the Caribbean—and now China over the South China Sea. Spykman called the Caribbean "the American Mediterranean" to underscore its importance to the United States. The South China Sea may become "the Asian Med-iterranean" and the heart of political geography in coming decades.

LIQUID INSECURITIES

There is, however, a contradiction at the heart of China's efforts to project power at sea in the Asian Mediterranean and beyond. On the one hand, China seems intent on denying U.S. vessels easy ac-cess to its coastal seas. On the other, it is still incapable of protect-ing its lines of communication at sea, which would make any attack on a U.S. warship futile, since the U.S. Navy could simply cut off Chinese energy supplies by interdicting Chinese ships in the Pa-cific and Indian oceans. Why even bother trying to deny access if you never intend to enforce it? According to the defense consultant Jacqueline Newmyer, Beijing aims to create "a disposition of power so favorable" that "it will not actually have to use force to secure its interests." Showcasing new weapons systems, building port facili-ties and listening posts in the Pacific and Indian oceans, giving military aid to littoral states located between Chinese territory and the Indian Ocean—none of these moves is secret; all are deliberate displays of power. Rather than fight the United States outright, the Chinese seek to influence U.S. behavior precisely so as to avoid a confrontation.

Nonetheless, there seems to be a hard edge to some of China's naval activities. China is constructing a major naval base on the southern tip of Hainan Island, smack in the heart of the South China Sea, with underground facilities that could accommodate up to 20 nuclear and diesel-electric submarines. This is an exercise of Monroe Doctrine-style sovereignty over nearby international waters. China may have no intention of going to war with the United States today or in the future, but motives can change. It is better to track capabilities instead.

The current security situation at the edges of Eurasia is fundamentally more complicated than it was in the first years after World War II. As American hegemony ebbs and the size of the U.S. Navy declines or plateaus, while China's economy and military grow, multipolarity will increasingly define power relationships in Asia. The United States is providing Taiwan with 114 Patriot air defense missiles and dozens of advanced military communications systems. China is building underground submarine pens on Hainan Island and developing antiship missiles. Japan and South Korea are continuing to modernize their fleets. India is building a great navy. Each of these states is seeking to adjust the balance of power in its favor.

This is why U.S. Secretary of State Hillary Clinton's rejection of balance-of-power politics as a relic of the past is either disingenuous or misguided. There is an arms race going on in Asia, and the United States will have to face this reality when it substantially reduces its forces in Afghanistan and Iraq. Although no Asian state has any incentive to go to war, the risk of miscalculations about the balance of power will increase with time and with the buildup of air and naval forces in the region (if only by China and India). Tensions on land may reinforce tensions at sea: the power vacuums that China is now filling will in due course bring it into uneasy contact with, at a minimum, India and Russia. Once-empty spaces are becoming crowded with people, roads, pipelines, ships—and missiles. The Yale political scientist Paul Bracken warned in 1999 that Asia was becoming a closed geography and faced a crisis of "room." That process has only continued since.

So can the United States work to preserve stability in Asia, protect its allies there, and limit the emergence of a Greater China while avoiding a conflict with Beijing? Offshore balancing may not be sufficient. As one former high-ranking Indian official told me early this year, major U.S. allies in Asia (such as India, Japan, Singapore, and South Korea) want the U.S. Navy and the U.S. Air Force to act in "concert" with their own forces—so that the United States will be an integral part of Asia's landscape and seascape, not merely a force lurking over the distant horizon. There is a big difference between haggling with the United States over basing rights, as the Japanese have been doing recently, and wanting a wholesale withdrawal of U.S. forces.

One plan that has been making the rounds in the Pentagon argues that the United States could "counter Chinese strategic power . . . without direct military confrontation" with a U.S. fleet of just 250 ships (down from the 280 it has now) and a 15 percent cut in defense spending. This plan, designed by the retired U.S. Marine colonel Pat Garrett, is significant because it introduces into the Eurasian equation the strategic significance of Oceania. Guam and the Caroline, Marshall, Northern Mariana, and Solomon islands are all U.S. territories, commonwealths with defense agreements with the United States, or independent states that would probably be open to such agreements. Oceania will grow in importance because it is both relatively close to East Asia and outside the zone in which China is eager to deny easy access to U.S. warships. Guam is only a four-hour flight from North Korea and a two-day sail from Taiwan. It would be less provocative for the United States to keep bases in Oceania in the future than it has been for it to keep troops in Japan, South Korea, and the Philippines.

Andersen Air Force Base, on Guam, already is the most commanding platform from which the United States projects hard power anywhere. With 100,000 bombs and missiles and a store of 66 million gallons of jet fuel, it is the U.S. Air Force's biggest strategic "gas-and-go" facility in the world. Long lines of C-17 Globemasters and F/A-18 Hornets fill the base's runways. Guam is also home to a U.S. submarine squadron and is expanding as a naval base. It and the nearby Northern Mariana Islands are both almost equidistant from Japan and the Strait of Malacca. And the southwestern tip of Oceania—namely, the offshore anchorages of the Australian-owned Ashmore Islands and Cartier Islet and the adjacent seaboard of western Australia itself (from Darwin to Perth)—looks out from below the Indonesian archipelago toward the Indian Ocean. Thus, under Garrett's plan, the U.S. Navy and the U.S. Air Force could take advantage of Oceania's geography to constitute a "regional presence in being" located "just over the horizon" from the informal borders of a Greater China and the main shipping lanes of Eurasia. (The phrase "regional presence in being" echoes the British naval historian Sir Julian Corbett's "fleet in being" of a hundred years ago, which referred to a dispersed collection of ships that can quickly coalesce into a unified fleet if necessary. "Just over the horizon" reflects a confluence of offshore balancing and participation in a concert of powers.)

Strengthening the U.S. air and sea presence in Oceania would be a compromise approach between resisting a Greater China at all cost and assenting to a future in which the Chinese navy policed the first island chain. This approach would ensure that China paid a steep price for any military aggression against Taiwan. It would also allow the United States to scale back its so-called legacy bases on the first island chain but nonetheless allow U.S. ships and planes to continue to patrol the area.

The Garrett plan also envisions a dramatic expansion of U.S. naval activity in the Indian Ocean. It does not envision enlarging existing U.S. bases, however; it anticipates relying on bare-bones facilities in the Andaman Islands, the Comoros, the Maldives, Mauritius, Réunion, and the Seychelles (some of which are run directly or indirectly by France and India), as well as on defense agreements with Brunei, Malaysia, and Singapore. This would ensure free navigation and unimpeded energy flows throughout

Robert D. Kaplan

Eurasia. And by both de-emphasizing the importance of existing U.S. bases in Japan and South Korea and diversifying the United States' footprint around Oceania, the plan would do away with easy-to-target "master" bases.

The United States' hold on the first island chain is beginning to be pried loose anyway. Local populations have become less agreeable to the presence of foreign troops in their midst. And the rise of China makes Beijing intimidating and appealing at once—mixed feelings that could complicate the United States' bilateral relations with its Pacific allies. It is about time. The current crisis in U.S.-Japanese relations—which has arisen because the inexperienced Hatoyama government wants to rewrite the rules of the bilateral relationship in its favor even as it talks of developing deeper ties with China—should have occurred years ago. The United States' still extraordinarily paramount position in the Pacific Ocean is an outdated legacy of World War II, a function of the devastation that China, Japan, and the Philippines suffered during the conflict. Nor can the United States' presence on the Korean Peninsula, a byproduct of a war that ended over half a century ago, last forever.

A Greater China may be emerging politically, economically, or militarily in Central Asia, on the Indian Ocean, in Southeast Asia, and in the western Pacific. But just beyond this new realm will be a stream of U.S. warships, many perhaps headquartered in Oceania and partnering with naval forces from India, Japan, and other democracies. And in time, as China's confidence grows, its blue-water force could develop a less territorial approach and itself be drawn into a large regional naval alliance.

In the meantime, it is worth noting that, as the political scientist Robert Ross pointed out in 1999, in military terms, the relationship between the United States and China will be more stable than was the one between the United States and the Soviet Union. This is because of the particular geography of East Asia. During the Cold War, U.S. maritime power alone was insufficient to contain the Soviet Union; a significant land force in Europe was also required. But no such land force will ever be required around the edge of

Eurasia, because even as the United States' land presence around the borders of a Greater China diminishes, the U.S. Navy will continue to be stronger than the Chinese navy.

Still, the very fact of China's rising economic and military power will exacerbate U.S.-Chinese tensions in the years ahead. To paraphrase Mearsheimer, the United States, the hegemon of the Western Hemisphere, will try to prevent China from becoming the hegemon of much of the Eastern Hemisphere. This could be the signal drama of the age.

*An earlier version of this article stated that the USS *Kitty Hawk* made a port visit to Hong Kong in 2010. This is incorrect, the USS *George Washington* did.

The Game Changer

Coping With China's Foreign Policy Revolution

Elizabeth C. Economy

After decades of following Deng Xiaoping's dictum "Hide brightness, cherish obscurity," China's leaders have realized that maintaining economic growth and political stability on the home front will come not from keeping their heads low but rather from actively managing events outside China's borders. As a result, Beijing has launched a "go out" strategy designed to remake global norms and institutions. China is transforming the world as it transforms itself. Never mind notions of a responsible stakeholder; China has become a revolutionary power.

China's leaders have spent most of the country's recent history proclaiming a lack of interest in shaping global affairs. Their rhetoric has been distinctly supportive of the status quo: China helping the world by helping itself; China's peaceful rise; and China's win-win policy are but a few examples. Beijing has been a reluctant host for the six-party talks on North Korea, it has tried to avoid negotiations over Iran's potential as a nuclear power, and it has generally not concerned itself with others' military and political conflicts. China's impact on the rest of the world has, in many respects, been unintentional—the result of revolutions within the country. As the Chinese people have changed how they live and how they manage their economy, they have had a profound impact on the rest of the

ELIZABETH C. ECONOMY is C. V. Starr Senior Fellow and Director for Asia Studies at the Council on Foreign Relations.

world. China's position as the world's largest contributor to global climate change is not by design; it is the result of extraordinary economic growth and 1.3 billion people relying on fossil fuels for their energy needs.

Yet all this is about to change. China's leaders once tried to insulate themselves from greater engagement with the outside world; they now realize that fulfilling their domestic needs demands a more activist global strategy. Rhetorically promoting a "peaceful international environment" in which to grow their economy while free-riding on the tough diplomatic work of others is no longer enough. Ensuring their supply lines for natural resources requires not only a well-organized trade and development agenda but also an expansive military strategy. The Chinese no longer want to be passive recipients of information from the outside world; they want to shape that information for consumption at home and abroad. And as their economic might expands, they want not only to assume a greater stake in international organizations but also to remake the rules of the game.

China's leaders recognize that they are at a crossroads and are struggling to articulate their new course. In an interview with the China News Service, the usually politically deft former ambassador Wu Jianmin tried to reconcile the old rhetoric with the new reality: "By the time the current financial crisis is completely over . . . there is no doubt that China will play a more significant role in the world," he declared. "What we have achieved is just a beginning. Deng Xiaoping's idea of 'keeping a low profile and trying to do something' will continue to be applicable for at least another 100 years." What Wu's somewhat ambiguous message in fact signals is that China is out to change the game.

For the rest of the world, China's new agenda will require far greater attention to the country's internal dynamics and a much more activist, coordinated foreign policy effort. The world needs to ensure that China respects the interests of others as it seeks to meet its needs. And if the United States wants to retain its preeminence, or at least maintain its role in shaping the norms and values that will guide the world in the twenty-first century, its China policy cannot merely be a reaction to Beijing's initiatives. It must be part of a broader, long-term global strategy that begins with a clear assertion of the United States' domestic priorities. As a first step, while Beijing searches for how to sell its revolution to the rest of the world, the rest of the world needs to move quickly to understand the shape of this revolution and anticipate its impact.

THE REVOLUTION WITHIN

In the late 1970s, the Chinese leader Deng began the process of "reform and openness," precipitating a series of reforms that, over three decades, produced revolutionary change. China's economic institutions, patterns of social mobility and interaction, and societal values and even the Communist Party were transformed. By almost any measure, Deng's revolution also produced one of the great economic success stories of the twentieth century. China is now the second-largest economy and exporting nation in the world. Through a booming export sector, a continuous flood of foreign capital, and a managed currency, its central bank and state investment institutions now hold the largest reserves of foreign currency in the world. In the process, hundreds of millions of Chinese have been lifted out of poverty in just a few decades.

Yet for China's current leaders, Deng's revolution has run its course. They must now confront the downside of 30 years of unfettered growth: skyrocketing rates of pollution and environmental degradation, rampant corruption, soaring unemployment (reports range from 9.4 percent to 20 percent), a social welfare net in tatters, and rising income inequalities. Together, these social ills contribute to over 100,000 protests annually. In response, China's leadership is poised to launch an equally dramatic set of reforms that will once again transform the country and its place in the world. If all goes according to plan, in 20 years or less, China will be unrecognizable: an urban-based, innovative, green, wired, and equitable society.

At the heart of this next revolution is Beijing's plan to urbanize 400 million people by 2030. In 1990, just 25 percent of all Chinese lived in cities; today, that number is almost 45 percent. By 2030, it will be 70 percent. Urbanizing China will allow for a more effective distribution of social services and help reduce income disparities. An urban China will also be knowledge-based. No longer content to have their country be the world's manufacturing powerhouse, China's leaders have embarked on an aggressive effort to transform the country into a leading center of innovation. Beijing is supporting research and development; recruiting Chinese-born, foreign-trained scientists to return to China to head labs and direct research centers; and carefully studying the models of innovation that have proved successful in the West.

China's new cities will also be green. Beijing is investing hundreds of billions of dollars in the clean-energy sector and is providing subsidies to domestic manufacturers to encourage the sale of clean-energy products. Already, China is among the world's leading manufacturers of wind turbines and photovoltaic panels, and it is poised to capture significant segments of the global market in clean-energy transport, including high-speed rail and electric vehicles. Finally, China's urban population will be wired. China is already in the midst of an information revolution. Over 30 percent of Chinese people use the Internet, and most of them are in cities. In a 2009 Gallup poll, 42 percent of urban Chinese reported having access to the Internet in their homes, representing a 14 percent jump since just 2008. In absolute terms, more people are wired in China than anywhere else in the world.

Even as China moves ahead with its bold plans to transform its economy and society, new pressures and challenges will emerge. The resource demands of rapid urbanization are substantial. Half of the world's new building construction occurs in China, and according to one estimate, the country will construct 20,000–50,000 new skyscrapers over the coming decades. Shanghai, already the country's most populous urban center, will soon be surrounded by ten satellite cities—each with half a million people or more.

Connecting all these and other new cities throughout the country will require 53,000 miles of highway. Once the cities are built and connected, the demand for resources will continue to grow: urban Chinese consume more resources than those in rural areas (roughly 3.5 times as much energy and 2.5 times as much water), placing significant stress on the country's already scarce resources. By 2050, China's city dwellers will likely account for around 20 percent of global energy consumption.

Urban Chinese also make more organized political demands—for a cleaner environment, broader cultural expression, and more transparent governance—than their rural counterparts. Civil society blossoms in China's cities: homeowners' associations, artists, and environmental and public health advocates all assert their rights and demand change with increasing frequency. Expanding China's middle class by 400 million people will bring only more demands and put more political pressure on China's leaders.

Expanding popular access to the Internet will further up the ante for China's leaders by significantly increasing the odds that political discontent will solidify into a broad-based challenge to Communist Party rule. Premier Wen Jiabao has admitted to "surfing the Net" daily to help him understand people's concerns, but President Hu Jintao has expressed some concern about what the Internet might mean for China: "Whether we can cope with the Internet is a matter that affects the development of socialist culture, the security of information, and the stability of the state." Hu's comment signals that China's leaders are aware of the political challenge the Internet could pose to their rule in the future.

Already, the Internet is evolving into a virtual political system in China: the Chinese people inform themselves, organize, and protest online. In July 2010, bloggers provided firsthand accounts of a large-scale pollution disaster in Jilin Province, contradicting official reports. Thousands of people ignored government officials, angrily accusing them of a cover-up, and rushed to buy bottled water. Chinese are also "voting" online.

In one instance, a journalist sought by the police on trumped-up charges of slander took his case to the Internet. Of the 33,000 people polled, 86 percent said they believed he was innocent. *The Economic Observer*, a Chinese financial weekly, then launched a broadside against the police, condemning their attempt to threaten a "media professional." The charges against the journalist were dropped.

Activists have also used the Internet to launch successful campaigns—some involving physical protests—to prevent the construction of dams and polluting factories and to oppose the removal of Cantonese on television programs airing in Guangdong. Most striking, perhaps, has been the emergence of iconic cultural figures who use the Internet for political purposes. The renowned artist Ai Weiwei, for example, has pursued justice for families whose children died in the Sichuan earthquake, even documenting his encounters with recalcitrant officials on YouTube. The racecar driver and novelist turned blogger Han Han, routinely calls for greater media and cultural freedom. Since its launch in 2006, his blog has received more than 410 million hits. Perhaps most significant, Twitter, which is banned in China, has emerged as the most vibrant underground forum for uncensored political debate—including a pathbreaking online conversation between Chinese netizens and the Dalai Lama in May 2010.

The core priorities of China's leaders today remain very much the same as those of Deng three decades ago: economic growth and political stability. Yet the domestic environment in which they operate and their understanding of the road to success are radically different. It is no longer enough to focus on the home front; China's leaders want to shape the international context in which they do business.

CHINA'S REVOLUTION GOES GLOBAL

In the 1990s, then Chinese President Jiang Zemin launched his country's first "go out" policy, encouraging the country's state-owned enterprises to go abroad in search of natural resources. As a result of Jiang's initiative, China's trade with the resource-rich countries of Southeast Asia, Latin America, and Africa exploded between 2001 and 2007, growing by 600 percent. Tens of thousands of Chinese companies now operate throughout the developing world, often rejuvenating previously moribund economies with their investments. Leaders from the Democratic Republic of the Congo to Venezuela and Cambodia have welcomed Chinese investment and infrastructure as the type of practical assistance their countries most need. In many instances, Chinese state-owned enterprises are willing—and able, with the support of the government—to take on projects that no other multinationals find financially prudent. The copper mines in Zambia had remained closed for more than a decade until the Chinese came to town. This economic outreach has been matched by an unparalleled diplomatic effort. China offers a vast menu of trade and aid deals, infrastructural support, and educational and technical training opportunities to countries rich in natural resources.

Chinese investors are generally welcomed for their implicit promise to bring some of the success of "the China model" to the host countries. The willingness of the Chinese government and its state-owned enterprises to do business anywhere, anytime, and at any price has become legendary. As Sahr Johnny, Sierra Leone's ambassador to Beijing, commented in an interview regarding Chinese construction projects in his country, "If a G-8 country had wanted to rebuild the stadium, for example, we'd still be holding meetings. The Chinese just come and do it. They don't start to hold meetings about environmental impact assessment, human rights, bad governance and good governance."

Yet not everyone is as sanguine about the way China does business. Chinese companies have encountered resistance in a number of countries, including Papua New Guinea, Peru, and Zambia. Poor environmental and safety practices, along with labor policies that overtly favor Chinese workers, have caused intense conflicts with local residents in all these countries. In Vietnam, a Chinese bauxite mining project that will bring in more than 2,000 Chinese workers has raised the ire of Vietnamese workers, religious leaders, and even military and government officials. A prominent Vietnamese lawyer has gone so far as to sue the prime minister, accusing him of breaking four different laws by expediting approval of the project.

China's urbanization push will only intensify the country's outward drive for more natural resources. More cities, more roads, and more infrastructure will mean more steel, more copper, and more bauxite. China accounts for approximately one-fourth of world demand for zinc, iron and steel, lead, copper, and aluminum. In mid-2010, according to the International Energy Agency, China surpassed the United States as the world's largest energy consumer. China has also become concerned about its access to sufficient water supplies. In China, the amount of water available per person is one-fourth the global average. China is water rich in absolute terms, but given the number of people, the levels of pollution, and the location of China's water resources, water is scarce throughout much of the country—and China's leaders fear serious future shortages due to rapidly growing household and industrial demand. Consequently, they are moving quietly but aggressively to dam and divert the water resources of the Qinghai-Tibetan plateau, a move that will affect millions of people outside the country's borders. China's river-diversion initiatives are generating significant concern in Bangladesh, India, and Kazakhstan, among other countries, and paving the way for future regional disputes: the economic livelihood of millions of people outside China's borders depends on access to these water resources.

The next wave of "going out," however, will take China far beyond investment in natural resources. As China becomes an innovative, knowledge-based economy, its leaders are encouraging their cash-rich state-owned enterprises and investment funds to take stakes in or acquire foreign companies, particularly those with desirable technologies. Where Chinese products are competitive, Chinese firms are jumping in feet first. China's Ministry of Commerce is an aggressive advocate for the country's companies, for example, promoting an "all-in-one" service for clean-technology exports: the provision of equipment, expertise, and services. The government will even provide the necessary loans, which can then be used to pay for Chinese-made equipment, workers, and technologies. Beijing has already promised 1,000 such clean-energy projects to countries in Africa.

Ensuring a fair deal for the countries in which Chinese firms invest will require that those countries engage Chinese companies head-on. For example, the Chinese Ministry of Railways, which is bidding with General Electric to build California's high-speed rail network, has promised to provide the financing, technology, equipment, and "many high-end engineers and high-end technicians," potentially raising questions about what role GE and American workers will play in the project. California and other U.S. states will need to ensure that Chinese investment satisfies multiple U.S. interests, including labor.

China's leaders are also making their voices heard in international financial and trade institutions, in an effort to ensure that their economic interests are protected. In March 2009, as the world struggled to cope with the global financial crisis, China's leaders issued a number of provocative statements regarding the future of the international financial system. China's well-respected central-bank governor, Zhou Xiaochuan, announced that it might be time to move away from the dollar as the world's global currency and develop a "super sovereign" currency based on a basket of currencies. Chinese President Hu similarly called for an overhaul of the global financial system at the G-20 summit in April 2009. The public reaction was swift: most international commentators stated that the time was not right for a move away from the dollar. Chinese officials quickly backtracked, assuring critics that their proposals were merely recommendations that could be implemented over the next decade rather than in the next year.

Yet China has quietly continued to push the issue within the International Monetary Fund, and as its voting share within the IMF continues to increase (it increased from 2.9 percent to

3.6 percent in 2006, and there is a pending increase to 3.8 percent in 2010), China will have more opportunities to press its case. Over time, China may also seek to upend other aspects of IMF governance, such as the annual review of countries' currency practices and the governance and transparency requirements for IMF loan recipients. Both practices are headaches for China: the IMF has both obliquely and directly criticized Beijing for keeping the yuan artificially low, and China's disregard for IMF-based transparency and good governance standards in its trade and aid deals in the developing world has earned it further criticism from the international community.

Although the expansion of China's economic reach may be the most noticeable manifestation of its new activist foreign policy, its efforts to limit foreign competition in key strategic sectors, such as clean-energy technology, will also have a major impact. China's initiative to support "indigenous innovation" has drawn significant criticism from the rest of the world. Consciously rejecting the Japanese and South Korean model of technology innovation, which was rooted in a long-term catch-up strategy of licensing foreign technologies, China is looking to develop its own technologies and product standards. And it is trying to use international institutions to promote its domestic standards as global standards. For example, it is currently engaged in trying to push its own standards for software encryption and wireless local area networks as global International Organization for Standardization standards. (The ISO has previously rejected Chinese proposals to adopt the new protocol globally largely due to its use of an undisclosed algorithm, which has raised concerns about unfair trade practices.) As Jeremie Waterman, a senior director at the U.S. Chamber of Commerce, noted in his testimony before the U.S. International Trade Commission in June 2010, Beijing has "recently begun to implement a medium-and long-term indigenous innovation plan via a growing web of discriminatory industrial policies, including in the areas of government procurement, information security, standards setting, tax, antitrust, intellectual property protection and enforcement and industrial espionage." In effect, rather than working to address the long-standing problems in its trade and investment sectors, China is using the weaknesses of its regulatory and enforcement regime to provide an even greater competitive advantage to its companies. Appropriating the intellectual property of other firms takes less time and is less costly than licensing it or creating one's own. As long as Chinese companies are unlikely to be sanctioned for taking the intellectual property of other firms, they are unlikely to change the way they do business.

China has also taken steps to protect its hold on strategic re-sources and, in some cases, to compel foreign companies to locate their manufacturing bases in China or be put out of business. In the process, Beijing is undermining global trade norms. In November 2009, the United States and the European Union launched a case in the World Trade Organization against China for using ex-port restraints on over 20 raw materials, such as bauxite and coke, that are essential for basic manufactured goods, including steel, semiconductors, and aircraft. Less than a year later, Beijing an-nounced another round of restrictive trade policies, this time for rare-earth metals, cutting its export quotas by 72 percent. These metals, over which China holds a near monopoly, are necessary to produce not only magnets, cell phones, and fiber-optic cables but also electric-vehicle batteries and wind turbines. If it is not re-scinded, China's action could force many clean-energy firms to manufacture significant components in China, given that the United States and many other countries would need several years to rebuild their rare-earth mining capacity.

The world has become accustomed to many of the global im-pacts of China's economic revolution. China is already a trade and investment powerhouse, a significant purchaser of U.S. debt, and a major player in global commodities markets. As Beijing now seeks to more actively shape international trade and investment norms to suit its next revolution, the rest of the world can draw on past ex-perience to negotiate with, and occasionally even redirect, China.

The same cannot be said, however, of China's efforts to expand its military reach.

NAVAL GAZING

In April 2010, Chinese Rear Admiral Zhang Huachen, deputy commander of the East Sea Fleet, baldly declared that the country's naval strategy had changed: "We are going from coastal defense to far sea defense. . . . With the expansion of the country's economic interests, the navy wants to better protect the country's transportation routes and the safety of our major sea-lanes." In reality, Zhang's pronouncement was merely the coming-out party for a strategy that had been on the books as early as 2007. The strategy envisions China's naval capacity as expanding in three stages: first, to a navy that can cover the "first island chain," which includes islands from Japan to Taiwan to the Philippines; then, to a regional naval force with capabilities extending to Guam, Indonesia, and Australia; and finally, to a global force by 2050. The state-owned *Global Times* reinforced the initial steps in describing the navy's strategic shift: "Naturally, the transformation of the Chinese navy will bring changes to the strategic pattern in East Asia and the west Pacific Ocean that has lasted for the last five decades."

The South China Sea has become the first battleground. In March, even before Rear Admiral Zhang's pronouncement, Chinese officials appeared to assert for the first time that the South China Sea—whose resources have long been claimed by a number of other countries, including Malaysia, the Philippines, and Vietnam—is a "core national interest," a term previously reserved only for Taiwan and Tibet. Shortly thereafter, in April, the navy followed up with an almost three-week exercise in the region.

The international community reacted swiftly. At the June 2010 Shangri-la Dialogue, in South Korea, which brought together defense ministers from throughout the Asia-Pacific region, U.S. Secretary of Defense Robert Gates asserted that the United States' interest in the South China Sea was ensuring "stability, freedom of navigation, and free and unhindered economic development." U.S.

Secretary of State Hillary Clinton followed suit at the July ASEAN Regional Forum, in Hanoi, by offering U.S. assistance in mediating the disputes surrounding the South China Sea's islands and resources. Her offer was immediately supported by several, although not all, of the claimants. And in August, Vietnam and the United States held their first joint naval exercises ever in the South China Sea.

More challenges will follow. In July 2010, one of China's foremost security scholars, Shen Dingli, laid out the rationale for establishing a more permanent Chinese military presence abroad through the establishment of military bases. Although retired Chinese naval officials and current senior political officials have offered differing perspectives on the idea, there appears to be political momentum behind such a move. The Chinese government has already pushed forward with the development of deep-water ports in Pakistan, Myanmar (also called Burma), and Sri Lanka and is openly discussing the potential of other sites in Bangladesh and Nigeria. It may take a decade or more for the capacity of China's navy to match its ambitions, but the contours of China's more activist security strategy are already evident.

GETTING THE STORY RIGHT

As the impact of China's transformational policies reverberate throughout the world, Beijing has recognized the need to match its economic and military expansionism with an equally aggressive media strategy. As the Internet is allowing foreign perspectives into China, Chinese officials have become convinced of the need for China to tell its own story to the rest of the world. As one senior propaganda official commented, "We must . . . initiate targeted international public opinion battles, and create an international public opinion environment that is objective, beneficial, and friendly to us."

The result is a Chinese media blitz, with a price tag upward of $80 billion. The Xinhua News Agency is launching a 24-hour global English-language television news service, headquartered in

New York City's Times Square, to compete with CNN and the BBC in order to "provide international and China news with a Chinese perspective to global audiences." Already, China's state media post 400 correspondents in 117 bureaus around the world, and they are planning for 180 bureaus by 2020. Chinese media companies—such as *Xinhua*, the *China Daily*, the *Global Times*, and the *People's Daily*—now routinely ask foreign experts for commentary on global affairs.

At the same time, Chinese officials remain committed to controlling the flow of information into and within the country. Censorship, Internet police who monitor and guide online discussions, new regulations for the registration of Internet Protocols, and arrests of Internet dissidents are all designed to prevent the Chinese people from straying too far outside acceptable political boundaries. Moreover, foreign media companies have been largely unsuccessful in capturing significant market share in China, and some—such as Google and the media magnate Rupert Murdoch—have scaled back their efforts or pulled out in the face of highly restrictive policies.

How successful Chinese media will ultimately be in winning the hearts and minds of the rest of the world will likely rest on their ability to change the way they do business. Other authoritarian states seek to emulate the Chinese model, restricting Internet access and controlling domestic media. However, gaining the respect and trust of the rest of the world will require China to adopt a very different strategy. An open and critical approach to reporting news about China will be essential. Ultimately, the impact of the Chinese media foray abroad may be less transformative globally than on the home front. As Chinese media companies remake themselves to compete in the international marketplace with more investigative and open reporting, the pressures will mount to adopt similar strategies in the domestic market.

Elizabeth C. Economy

AMERICA FIRST

China has been remarkably consistent over the past three decades in defining its core interests as economic growth and political stability. What has changed is the leadership's understanding of what is required to achieve these goals. China's drive to remake global norms is also fueled by a resurgent nationalism that hearkens back to the days when China was a world trading power. For some Chinese officials, the past century—in which China has been largely absent as an economic and military force—was merely a historical aberration. In their eyes, things are now returning to normal.

In the United States, China's more activist foreign policy necessitates a strategic reevaluation. Buzzwords such as "containment," "engagement," and "congagement" and the notion of a "G-2" will not be useful concepts in the years to come. Instead, the White House needs to consider its policy on three different planes.

First, rather than relying primarily on bilateral engagement (an effort attempted and later discarded in the face of Chinese lack of interest), the Obama administration should continue to work with others to help influence Beijing. The United States, the European Union, and Japan often coordinate their trade policies toward China; U.S. cooperation with Russia brought China along on a round of UN sanctions against North Korea; and the United States and a number of Southeast Asian nations have found common cause in pressing Beijing to come to the negotiating table over the South China Sea. As China expands its naval activities in the coming decades, such multilateral cooperation—and pressure—will be essential in convincing China to discuss military transparency and the rules of the road in maritime security.

The White House must also continue to make clear that it believes certain core values should underpin the international system. These values above all reflect an American commitment to freedom—freedom of the seas, the air, space, and the Internet; free trade; the rule of law; and the political freedoms associated with basic human rights. The degree to which these values conflict with those espoused by China helps explain why the road to trust and cooperation between the two countries remains so challenging. Within China, there are political thinkers, activists, and even officials who share the ideals espoused by the United States. Until such views become more prevalent, however, it is essential that the United States be willing to advance them through both its diplomatic and its policy initiatives.

U.S. policy toward China cannot consist merely of blocking and parrying Chinese initiatives and promoting American ideals. Nor can Washington rely on annual dialogues designed to hash over a laundry list of issues that, in the end, simply delineate where the United States and China disagree and contribute little to attaining U.S. interests.

The third plane of U.S. policy should concern the United States' domestic interests and objectives. The Obama administration should begin by taking a page from China's playbook. Like China, the United States should derive its foreign policy first from a clear articulation of its objectives and strategy for its own future: What does the United States want to look like 50 years from now, and how is it going to get there? From such a vantage point, policy toward China becomes an instrument of achieving U.S. goals rather than an end in itself.

If the United States wants to be the global leader in clean-energy technology by 2050, for example, it should now be developing the intellectual, financial, and political infrastructure to get there. And when Chinese clean-energy investment interests come knocking, as they are doing, the United States will be well positioned to determine what types of investment should be welcomed. When done right, such deals have the potential to result in equitable partnerships and successful cooperation. In August 2010, for example, the United Steelworkers union struck a deal with the Chinese companies A-Power Energy Generation Systems and Shenyang Power Group to develop a $1.5 billion wind-farm venture in Texas that will create 1,000 jobs for U.S. workers—up from 330 U.S. jobs when the project was first proposed—and use about 50,000 tons of U.S.-made steel.

Similarly, China's efforts to move the international financial system away from the dollar as the world's reserve currency, although potentially costly if done abruptly, might nonetheless be advantageous for Washington over the long run. If the United States were no longer able to borrow money at a better rate than other countries or run greater trade deficits with the benefit of a much-delayed economic impact, for example, it would impose a potentially helpful fiscal discipline on the U.S. economy.

Paying close attention to transformations within China will pay significant dividends for U.S. policymakers seeking to predict what China might do next. Growing water scarcity in China, for example, will likely shape and perhaps even limit agricultural and industrial opportunities there over the coming decades. Listening to early signals of policy shifts, such as the recent scholarly but public commentary on the future of Chinese military bases abroad, is also important. Finally, China's own leadership will be replaced in 2012. Five of the seven top leaders in the Standing Committee of the Politburo, including President Hu and Premier Wen, will retire. These relatively insular engineers will be replaced by a leadership class dominated by more confident, well-traveled, and politically entrepreneurial social scientists. Bold political change may not be on their agenda, but a few of them initiated political experiments or reforms as provincial leaders. It is a group of leaders that, when given the reins, will certainly bring more change and perhaps even a few surprises. Although China's leaders have laid out their vision and put change in motion, both domestic and international pressures may well produce an outcome far different from the one they anticipate. All revolutions are inherently unstable, and China's is no exception. The United States needs to be ready, and that requires more than simply reacting to Beijing's more active foreign policy; it demands a U.S. policy toward China that looks inside China's domestic revolution to anticipate the future challenges and opportunities for the international community that will arise as a result of it.

As China seeks to remake global norms and institutions, it is also essential that the United States continue to assert its own ideals and strategic priorities and continue to work closely with other like-minded nations. Ultimately, however, the United States will succeed only when it can clearly articulate its own economic and political priorities and then ascertain how China can best help meet those objectives. The United States' China policy should be a means to an end, not an end in itself.

How China Sees America

The Sum of Beijing's Fears

Andrew J. Nathan and Andrew Scobell

"Great power" is a vague term, but China deserves it by any measure: the extent and strategic location of its territory, the size and dynamism of its population, the value and growth rate of its economy, the massive size of its share of global trade, and the strength of its military. China has become one of a small number of countries that have significant national interests in every part of the world and that command the attention, whether willingly or grudgingly, of every other country and every international organization. And perhaps most important, China is the only country widely seen as a possible threat to U.S. predominance. Indeed, China's rise has led to fears that the country will soon overwhelm its neighbors and one day supplant the United States as a global hegemon.

But widespread perceptions of China as an aggressive, expansionist power are off base. Although China's relative power has grown significantly in recent decades, the main tasks of Chinese foreign policy are defensive and have not changed much since the Cold War era: to blunt destabilizing influences from abroad, to avoid territorial losses, to reduce its neighbors' suspicions, and to

ANDREW J. NATHAN is Class of 1919 Professor of Political Science at Columbia University. Andrew Scobell is Senior Political Scientist at the RAND Corporation. This essay is adapted from their forthcoming book, *China's Search for Security* (Columbia University Press, 2012). © Andrew J. Nathan and Andrew Scobell.

sustain economic growth. What has changed in the past two decades is that China is now so deeply integrated into the world economic system that its internal and regional priorities have become
part of a larger quest: to define a global role that serves Chinese
interests but also wins acceptance from other powers.

Chief among those powers, of course, is the United States, and
managing the fraught U.S.-Chinese relationship is Beijing's foremost foreign policy challenge. And just as Americans wonder
whether China's rise is good for U.S. interests or represents a
looming threat, Chinese policymakers puzzle over whether the
United States intends to use its power to help or hurt China.

Americans sometimes view the Chinese state as inscrutable. But
given the way that power is divided in the U.S. political system and
the frequent power turnovers between the two main parties in the
United States, the Chinese also have a hard time determining
U.S. intentions. Nevertheless, over recent decades, a long-term U.S.
strategy seems to have emerged out of a series of American actions
toward China. So it is not a hopeless exercise—indeed, it is
necessary—for the Chinese to try to analyze the United States.

Most Americans would be surprised to learn the degree to which
the Chinese believe the United States is a revisionist power that
seeks to curtail China's political influence and harm China's interests. This view is shaped not only by Beijing's understanding of
Washington but also by the broader Chinese view of the international system and China's place in it, a view determined in large
part by China's acute sense of its own vulnerability.

THE FOUR RINGS

The world as seen from Beijing is a terrain of hazards, beginning
with the streets outside the policymaker's window, to land borders
and sea-lanes thousands of miles away, to the mines and oil fields
of distant continents. These threats can be described in four con-
centric rings. In the first ring, the entire territory that China ad-
ministers or claims, Beijing believes that China's political stability
and territorial integrity are threatened by foreign actors and forces.

Compared with other large countries, China must deal with an unparalleled number of outside actors trying to influence its evolution, often in ways the regime considers detrimental to its survival. Foreign investors, development advisers, tourists, and students swarm the country, all with their own ideas about how China should change. Foreign foundations and governments give financial and technical support to Chinese groups promoting civil society. Dissidents in Tibet and Xinjiang receive moral and diplomatic support and sometimes material assistance from ethnic diasporas and sympathetic governments abroad. Along the coast, neighbors contest maritime territories that Beijing claims. Taiwan is ruled by its own government, which enjoys diplomatic recognition from 23 states and a security guarantee from the United States.

At China's borders, policymakers face a second ring of security concerns, involving China's relations with 14 adjacent countries. No other country except Russia has as many contiguous neighbors. They include five countries with which China has fought wars in the past 70 years (India, Japan, Russia, South Korea, and Vietnam) and a number of states ruled by unstable regimes. None of China's neighbors perceives its core national interests as congruent with Beijing's.

But China seldom has the luxury of dealing with any of its neighbors in a purely bilateral context. The third ring of Chinese security concerns consists of the politics of the six distinct geopolitical regions that surround China: Northeast Asia, Oceania, continental Southeast Asia, maritime Southeast Asia, South Asia, and Central Asia. Each of these areas presents complex regional diplomatic and security problems.

Finally, there is the fourth ring: the world far beyond China's immediate neighborhood. China has truly entered this farthest circle only since the late 1990s and so far for limited purposes: to secure sources of commodities, such as petroleum; to gain access to markets and investments; to get diplomatic support for isolating Taiwan and Tibet's Dalai Lama; and to recruit allies for China's positions on international norms and legal regimes.

INSCRUTABLE AMERICA

In each of China's four security rings, the United States is omnipresent. It is the most intrusive outside actor in China's internal affairs, the guarantor of the status quo in Taiwan, the largest naval presence in the East China and South China seas, the formal or informal military ally of many of China's neighbors, and the primary framer and defender of existing international legal regimes. This omnipresence means that China's understanding of American motives determines how the Chinese deal with most of their security issues.

Beginning with President Richard Nixon, who visited China in 1972, a succession of American leaders have assured China of their goodwill. Every U.S. presidential administration says that China's prosperity and stability are in the interest of the United States. And in practice, the United States has done more than any other power to contribute to China's modernization. It has drawn China into the global economy; given the Chinese access to markets, capital, and technology; trained Chinese experts in science, technology, and international law; prevented the full remilitarization of Japan; maintained the peace on the Korean Peninsula; and helped avoid a war over Taiwan.

Yet Chinese policymakers are more impressed by policies and behaviors that they perceive as less benevolent. The American military is deployed all around China's periphery, and the United States maintains a wide network of defense relationships with China's neighbors. Washington continues to frustrate Beijing's efforts to gain control over Taiwan. The United States constantly pressures China over its economic policies and maintains a host of government and private programs that seek to influence Chinese civil society and politics.

Beijing views this seemingly contradictory set of American actions through three reinforcing perspectives. First, Chinese analysts see their country as heir to an agrarian, eastern strategic tradition that is pacifistic, defense-minded, nonexpansionist, and ethical. In contrast, they see Western strategic culture—especially

177

that of the United States—as militaristic, offense-minded, expansionist, and selfish.

Second, although China has embraced state capitalism with vigor, the Chinese view of the United States is still informed by Marxist political thought, which posits that capitalist powers seek to exploit the rest of the world. China expects Western powers to resist Chinese competition for resources and higher-value-added markets. And although China runs trade surpluses with the United States and holds a large amount of U.S. debt, China's leading political analysts believe the Americans get the better end of the deal by using cheap Chinese labor and credit to live beyond their means.

Third, American theories of international relations have become popular among younger Chinese policy analysts, many of whom have earned advanced degrees in the United States. The most influential body of international relations theory in China is so-called offensive realism, which holds that a country will try to control its security environment to the full extent that its capabilities permit. According to this theory, the United States cannot be satisfied with the existence of a powerful China and therefore seeks to make the ruling regime there weaker and more pro-American. Chinese analysts see evidence of this intent in Washington's calls for democracy and its support for what China sees as separatist movements in Taiwan, Tibet, and Xinjiang.

Whether they see the United States primarily through a culturalist, Marxist, or realist lens, most Chinese strategists assume that a country as powerful as the United States will use its power to preserve and enhance its privileges and will treat efforts by other countries to protect their interests as threats to its own security. This assumption leads to a pessimistic conclusion: as China rises, the United States will resist. The United States uses soothing words; casts its actions as a search for peace, human rights, and a level playing field; and sometimes offers China genuine assistance. But the United States is two-faced. It intends to remain the global hegemon and prevent China from growing strong enough to challenge it. In a 2011 interview with *Liaowang*, a state-run Chinese newsmagazine, Ni Feng, the deputy director of the Chinese Academy of Social Sciences' Institute of American Studies, summed up this view. "On the one hand, the United States realizes that it needs China's help on many regional and global issues," he said. "On the other hand, the United States is worried about a more powerful China and uses multiple means to delay its development and to remake China with U.S. values."

A small group of mostly younger Chinese analysts who have closely studied the United States argues that Chinese and American interests are not totally at odds. In their view, the two countries are sufficiently remote from each other that their core security interests need not clash. They can gain mutual benefit from trade and other common interests.

But those holding such views are outnumbered by strategists on the other side of the spectrum, mostly personnel from the military and security agencies, who take a dim view of U.S. policy and have more confrontational ideas about how China should respond to it. They believe that China must stand up to the United States militarily and that it can win a conflict, should one occur, by outpacing U.S. military technology and taking advantage of what they believe to be superior morale within China's armed forces. Their views are usually kept out of sight to avoid frightening both China's rivals and its friends.

WHO IS THE REVISIONIST?

To peer more deeply into the logic of the United States' China strategy, Chinese analysts, like analysts everywhere, look at capabilities and intentions. Although U.S. intentions might be subject to interpretation, U.S. military, economic, ideological, and diplomatic capabilities are relatively easy to discover—and from the Chinese point of view, they are potentially devastating.

U.S. military forces are globally deployed and technologically advanced, with massive concentrations of firepower all around the Chinese rim. The U.S. Pacific Command (PACOM) is the largest of the United States' six regional combatant commands in terms of its geographic scope and nonwartime manpower. PACOM's assets include about 325,000 military and civilian personnel, along with some 180 ships and 1,900 aircraft. To the west, PACOM gives way to the U.S. Central Command (CENTCOM), which is responsible for an area stretching from Central Asia to Egypt. Before September 11, 2001, CENTCOM had no forces stationed directly on China's borders except for its training and supply missions in Pakistan. But with the beginning of the "war on terror," CENTCOM placed tens of thousands of troops in Afghanistan and gained extended access to an air base in Kyrgyzstan.

The operational capabilities of U.S. forces in the Asia-Pacific are magnified by bilateral defense treaties with Australia, Japan, New Zealand, the Philippines, and South Korea and cooperative arrangements with other partners. And to top it off, the United States possesses some 5,200 nuclear warheads deployed in an invulnerable sea, land, and air triad. Taken together, this U.S. defense posture creates what Qian Wenrong of the Xinhua News Agency's Research Center for International Issue Studies has called a "strategic ring of encirclement."

Chinese security analysts also take note of the United States' extensive capability to damage Chinese economic interests. The United States is still China's single most important market, unless one counts the European Union as a single entity. And the United States is one of China's largest sources of foreign direct investment and advanced technology. From time to time, Washington has entertained the idea of wielding its economic power coercively. After the 1989 Tiananmen Square crackdown, the United States imposed some limited diplomatic and economic sanctions on China, including an embargo, which is still in effect, on the sale of advanced arms. For several years after that, Congress debated whether to punish China further for human rights violations by canceling the low most-favored-nation tariff rates enjoyed by Chinese imports, although proponents of the plan could never muster a majority. More recently, U.S. legislators have proposed sanctioning China for artificially keeping the value of the yuan low to the benefit of

Chinese exporters, and the Republican presidential candidate Mitt Romney has promised that if elected, he will label China a currency manipulator on "day one" of his presidency.

Although trade hawks in Washington seldom prevail, flare-ups such as these remind Beijing how vulnerable China would be if the United States decided to punish it economically. Chinese strategists believe that the United States and its allies would deny supplies of oil and metal ores to China during a military or economic crisis and that the U.S. Navy could block China's access to strategically crucial sea-lanes. The ubiquity of the dollar in international trade and finance also gives the United States the ability to damage Chinese interests, either on purpose or as a result of attempts by the U.S. government to address its fiscal problems by printing dollars and increasing borrowing, acts that drive down the value of China's dollar-denominated exports and foreign exchange reserves.

Chinese analysts also believe that the United States possesses potent ideological weapons and the willingness to use them. After World War II, the United States took advantage of its position as the dominant power to enshrine American principles in the Universal Declaration of Human Rights and other international human rights instruments and to install what China sees as Western-style democracies in Japan and, eventually, South Korea, Taiwan, and other countries. Chinese officials contend that the United States uses the ideas of democracy and human rights to delegitimize and destabilize regimes that espouse alternative values, such as socialism and Asian-style developmental authoritarianism. In the words of Li Qun, a member of the Shandong Provincial Party Committee and a rising star in the Communist Party, the Americans' "real purpose is not to protect so-called human rights but to use this pretext to influence and limit China's healthy economic growth and to prevent China's wealth and power from threatening [their] world hegemony."

In the eyes of many Chinese analysts, since the end of the Cold War the United States has revealed itself to be a revisionist power that tries to reshape the global environment even further in its favor. They see evidence of this reality everywhere: in the expansion of NATO; the U.S. interventions in Panama, Haiti, Bosnia, and Kosovo; the Gulf War; the war in Afghanistan; and the invasion of Iraq. In the economic realm, the United States has tried to enhance its advantages by pushing for free trade, running down the value of the dollar while forcing other countries to use it as a reserve currency, and trying to make developing countries bear an unfair share of the cost of mitigating global climate change. And perhaps most disturbing to the Chinese, the United States has shown its aggressive designs by promoting so-called color revolutions in Georgia, Ukraine, and Kyrgyzstan. As Liu Jianfei, director of the foreign affairs division of the Central Party School of the Chinese Communist Party, wrote in 2005, "The U.S. has always opposed communist 'red revolutions' and hates the 'green revolutions' in Iran and other Islamic states. What it cares about is not 'revolution' but 'color.' It supported the 'rose,' 'orange', and 'tulip' revolutions because they served its democracy promotion strategy." As Liu and other top Chinese analysts see it, the United States hopes "to spread democracy further and turn the whole globe 'blue.'"

EXPLOITING TAIWAN

Although American scholars and commentators typically see U.S.-Chinese relations in the postwar period as a long, slow thaw, in Beijing's view, the United States has always treated China harshly. From 1950 to 1972, the United States tried to contain and isolate China. Among other actions, it prevailed on most of its allies to withhold diplomatic recognition of mainland China, organized a trade embargo against the mainland, built up the Japanese military, intervened in the Korean War, propped up the rival regime in Taiwan, supported Tibetan guerillas fighting Chinese control, and even threatened to use nuclear weapons during both the Korean War and the 1958 Taiwan Strait crisis. Chinese analysts concede that the United States' China policy changed after 1972. But they assert that the change was purely the result of an effort to counter the Soviet Union and, later, to gain economic benefits by doing business in China. Even then, the United States continued to hedge against China's rise by maintaining Taiwan as a strategic distraction, aiding the growth of Japan's military, modernizing its naval forces, and pressuring China on human rights.

The Chinese have drawn lessons about U.S. China policy from several sets of negotiations with Washington. During ambassadorial talks during the 1950s and 1960s, negotiations over arms control in the 1980s and 1990s, discussions over China's accession to the World Trade Organization in the 1990s, and negotiations over climate change during the decade that followed, the Chinese consistently saw the Americans as demanding and unyielding. But most decisive for Chinese understandings of U.S. policy were the three rounds of negotiations that took place over Taiwan in 1971–72, 1978–79, and 1982, which created the "communiqué framework" that governs U.S. Taiwan policy to this day. When the U.S.-Chinese rapprochement began, Chinese policymakers assumed that Washington would give up its support for Taipei in exchange for the benefits of normal state-to-state relations with Beijing. At each stage of the negotiations, the Americans seemed willing to do so. Yet decades later, the United States remains, in Beijing's view, the chief obstacle to reunification.

When Nixon went to China in 1972, he told the Chinese that he was willing to sacrifice Taiwan because it was no longer strategically important to the United States, but that he could not do so until his second term. On this basis, the Chinese agreed to the 1972 Shanghai Communiqué, even though it contained a unilateral declaration by the United States that "reaffirm[ed] its interest in a peaceful settlement of the Taiwan question," which was diplomatic code for a U.S. commitment to deter any effort by the mainland to take Taiwan by force. As events played out, Nixon resigned before he was able to normalize relations with Beijing, and his successor, Gerald Ford, was too weak politically to fulfill Nixon's promise.

When the next president, Jimmy Carter, wanted to normalize relations with China, the Chinese insisted on a clean break with

Taiwan. In 1979, the United States ended its defense treaty with Taiwan but again issued a unilateral statement restating its commitment to a "peaceful resolution of the Taiwan issue." Congress then surprised both the Chinese and the administration by adopting the Taiwan Relations Act, which required the United States to "maintain [its] capacity . . . to resist any resort to force or other forms of coercion that would jeopardize the security . . . of the people on Taiwan." Once again, the deterrent intent was clear.

In 1982, when President Ronald Reagan sought closer relations with Beijing to ramp up pressure on Moscow, China prevailed on the United States to sign another communiqué, which committed Washington to gradually reducing its weapons sales to Taiwan. But once the agreement was in place, the Americans set the benchmark year at 1979, when arms sales had reached their highest level; calculated annual reductions at a small marginal rate, adjusting for inflation so that they were actually increases; claimed that the more advanced weapons systems that they sold Taiwan were the qualitative equivalents of older systems; and allowed commercial firms to cooperate with the Taiwanese armaments industry under the rubric of technology transfers rather than arms sales. By the time President George W. Bush approved a large package of advanced arms to Taiwan in April 2001, the 1982 communiqué was a dead letter. Meanwhile, as the United States prolonged its involvement with Taiwan, a democratic transition took place there, putting unification even further out of Beijing's reach.

Reviewing this history, Chinese strategists ask themselves why the United States remains so committed to Taiwan. Although Americans often argue that they are simply defending a loyal democratic ally, most Chinese see strategic motives at the root of Washington's behavior. They believe that keeping the Taiwan problem going helps the United States tie China down. In the words of Luo Yuan, a retired general and deputy secretary-general of the Chinese Society of Military Science, the United States has long used Taiwan "as a chess piece to check China's rise."

THE PERILS OF PLURALISM

The Taiwan Relations Act marked the beginning of a trend toward congressional assertiveness on U.S. China policy, and this continues to complicate Washington's relationship with Beijing. Ten years later, the 1989 Tiananmen incident, followed by the end of the Cold War, shifted the terms of debate in the United States. China had been perceived as a liberalizing regime; after Tiananmen, China morphed into an atavistic dictatorship. And the collapse of the Soviet Union vitiated the strategic imperative to cooperate with Beijing. What is more, growing U.S.-Chinese economic ties began to create frictions over issues such as the dumping of cheap manufactured Chinese goods on the U.S. market and the piracy of U.S. intellectual property. After decades of consensus in the United States, China quickly became one of the most divisive issues in U.S. foreign policy, partially due to the intense advocacy efforts of interest groups that make sure China stays on the agenda on Capitol Hill.

Indeed, since Tiananmen, China has attracted the attention of more American interest groups than any other country. China's political system elicits opposition from human rights organizations; its population-control policies anger the antiabortion movement; its repression of churches offends American Christians; its inexpensive exports trigger demands for protection from organized labor; its reliance on coal and massive dams for energy upsets environmental groups; and its rampant piracy and counterfeiting infuriate the film, software, and pharmaceutical industries. These specific complaints add strength to the broader fear of a "China threat," which permeates American political discourse—a fear that, in Chinese eyes, not only denies the legitimacy of Chinese aspirations but itself constitutes a kind of threat to China.

Of course, there are also those in Congress, think tanks, the media, and academia who support positions favorable to China, on the basis that cooperation is important for American farmers, exporters, and banks, and for Wall Street, or that issues such as North Korea and climate change are more important than disputes over

Andrew J. Nathan and Andrew Scobell

rights or religion. Those advocates may be more powerful in the long run than those critical of China, but they tend to work behind the scenes. To Chinese analysts trying to make sense of the cacophony of views expressed in the U.S. policy community, the loudest voices are the easiest to hear, and the signals are alarming.

SUGARCOATED THREATS

In trying to ascertain U.S. intentions, Chinese analysts also look at policy statements made by senior figures in the executive branch. Coming from a political system where the executive dominates, Chinese analysts consider such statements reliable guides to U.S. strategy. They find that the statements often do two things: they seek to reassure Beijing that Washington's intentions are benign, and at the same time, they seek to reassure the American public that the United States will never allow China's rise to threaten U.S. interests. This combination of themes produces what Chinese analysts perceive as sugarcoated threats.

For example, in 2005, Robert Zoellick, the U.S. deputy secretary of state, delivered a major China policy statement on behalf of the George W. Bush administration. He reassured his American audience that the United States would "attempt to dissuade any military competitor from developing disruptive or other capabilities that could enable regional hegemony or hostile action against the United States or other friendly countries." But he also explained that China's rise was not a threat because China "does not seek to spread radical, anti-American ideologies," "does not see itself in a death struggle with capitalism," and "does not believe that its future depends on overturning the fundamental order of the international system." On that basis, he said, the two sides could have "a cooperative relationship." But cooperation would depend on certain conditions. China should calm what he called a "cauldron of anxiety" in the United States about its rise. It should "explain its defense spending, intentions, doctrine, and military exercises"; reduce its trade surplus with the United States; and cooperate with Washington on Iran and North Korea. Above all,

186 FOREIGN AFFAIRS

Zoellick advised, China should give up "closed politics." In the U.S. view, he said, "China needs a peaceful political transition to make its government responsible and accountable to its people."

The same ideas have been repeated in slightly gentler language by the Obama administration. In the administration's first major policy speech on China, in September 2009, James Steinberg, then deputy secretary of state, introduced the idea of "strategic reassurance." Steinberg defined the principle in the following way: "Just as we and our allies must make clear that we are prepared to welcome China's 'arrival' . . . as a prosperous and successful power, China must reassure the rest of the world that its development and growing global role will not come at the expense of [the] security and well-being of others." China would need to "reassure others that this buildup does not present a threat"; it would need to "increase its military transparency in order to reassure all the countries in the rest of Asia and globally about its intentions" and demonstrate that it "respects the rule of law and universal norms." To Chinese analysts, such statements send the message that Washington wants cooperation on its own terms, seeks to deter Beijing from developing a military capability adequate to defend its interests, and intends to promote change in the character of the Chinese regime.

To be sure, Beijing's suspicion of Washington must contend with the fact that the United States has done so much to promote China's rise. But for Chinese analysts, history provides an answer to this puzzle. As they see it, the United States contained China for as long as it could. When the Soviet Union's rising strength made doing so necessary, the United States was forced to engage with China in order to reinforce its hand against Moscow. Once the United States started to engage with China, it came to believe that engagement would turn China toward democracy and would win back for the United States the strategic base on the mainland of Asia that Washington lost in 1949, when the Communists triumphed in the Chinese Civil War.

In the Chinese view, Washington's slow rapprochement with Beijing was not born of idealism and generosity; instead, it was pursued so that the United States could profit from China's economic opening by squeezing profits from U.S. investments, consuming cheap Chinese goods, and borrowing money to support the U.S. trade and fiscal deficits. While busy feasting at the Chinese table, U.S. strategists overlooked the risk of China's rise until the late 1990s. Now that the United States perceives China as a threat, these Chinese analysts believe, it no longer has any realistic way to prevent it from continuing to develop. In this sense, the U.S. strategy of engagement failed, vindicating the advice of Chinese leader Deng Xiaoping, who in 1991 advocated a strategy of "hiding our light and nurturing our strength." Faced with a China that has risen too far to be stopped, the United States can do no more than it is doing: demand cooperation on U.S. terms, threaten China, hedge militarily, and continue to try to change the regime.

HOW DO YOU HANDLE AN OFFENSIVE REALIST?

Despite these views, mainstream Chinese strategists do not advise China to challenge the United States in the foreseeable future. They expect the United States to remain the global hegemon for several decades, despite what they perceive as initial signs of decline. For the time being, as described by Wang Jisi, dean of Peking University's School of International Studies, "the superpower is more super, and the many great powers less great." Meanwhile, the two countries are increasingly interdependent economically and have the military capability to cause each other harm. It is this mutual vulnerability that carries the best medium-term hope for cooperation. Fear of each other keeps alive the imperative to work together.

In the long run, however, the better alternative for both China and the West is to create a new equilibrium of power that maintains the current world system, but with a larger role for China. China has good reasons to seek that outcome. Even after it becomes the world's largest economy, its prosperity will remain dependent on the prosperity of its global rivals (and vice versa), including the United States and Japan. The richer China becomes, the greater will be its stake in the security of sea-lanes, the stability of the world trade and financial regimes, nonproliferation, the control of global climate change, and cooperation on public health. China will not get ahead if its rivals do not also prosper. And Chinese strategists must come to understand that core U.S. interests—in the rule of law, regional stability, and open economic competition—do not threaten China's security.

The United States should encourage China to accept this new equilibrium by drawing clear policy lines that meet its own security needs without threatening China's. As China rises, it will push against U.S. power to find the boundaries of the United States' will. Washington must push back to establish boundaries for the growth of Chinese power. But this must be done with cool professionalism, not rhetorical belligerence. Hawkish campaign talk about trade wars and strategic competition plays into Beijing's fears while undercutting the necessary effort to agree on common interests. And in any case, putting such rhetoric into action is not a realistic option. To do so would require a break in mutually beneficial economic ties and enormous expenditures to encircle China strategically, and it would force China into antagonistic reactions.

Nevertheless, U.S. interests in relation to China are uncontroversial and should be affirmed: a stable and prosperous China, resolution of the Taiwan issue on terms Taiwan's residents are willing to accept, freedom of navigation in the seas surrounding China, the security of Japan and other Asian allies, an open world economy, and the protection of human rights. The United States must back these preferences with credible U.S. power, in two domains in particular. First, the United States must maintain its military predominance in the western Pacific, including the East China and South China seas. To do so, Washington will have to continue to upgrade its military capabilities, maintain its regional defense alliances, and respond confidently to challenges. Washington should reassure Beijing that these moves are intended to create a balance of common interests rather than to threaten China. That reassurance can be achieved by strengthening existing mechanisms for managing U.S.-Chinese military interactions. For example, the existing Military Maritime Consultative Agreement should be used to design procedures that would allow U.S. and Chinese aircraft and naval vessels to operate safely when in close proximity.

Second, the United States should continue to push back against Chinese efforts to remake global legal regimes in ways that do not serve the interests of the West. This is especially important in the case of the human rights regime, a set of global rules and institutions that will help determine the durability of the liberal world order the United States has long sought to uphold.

China has not earned a voice equal to that of the United States in a hypothetical Pacific Community or a role in a global condominium as one member of a "G-2." China will not rule the world unless the United States withdraws from it, and China's rise will be a threat to the United States and the world only if Washington allows it to become one. For the United States, the right China strategy begins at home. Washington must sustain the country's military innovation and renewal, nurture its relationships with its allies and other cooperating powers, continue to support a preeminent higher-education sector, protect U.S. intellectual property from espionage and theft, and regain the respect of people around the world. As long as the United States addresses its problems at home and holds tight to its own values, it can manage China's rise.

Beijing's Brand Ambassador

A Conversation With Cui Tiankai

Cui Tiankai

C ui Tiankai, 60, arrived in Washington, D.C., on April 2 to take up his new post as China's ambassador to the United States. A fluent English speaker with a master's degree from Johns Hopkins' School of Advanced International Studies, Cui spent five years as a farm hand during the Cultural Revolution before entering Shanghai Normal University. During his extensive diplomatic career, he has also served as China's ambassador to Japan and vice minister of foreign affairs. He spoke with *Foreign Affairs* managing editor Jonathan Tepperman in China's new I. M. Pei–designed embassy a few weeks after presenting his credentials to President Barack Obama.

Having just arrived in Washington, what's your assessment of the state of U.S.-Chinese relations?

For the last four years or so, relations have been moving forward steadily, although we sometimes wish they could move even faster. President Hu Jintao and President Obama met 12 times in the last four years. This is quite rare, even between the U.S. and its allies; it's certainly rare for China's relations with other countries.

Now that we have a new leadership in China, we have to spend time on the transition. President Xi Jinping and President Obama had a very good conversation on the phone [shortly after Xi took office] and reaffirmed that they will make every effort to have a cooperative partnership.

Cui Tiankai

What are your priorities as ambassador?

First, I have to make sure that the frequency of the high-level contacts continues and the mechanisms that we have set up between the two countries also continue and, where necessary, improve.

Many people seem worried that the relationship is drifting. President Xi has come up with what sounds like a new paradigm, what he calls "a new type of great-power relationship," to address this. What does he mean?

I think there is a clear mutual understanding between the two governments about the need to have a constructive and steady relationship—to base our partnership on mutual respect and mutual benefit. This is our goal. As for the concept of a new type of relationship between our two countries, that is also our goal. But of course, this is a long-term goal, which means that we have to give more substance to it.

In the past, when one big country developed very fast and gained international influence, it was seen as being in a kind of a zero-sum game vis-à-vis the existing powers. This often led to conflict or even war. Now, there is a determination both in China and in the United States to not allow history to repeat itself. We'll have to find a new way for a developing power and an existing power to work with each other, not against each other.

Scholars sometimes distinguish between status quo and revisionist powers, arguing that problems arise only if the new power is the latter and wants to change the rules of the game. Which is China?

It is an oversimplification to put China and the United States in the same category of power. The U.S. is still much more developed, much stronger. China is huge but still a developing country, whether in terms of the economy, science and technology, or military power. In many respects, we still have a long way to go before we can really be seen as on par with the United States.

As for whether we are trying to change the rules of the game, if you look at recent history since China reformed and opened up, there has been a clear integration of China into the existing global order. We are now members of many international institutions, not only the United Nations but also the World Bank and the International Monetary Fund. We have joined the World Trade Organization. We are taking part in many regional mechanisms.

So we are ready to integrate ourselves into the global system, and we are ready to follow the international rules. Of course, these rules were set without much participation by China, and the world is changing. You cannot say that the rules that were set up half a century ago can be applied without any change today. But what we want is not a revolution. We stand for necessary reform of the international system, but we have no intention of overthrowing it or setting up an entirely new one.

What sort of rules does China feel need to be adjusted?

For the last few years, we've had the G-20. This mechanism is quite new. It's different from the G-7 or the G-8. The G-20 has all the existing powers and also countries like India, Brazil, South Africa, Russia. China is also a member of the G-20, and we are playing a very important role in it. For the first time in history, these countries are sitting together around the same table as equals and discussing major international financial and economic issues. This is the kind of change we want to have.

Americans sometimes wonder whether China is really willing to help solve key international problems. Take Syria: the U.S. government is trying to build an international coalition to deal with the civil war there, and it feels that China has not been very cooperative.

If we are really serious about building a new type of relationship, we have to have mutual accommodation and mutual understanding. It's not that we are just helping the United States, or that the United States is just helping us. We have to help each other. We must make efforts to see issues from the other guy's point of view.

We certainly don't want chaos and civil war in Syria or anywhere in the world. We understand there are political differences in the country. But we always follow the principle that the affairs of a particular country should be determined by its own people, not by us, not by outsiders. It's not up to China or the United States to decide the future of the country.

But under the "responsibility to protect" doctrine, which most UN members have endorsed, when a leader is slaughtering his people in large numbers, the international community now has a responsibility, or at least a right, to intervene. You say the Syrian people should determine their own form of government. But the Syrian people have tried that, and their government is killing them.

To be very frank with you, this kind of theory has not always proved successful. When the United States started the war in Iraq, people were also talking about the responsibility to protect the Iraqi people, or to eliminate weapons of mass destruction, but the end result is obvious. Who is protecting whom, and who is protecting what? This is still open to debate.

Both Beijing and Washington want the Korean Peninsula to be peaceful and nuclear free. Yet China and the United States don't seem to be cooperating as closely as they could there. Why not?

China and the United States have many common interests on North Korea, but we might also have slightly different approaches on how to reach our common goals.

As far as China is concerned, we have three key elements to our policy on the Korean Peninsula. First, we stand for stability. Second, we stand for denuclearization of the Korean Peninsula. Third, we stand for peaceful means. These three elements are interrelated; you cannot have one at the expense of the other two.

It seems that Beijing has recently become more frustrated with Pyongyang and more willing to put real pressure on it. Is this true, and is China starting to distance itself from North Korea?

We just cannot distance ourselves from North Korea geographically. That's our problem—it's so close to us. Any chaos or armed conflict on the Korean Peninsula would have a major impact on China's national security interests. We have to keep that in mind all the time.

And our influence over the DPRK [Democratic People's Republic of Korea] may not be as real as what is reported in the media. Of course, as neighbors and long-standing friends, we do have some influence there. But the DPRK is a sovereign state. It could choose not to listen to us. It could decline whatever we might suggest.

But China has unique ways of putting pressure on North Korea, for example by turning off its energy supplies.

We provide, and are still providing, humanitarian assistance to North Korea. That has a lot to do with the Korean people and has almost nothing to do with [the leadership's] ambitions, particularly the nuclear program. We are against that. They know this quite clearly. They know China will never accept their nuclear program. We are against their nuclear tests. That's why we voted in favor of un sanctions in the Security Council.

So will China be prepared to take stronger measures if North Korea continues to act in an aggressive way?

We'll do whatever is necessary to achieve our goal of denuclearization and stability. But we have to think about how whatever we do serves our long-term goals. If we do something that leads to an escalation of the situation, it would defeat our own purposes.

Yet China is so much more powerful than North Korea.

Well, the United States is even more powerful, and has it managed to change North Korea's behavior? I don't think it has been very successful so far.

Do you think Washington's "pivot" to Asia actually represents anything new, and is it damaging U.S.-Chinese ties?

The United States has a long-standing interest in the Asia-Pacific. Maybe in the last decade or so, the United States focused so much on the Middle East—on Iraq and Afghanistan—that some people in the United States came to believe it was done at the expense of U.S.

interests in the Asia-Pacific. But the United States never removed its bases from the region, so it doesn't need to pivot. It's already there.

But some in the United States argue that talk of the pivot, sending U.S. troops to Australia, working out a new trade partnership that excludes China, and so forth have been a mistake, because these moves will create the impression that the United States is hostile to and is trying to encircle China. Do the Chinese feel that way?

Some Chinese do have this view. But today's China is a much more diversified society. You can find all kinds of views.

Over the last year or so, there has been a serious effort on the U.S. side to try to elaborate its Asia-Pacific policy in a more comprehensive way. Visiting U.S. officials to Beijing always try to explain to us that what you might call the pivot, or "rebalancing," is not against China and that China will be an essential part of this new approach. We listen to these statements very carefully. But of course, we have to wait and see what will happen in reality. For instance, we are following the Trans-Pacific Partnership negotiations very closely, but it's too early to come to the conclusion that the TPP is against any particular country.

America's top military official, General Martin Dempsey, went to Beijing recently to talk with his Chinese counterpart about cyber-space, which has become a big source of tension between the two countries. Americans feel that China is either not doing enough to stop cyberattacks aimed at the United States or is actually direct-ing those attacks. Is China willing to shut them down, and if so, what would it want in return?

Cybersecurity is a new issue for the international community at large. First of all, the technologies are new, and the attacks are in-visible. Traditionally, if you perceived a threat, it could be seen. It was physical. But not in cyberspace.

Second, very few international rules have been designed for these kind of problems. So we have to work out a new set of inter-national rules for everybody to follow.

Third, if we look at the development of IT and at the industry itself, the United States is much more advanced than China. So logically, I think the weaker should be more concerned about the stronger. The stronger is in a better position both to defend itself and to maybe go on the offensive against others.

Yet U.S. commercial and military computers are attacked all the time from abroad, and many of these attacks seem to be coming from China. *The New York Times* traced a number of these attacks to a specific building in Shanghai that is connected to the Chinese military. So many people have concluded that the Chinese government, or some forces within it, is involved in these attacks.

I don't think anybody has so far presented any hard evidence, evidence that could stand up in court, to prove that there is really somebody in China, Chinese nationals, that are doing these things. Cyberattacks can come from anywhere in the world. Even if you could locate a computer, you cannot say that computer belongs to the government of that particular country or even that the people who are doing this are nationals of that country. It's very hard to prove.

A huge number of Chinese computers, Chinese companies, and Chinese government agencies have also been attacked by hackers. If we trace these attacks, maybe some of them, or even most of them, would come from the United States. But we are not in the position to come to the conclusion that these attacks are sponsored or supported by the U.S. government. This is not a very responsible way of making such claims.

So do you deny the American accusations?

I think if they make the accusation, they have to give us proof, hard evidence. Nobody has done that. What is important is for the two governments to sit down, work out a new set of rules, and find out ways that we can work together to prevent such attacks from happening again.

Relations between Japan and China are in a very dangerous downward spiral at the moment. Armed Chinese ships have started regularly confronting armed Japanese ships surrounding the disputed Diaoyu/Senkaku Islands, risking a violent confrontation.

China and Japan share close economic ties, and yet neither country seems to be willing to resolve the issue. Why?

This issue has a long history. These islands were originally Chinese territory, but at the end of the nineteenth century, because of the war between China and Japan, Japan took action to put these islands in its own territorial jurisdiction. When the United States returned Okinawa to Japan [in 1972], it also included the Diaoyu Islands. We were against that and made it very clear at the time. So there has been a consistent Chinese position on the sovereignty of the islands. There is no doubt about that.

On the other hand, we also understand such issues will take time to resolve, and we are not in a hurry to resolve them overnight. When China and Japan normalized relations with each other [also in 1972], the leaders of both countries decided to put such disputes aside. And I think that was a very wise policy. We had tranquility over these islands for many years, until the Japanese government decided to nationalize the islands last year.

But they only did that to prevent a bigger problem, which was the nationalist governor of Tokyo buying the islands himself to build on them.

Well, it's quite clear Japan's decision will lead to very serious consequences under international law—even more serious than whatever the governor of Tokyo tried to do.

So China has strong historical claims. Japan also says it has strong historical claims. At a certain point, doesn't it become necessary to say, OK, history is history, but we live in the present, and we have to think about the future. Can you see a solution here that both countries can live with?

What you said is very wise, but no side should take action to upset this kind of balance. The legal action taken by the Japanese government really provoked everything.

I think the two sides have to engage in very serious negotiation. We approached the Japanese side last year. But I don't think that they were quite prepared at that time. Now, they have a new ruling party—the new old ruling party. The LDP [Liberal Democratic Party] is back. But I don't see any serious efforts by them to sit down with us and start very serious talks.

Is China concerned that Prime Minister Shinzo Abe's history as a nationalist will make resolution of the issue even more difficult?

It will depend on his choices. We know his political attitudes. But on the other hand, when he was prime minister last time [in 2006–7], he made the right decision not to visit the Yasukuni Shrine [a memorial for Japanese soldiers where a number of war criminals are also buried]. So he could do the right thing here.

China and Japan have enormous common interests, economic and otherwise. There is a huge potential for close cooperation, but we have to remove the political obstacle.

Is there a role for the United States to play?

The most helpful thing the U.S. could do is to remain truly neutral, to take no side.

What about helping the two sides communicate? Sometimes, a third party can be a useful mediator.

If that happens, I think it would be welcome. But it would really depend on how the third party acted. Is it really fair? When the United States talks to us, they say they'll take no side, but sometimes, when they talk to the Japanese or when they make public statements, we hear something different.

Some have argued that as the United States is pivoting east, China is pivoting west, getting more involved in Russia, Central Asia, the Middle East, and Africa. Could this someday threaten American interests?

The United States is lucky: it has only two neighboring countries and oceans on both sides. We have over a dozen neighboring countries, and we have a long and complicated history with them. So China really has to take care in its relations with its neighbors. It's not just in one direction, east or west. We certainly want to develop economic cooperation in all directions, because we need more trade, we need to export more and import more, and we need to have more sources of energy. I don't think that we are pivoting in any particular direction. And I don't think whatever we are doing will hurt U.S. interests, because if we can have mutually beneficial relations with all our neighbors, that will help guarantee the stability of the region.

Let me ask you about those neighbors. For about ten years, China worked very hard to convince the whole region, indeed the world, that it was interested in a "peaceful rise." Then, in the last year or so of the Hu Jintao administration, it seemed to start behaving more aggressively, which made a lot of its neighbors nervous. What happened?

We never provoked anything. We are still on the path of peaceful development. If you look carefully at what happened in the last couple of years, you will see that the others started all the disputes. We did not start them, but we had to respond because these issues concern China's sovereignty and territorial integrity, and there is strong public sentiment on these issues.

So why then is there this perception that it was China that was assertively pressing its territorial claims?

As I said, we never started the incidents. We only reacted to them. China has to safeguard its interests. In the meanwhile, we have been calling for dialogue. China always promotes the principle of "shelving differences and seeking joint development." We did a lot in the past years to implement this principle, and I hope that others will do the same.

How has the United States changed since your last posting here?

I was posted in New York at our UN mission from late 1997 until early 2000. This was before 9/11, so I see a big difference. There seems to be a strong sense of insecurity in America, although I do not fully understand that, because if the most powerful country in the world feels insecure, how can other countries feel secure?

But on the whole, I don't think there is fundamental change in the United States with regard to its strength, vitality, or its status internationally.

If you look at the world, you see the emergence of what people used to call new poles, or the rapid development of countries like China, India, and so on. To some extent, you could say—and only in relative terms—that the United States is not as powerful as before, but this only means that others are trying to catch up. It does not mean that the U.S. is declining.

But it seems to many people that the American political system is broken, or at least deeply dysfunctional. How does that look from a Chinese perspective?

We have our own problems. Yes, there are big problems here, and in politics, people go to the extremes. But still, I believe America is capable of resolving these issues and moving forward. There is no evidence that because of [domestic] problems, the United States is losing its position globally.

You spoke a moment ago about American insecurity. What about China's? China has now been on an incredible growth path for over 30 years; in many ways, it is the envy of countries all around the world. Yet China still seems to feel insecure. Can you imagine a time when China acts more like a "normal" country, one that has arrived, as opposed to a country that is still striving to become and is battling with its past?

I think normal people always have things to worry about. So I think it's only normal for countries to worry, too. Besides, China still faces mountains of problems. Some are historical legacies. Others might be the byproducts of our rapid development. We have to move forward and make great efforts to respond to these challenges so that the whole Chinese nation can modernize. This is a long-term process. We still have a long, long way to go. Maybe sometimes it's even good for individuals or nations to have a certain sense of insecurity. This can turn into motivation to work hard.

The Inevitable Superpower

Why China's Dominance Is a Sure Thing

Arvind Subramanian

To debtors, creditors can be like dictators. Governments in financial trouble often turn to the International Monetary Fund as supplicants, and acting at the behest of its own major creditors, the IMF often imposes tough conditions on them. After the Asian financial crisis of the late 1990s, Mickey Kantor, U.S. trade representative under President Bill Clinton, called the organization "a battering ram," because it had served to open up Asian markets to U.S. products. During the 1956 Suez crisis, the United States threatened to withhold financing that the United Kingdom desperately needed unless British forces withdrew from the Suez Canal. Harold Macmillan, who, as the British chancellor of the exchequer, presided over the last, humiliating stages of the crisis, would later recall that it was "the last gasp of a declining power." He added, "perhaps in 200 years the United States would know how we felt."

Is that time already fast approaching, with China poised to take over from the United States? This is an essential question, and yet it

ARVIND SUBRAMANIAN is a Senior Fellow at the Peterson Institute for International Economics and at the Center for Global Development. This article is adapted from his forthcoming book *Eclipse: Living in the Shadow of China's Economic Dominance* (Peterson Institute for International Economics, 2011).
© Peterson Institute for International Economics.

has not yet been taken seriously enough in the United States. There, this central conceit still reigns: the United States' economic preeminence cannot be seriously threatened because it is the United States' to lose, and sooner or later, the United States will rise to the challenge of not losing it. China may be on its way to becoming an economic superpower, and the United States may have to share the global stage with it in the future. But, the argument goes, the threat from China is not so imminent, so great, or so multifaceted that it can push the United States out of the driver's seat.

Thus, the economist Barry Eichengreen concludes in his recent history of different reserve currencies, *Exorbitant Privilege*, "The good news, such as it is, is that the fate of the dollar is in our hands, not those of the Chinese." And in December 2010, as he was leaving the White House as President Barack Obama's national economic adviser, Larry Summers said, "Predictions of America's decline are as old as the republic. But they perform a crucial function in driving the kind of renewal that is required of each generation of Americans. I submit to you that as long as we're worried about the future, the future will be better. We have our challenges. But we also have the most flexible, dynamic, entrepreneurial society the world has ever seen." In other words, if the United States can get its economic house in order, it can head off the Chinese threat.

But such views underestimate the probability that China will be economically dominant in 20 years. And they reveal a one-sided, U.S.-centric perspective: that world dominance will be determined mostly by the actions of the United States, not those of China. In fact, the outcome of this race is far more likely to be shaped by China.

THE WORLD IN 2030

Broadly speaking, economic dominance is the ability of a state to use economic means to get other countries to do what it wants or to prevent them from forcing it to do what it does not want. Such means include the size of a country's economy, its trade, the health of its external and internal finances, its military prowess, its technological dynamism, and the international status that its currency enjoys. My forthcoming book develops an index of dominance combining just three key factors: a country's GDP, its trade (measured as the sum of its exports and imports of goods), and the extent to which it is a net creditor to the rest of the world. GDP matters because it determines the overall resources that a country can muster to project power against potential rivals or otherwise have its way. Trade, and especially imports, determines how much leverage a country can get from offering or denying other countries access to its markets. And being a leading financier confers extraordinary influence over other countries that need funds, especially in times of crisis. No other gauge of dominance is as instructive as these three: the others are largely derivative (military strength, for example, depends on the overall health and size of an economy in the long run), marginal (currency dominance), or difficult to measure consistently across countries (fiscal strength).

I computed this index going back to 1870 (focusing on the United Kingdom's and the United States' economic positions then) and projected it to 2030 (focusing on the United States' and China's positions then). The projections are based on fairly conservative assumptions about China's future growth, acknowledging that China faces several major challenges going forward. For starters, its population will begin to age over the coming decade. And its economy is severely distorted in several respects: overly cheap capital has led to excessive investment; the exchange rate has been undervalued, which has led to the overdevelopment of exports; and energy is subsidized, leading to its inefficient use and pollution. Correcting these distortions will impose costly dislocations. To take account of these costs, I project that China's growth will slow down considerably: it will average seven percent a year over the next 20 years, compared with the approximately 11 percent it has registered over the last decade. History suggests that plenty of economies—Germany, Japan, Singapore, South Korea, and Taiwan—grew at the pace I project for China after they reached China's current level of development. Meanwhile, I assume that the U.S. economy will grow at about 2.5 percent per year, as it has over the last 30 years. This is slightly optimistic compared with the Congressional Budget Office's latest long-term growth forecast of 2.2 percent, a forecast that the CBO lowers occasionally because of the negative impact of the country's accumulating public and private debt and sustained high unemployment on the U.S. economy.

The upshot of my analysis is that by 2030, relative U.S. decline will have yielded not a multipolar world but a near-unipolar one dominated by China. China will account for close to 20 percent of global GDP (measured half in dollars and half in terms of real purchasing power), compared with just under 15 percent for the United States. At that point, China's per capita GDP will be about $33,000, or about half of U.S. GDP. In other words, China will not be dirt poor, as is commonly believed. Moreover, it will generate 15 percent of world trade—twice as much as will the United States. By 2030, China will be dominant whether one thinks GDP is more important than trade or the other way around; it will be ahead on both counts.

According to this index and these projections, China's ascendancy is imminent. Although the United States' GDP is greater than China's today and the two countries' respective trade levels are close, the United States is a very large and vulnerable debtor—it hogs about 50 percent of the world's net capital flows—whereas China is a substantial net creditor to the world. In 2010, the United States' lead over China was marginal: there was less than one percentage point difference between their respective indices of dominance. In fact, if one weighed these factors slightly differently, giving slightly less weight to the size of the economy relative to trade, China was already ahead of the United States in 2010.

China's ascendancy in the future will also apply to many more issues than is recognized today. The Chinese economy will be larger than the economy of the United States and larger than that of any other country, and so will its trade and supplies of capital.

The yuan will be a credible rival to the dollar as the world's premier reserve currency.

What is more, the gap between China and the United States will be far greater than expected. In 2010, the U.S. National Intelligence Council assessed that in 2025, "the U.S. will remain the preeminent power, but that American dominance will be much diminished." This is unduly optimistic. My projections suggest that the gap between China and the United States in 2030 will be similar to that between the United States and its rivals in the mid-1970s, the heyday of U.S. hegemony, and greater than that between the United Kingdom and its rivals during the halcyon days of the British Empire, in 1870. In short, China's future economic dominance is more imminent and will be both greater and more varied than is currently supposed.

STRONG LIKE A BULL

Martin Wolf, the *Financial Times* columnist, has used the term "premature superpower" to describe China's unique ability to wield power despite being poor. According to my projections, however, by 2030, China will not be so badly off. Rather, its GDP per capita (in terms of purchasing power parity) will be more than half that of the United States and greater than the average per capita GDP around the world. Still, China's economic dominance will be singular: unlike in the past, when the dominant powers—the United Kingdom and the United States—were very rich relative to their competitors, China will be just a middle-or upper-middle-income country. And can a country be dominant even when it is not among the richest?

There are three plausible reasons for thinking that it cannot. First, a relatively poor country might have to subordinate its hopes of projecting power internationally to its need to address more pressing domestic challenges, such as achieving higher standards of living and greater social stability. Second, it might not be able to reliably raise the resources it needs to project power abroad. Military assets, for one thing, have to be financed, and poorer countries have more difficulty taxing their citizens than do rich countries. Third, a poor country can have only so much influence abroad if it does not have soft power, such as democracy, an open society, or pluralistic values. The leadership that comes with dominance lasts only if it inspires followers: only those who stand for something that commands universal or near-universal appeal are inspiring. Likewise, only a rich country—one on the economic and techno- logical edge—can be a fount of ideas, technology, institutions, and practices for others.

That said, even if dominance is generally inconsistent with pov- erty, one can be dominant without being among the richest coun- tries. Even a middle-income power, which China is likely to be by 2030, can be internally cohesive, raise resources for external pur- poses (such as military expenditures), and possess some inspiring national ideals. In fact, despite China's relatively low per capita GDP today, it is already dominant in several ways. China convinced the African countries in which it invests heavily to close down the Tai- wanese embassies they were hosting. With $3 trillion in foreign re- serves, it has offered to buy Greek, Irish, Portuguese, and Spanish debt to forestall or mitigate financial chaos in Europe. ("China is Spain's best friend," said Spanish Prime Minister José Luis Rodrí- guez Zapatero in April on the occasion of the Chinese president's visit.) China has also used its size to strengthen its trade and finan- cial relationships in Asia and Latin America: for example, trade transactions among several countries in both regions can now be settled in yuan.

Above all, China's exchange-rate policy has affected economies throughout the world, hurting developing countries as much as the United States: by keeping its currency cheap, China has managed to keep its exports more competitive than those from countries such as Bangladesh, India, Mexico, and Vietnam. Yet these coun- tries have stood on the sidelines, leaving Washington to wage a crusade against Beijing on its own—and for that reason, it has not done so very successfully. China, meanwhile, has been able to buy off the opposition. Although many countries chafe at seeing their competitiveness undermined by an undervalued yuan, they remain silent, either for fear of China's political muscle or because China offers them financial assistance or trading opportunities. Even within the United States, few groups have really been critical. China is a large market for U.S. companies, and so it is the liberal left, not the holders of U.S. capital, that has condemned China's exchange-rate policy, on behalf of U.S. workers.

Even if China is unlikely to muster anytime soon the kind of dominance that naturally inspires or might be necessary to build international systems and institutions like those the United States created after World War II, Beijing is already exercising other forms of dominance. For example, it can require that U.S. and European firms share their technology with Chinese firms before granting them access to its market. And it can pursue policies that have systemic effects, despite opposition from much of the world. Its policy of undervaluing its exchange rate is a classic beggar-thy-neighbor strategy that undermines the openness of the world's trading and financial systems while also creating the conditions for easy liquidity, which contributed to the recent global economic crisis. Chinese dominance is not looming. In some ways, it is already here.

DROWNING BY NUMBERS

Can the United States reverse this trend? Its economic future inspires angst: the country has a fiscal problem, a growth problem, and, perhaps most intractable of all, a middle-class problem. Repeated tax cuts and two wars, the financial and economic crisis of 2008–10, the inexorable growth of long-term entitlements (especially related to health), and the possible buildup of bad assets for which the government might eventually be responsible have created serious doubts about the U.S. public sector's balance sheet. High public and private debt and long-term unemployment will depress long-term growth. And a combination of stagnating middle-class incomes, growing inequality, declining mobility, and, more recently, falling prospects for even the college educated has created big distributional problems. The middle class is feeling beleaguered: it does not want to have to move down the skill ladder, but its upward prospects are increasingly limited by competition from China and India.

The United States' continued strength comes from its can-do attitude about fixing its economic problems and its confidence that sound economic fundamentals can ensure its enduring economic dominance. Most notably, the United States affords unique opportunities for entrepreneurship "because it has a favorable business culture, the most mature venture capital industry, close relations between universities and industry, and an open immigration policy," according to the Global Entrepreneurship Monitor, an academic consortium that studies entrepreneurial activity worldwide. In a 2009 survey, GEM ranked the United States first in the world in providing such opportunities. Nearly all the major commercially successful companies that have made technological breakthroughs in the last three decades—Apple and Microsoft, Google and Facebook—were founded and are based in the United States. In fact, it was by finding new and dynamic sources of growth in the 1990s that the United States was able to head off the economic challenge posed by that era's rising power, Japan. Today, optimists argue that the United States can replicate that experience with China. It is true that if the U.S. economy were to grow consistently at a rate of 3.5 percent over the next 20 years, as it did in the 1990s, investor sentiment and confidence in the dollar as a reserve currency could be buoyed.

But some key differences today should dampen any such hope. The United States headed into the 1990s with far less government debt than it will have in the future. In 1990, the ratio of public debt to GDP was about 42 percent, whereas the COB's latest projected figure for 2020 is close to 100 percent. The external position of the United States was also less vulnerable two decades ago. For example, in 1990, foreign holdings of U.S. government debt amounted to 19 percent; today, they are close to 50 percent, and a majority are in China's hands. In the 1990s, the country was also considerably further away from the date at which it would have to reckon with the cost of entitlements.

And then there is the United States' beleaguered middle class. Over the last 20 years, several related pathologies that have squeezed the American middle class, such as a stagnating median income, have become more entrenched and more intractable. Even a 3.5 percent growth rate, which would be well above current expectations, may not be adequate to maintain confidence in the U.S. model, which is based on the hope of a better future for many.

In other words, the United States cannot escape the inexorable logic of demography and the fact that poor countries, especially China, are catching up with it. China, which is four times as populous as the United States, will be a bigger economy as soon as its average standard of living (measure in per capita GDP) exceeds one-quarter of the United States'. By some measures, including my own, this has already occurred, and as China continues to grow, the gap will only widen. A resurgent United States might be able to slow down that process, but it will not be able to prevent it. Growing by 3.5 percent, rather than 2.5 percent, over the next 20 years might boost the United States' economic performance, social stability, and national mood. But it would not make a significant difference in its position relative to China in the face of, say, a seven percent growth rate there.

These projections undermine the dominant belief that the United States' economic preeminence is its own to lose. It is China's actions that will largely determine whether the differential in growth between China and the United States is modest or great. China can radically mess up, for example, if it allows asset bubbles to build or if it fails to stave off political upheaval. Or it can surge ahead by correcting existing economic distortions, especially by moving away from an export-intensive growth strategy toward one that develops demand at home. The United States' range of action is much narrower. If the United States is unlikely to grow significantly slower than by 2.0–2.5 percent, it is even more unlikely to grow faster than by 3.5 percent. This is the curse of being at the frontier of economic development: both the potential downsides and the potential upsides are limited.

Even if the United States grows fast—say, by 3.5 percent—other countries, such as China, may grow faster, too, leaving the basic picture of their relative economic power unaffected. In fact, when the pace of technological innovation in leading countries, such as the United States, quickens, the new technologies become quickly available to poorer countries, providing a stimulus to their growth, too. Even more important than producing new technologies is having the human capital and the skills to use them. According to the National Science Foundation, in 2006 there were nearly twice as many undergraduates in science and engineering in China as in the United States. This differential is likely only to grow. Despite having a considerably worse educational system than the United States, China seems well positioned to absorb new technologies. There were six times as many peer-reviewed scientific publications in the United States as in China in 2002—and just 2.5 times as many in 2008. The ability of rich countries to stay ahead in terms of growth is inherently limited because China is better able to absorb and use new technologies. China's technological sophistication is growing: the United States, Europe, and Japan export very few products that China does not also export. More generally, if growth in the United States slows, China's growth might be unaffected, but if it accelerates, China's growth might, too. Either way, the United States cannot pull away.

BACK TO SUEZ

Even a resurgent United States could not exercise power and dominance over a rising China. China is already able to do what the rest of the world does not want it to do. Might it soon be able to get the United States to do what the United States does not want to do? Is another Suez crisis possible?

In 1956, with sterling under pressure because of Egypt's blockade of the Suez Canal, the United Kingdom turned to the United States for financial assistance, invoking their "special relationship." But U.S. President Dwight Eisenhower refused. He was furious that the British (and the French) had attacked Egypt after

President Gamal Abdel Nasser nationalized the canal, just as he was campaigning for reelection as the man of peace who had ended the fighting on the Korean Peninsula. He demanded that the United Kingdom comply with a U.S.-sponsored UN resolution requiring the prompt and unconditional withdrawal of British troops. If it did not, Washington would block the United Kingdom's access to resources from the IMF. But if it did, it would get substantial financial assistance. The United Kingdom agreed, and the United States supported a massive financial package, including an unprecedented IMF loan worth $1.3 billion and a $500 million loan from the U.S. Export-Import Bank.

Now, imagine a not-so-distant future in which the United States has recovered from the crisis of 2008–10 but remains saddled with structural problems: widening income gaps, a squeezed middle class, and reduced economic and social mobility. Its financial system is still as fragile as before the crisis, and the government has yet to come to grips with the rising costs of entitlements and the buildup of bad assets in the financial system, which the government might have to take over. Inflation is a major global problem because commodity prices are skyrocketing as a result of rapid growth in emerging markets. China has an economy and a trade flow twice as large as the United States'. The dollar has lost its sheen; demand for the yuan as a reserve currency is growing.

Much as in 1956, when Washington was suspected of orchestrating massive sales of sterling in New York to force the British government to withdraw its troops from the Suez Canal, rumors are swirling that China is planning to wield its financial power; it has had enough of the United States' naval presence in the Pacific Ocean. Beijing starts selling some of its currency reserves (by then likely to amount to $4 trillion). Investors grow skittish, fearing that the dollar might collapse, and bond markets turn on U.S. government paper. The United States soon loses its AAA credit rating. Auctions for U.S. Treasury bonds find no buyers. To maintain confidence, the U.S. Federal Reserve sharply raises interest rates. Before long, interest rates substantially exceed growth rates, and the

United States urgently needs cheap financing. It turns to oil exporters, but the friendly autocrats of yore have been replaced by illiberal democrats of various Islamic persuasions, ranging from moderate to extreme, and all with long memories of U.S. intervention in the Middle East. Much as for Greece, Ireland, and Portugal recently, seeking help from the IMF seems unavoidable: defaulting on U.S. debt obligations would be fatal to the effort to preserve what is left of the United States' global role.

But by this time, China, already the world's largest banker since 2000, controls the spigot. Although it, too, deems that an IMF bailout is necessary, it has a precondition: the withdrawal of the United States' naval presence in the western Pacific. The request has bite because China, as the IMF's largest contributor and a benefactor to many of its members, can easily block the United States' request for financing. By then, China may even have acquired veto power thanks to the governance reforms scheduled for 2018.

Some will say this scenario is pure fantasy. After all, the United States could easily withhold financing from the United Kingdom in 1956 because doing so had no serious consequences for the dollar or the U.S. economy. But if tomorrow, China sold, or just stopped buying, U.S. Treasury bonds, the dollar would decline and the yuan would appreciate—the very outcome that China has steadfastly been trying to prevent. China is unlikely to suddenly undermine its mercantilist growth strategy and risk large capital losses on its stock of foreign exchange reserves. Others might say that even if China were willing to do so, if the U.S. economy were depressed, the Federal Reserve might be only too happy to buy up any U.S. Treasuries dumped by China.

But all this leaves out that China's incentives might be very different in the future. Ten years on, China might be less wedded to keeping the yuan weak. If it continues to slowly internationalize its currency, both its ability to maintain a weak yuan and its interest in doing so may soon disappear. And when they do, China's power over the United States will become considerable. In 1956, the United Kingdom's financiers were dispersed across the public and private sectors. But the Chinese government is the largest net supplier of capital to the United States: it holds many U.S. Treasury bonds and finances the U.S. deficit. Leverage over the United States is concentrated in Beijing's hands.

Of course, the prospects of a dollar devaluation would probably be less painful for the United States in this hypothetical future than the prospects of a weakening sterling was for the United Kingdom in 1956. Back then, a devaluation of sterling would have inflicted heavy losses on the currencies of the United Kingdom's former colonies that held large sterling-denominated assets. These colonies would have sold their sterling assets, weakening their economic links with the United Kingdom. Preventing this was important to the government in London in order to preserve what was left of the British Empire. A devaluation of the dollar would be less of a problem partly because the United States' foreign liabilities are denominated in dollars.

A repeat of the Suez crisis may seem improbable today. But the United States' current economic situation does leave the country fundamentally vulnerable in the face of China's inescapable dominance. The United Kingdom was playing with a weak hand during the Suez crisis not just because it was in debt and its economy was weakening but also because another great economic power had emerged. Today, even as the United States' economy is structurally weak, its addiction to debt has made the country dependent on foreigners, and its prospects for growth are minimal, a strong rival has emerged. China may not quite be an adversary, but it is not an ally, either. Macmillan's 1971 prophecy that the United States might decline "in 200 years" betrayed a mechanical interpretation of history: it projected enduring dominance for the United States, much like his own country had enjoyed. But China could accelerate the patterns of history—and make the United States confront its decline much sooner than Macmillan anticipated or even than most people expect today.

The Middling Kingdom

The Hype and the Reality of China's Rise

Salvatore Babones

B y any measure, China's economic growth has been unprecedented, even miraculous. According to the International Monetary Fund, the Chinese economy grew by an average of
9.6 percent per year between 1990 and 2010. At the beginning of the
recent global financial crisis, many feared that the Chinese growth
engine would grind to a halt. In late 2008, Chinese exports collapsed,
triggering fears of political instability and popular revolt in the country. In the end, however, the global economic crisis turned out to be
little more than a pothole on the road of China's economic growth.
Inflationary pressures may now be building up in China, and China's
property bubble may be threatening to burst, but most economists
continue to predict rapid growth for the country well into the future.
Although their forecasts vary widely, they seem to share the view that
China's growth will be fast—if not as fast as it has been—and that this
rate of growth will continue for decades. These predictions are at once
cautious about the near future (China's performance will not be as
extraordinary as it has been) and optimistic about the distant future
(they see no end to China's upward trajectory). By coincidence or
design, they are moderated extrapolations of current trends.

For example, the Nobel Prize-winning economist Robert Fogel
believes that China will grow at an average annual rate of eight

SALVATORE BABONES is Senior Lecturer in Sociology and Social Policy at
the University of Sydney, in Australia.

percent until 2040, by which time it will be twice as rich as Europe (in per capita terms) and its share of global GDP will be 40 percent (compared with 14 percent for the United States and five percent for the European Union). Other economists are slightly more cautious: Uri Dadush and Bennett Stancil of the Carnegie Endowment for International Peace predict that China will grow by 5.6 percent per year through 2050.

Like many other forecasts of China's continued rise, these projections are based on careful formal economic modeling. But are they convincing? Extrapolating from current trends may make sense when predicting growth in the next year and the year after that, but once the years turn into decades, such assumptions seem more questionable. If my ancestors had invested a penny in my name in 1800 at a real compound interest rate of six percent per year above inflation, that penny would now be worth about $280,000. That does not mean, however, that reliably high-yielding 211-year investments are easy to find. Things change; things go wrong. Past returns are no guarantee of future performance.

When it comes to gauging China's future growth, economic modeling can offer only so much guidance. The models predict future economic outputs on the basis of projected future levels of economic inputs, but future economic inputs are impossible to predict. In the end, there is little to do but extrapolate from current inputs. But inputs, as well as other key features of any economy, change over time. China's economy is evolving rapidly: from subsistence agriculture to smokestack industries to the latest electronics to consumer services. And at some point in the future, perhaps in the not-too-distant future, China's excess growth rates will level out and its economic growth will slow down, returning to rates more like those experienced by comparable countries.

WHEN THE GROWING GETS TOUGH

It may seem foolish in 2011 to even talk about calling a top to the Chinese market. Judging by the Fogel and Dadush-Stancil models, there seem to be no medium-term barriers to China's growth. So long as the country's urban labor force continues to expand, its educational levels continue to rise, and capital continues to move into China, the Chinese economy should continue to grow.

But are things as simple as that? For one thing, economic models tend to downplay the fact that as countries grow, growth gets harder. When economies move up global value chains, graduating from the production of simple manufactured goods to a reliance on the creativity of their citizens to develop new industries, they rise less and less rapidly. It took South Korea 30 years, from 1960 to 1990, to raise its GDP per capita from one-thirtieth of U.S. GDP per capita to one-third—but then it took another 20 years to nudge its way up from one-third to one-half. And South Korea today is still a long way from catching up with the United States. Japan caught up with the West (and by some accounts exceeded it) in the 1980s, but then the bubble burst, and since 1990 its economy has grown by an average of just one percent per year.

What is more, these two states have been vastly more successful than most others. No other medium sized or large country with a diversified economy has even come close to Japan's accomplishments. Of the four "Asian tigers," the richest two (Hong Kong and Singapore) are cities, and the other two (South Korea and Taiwan) are basically cities-plus and are much farther behind economically. Other poor countries that have become rich are either offshore financial centers or small petro-sheikdoms. None of them is a full-sized country with multiple cities and regions, a large rural population, and competing political constituencies. Even Japan represents a questionable model of a state recently and rapidly catching up to the West, if only because it had already achieved much of its progress before World War II. Like the leading Western countries, it industrialized in the late nineteenth century and early twentieth century, partly through ruthless colonial exploitation. Its economy was then bombed into oblivion during World War II; thus, its rapid postwar growth was to some extent a return to prewar levels. In other words, there is no example to date of a state taking a very rapid growth trajectory to the top of the world economy, raising doubts about whether China can be the unlikely exception.

China's recent growth is often characterized as the country's natural, deserved return to its historical place in the global economy, but this argument is more clever than correct. According to the late economic historian Angus Maddison, China last reached parity with the West around the time of Marco Polo. China's subsequent decline relative to the West long predates the Industrial Revolution, Western colonialism, and even China's sixteenth-century inward turn. The overarching story of the past five centuries is not about China's absolute decline so much as about the West's relative advance. European economies grew substantially between 1500 and 1800. According to Maddison, by 1820—before the advent of the railroad, the telegraph, and the modern steel industry, and before the Opium Wars, the colonization of Hong Kong, and the Boxer Rebellion— China's national income per capita was less than half that of the average for European countries. By 1870, it had dropped to 25 percent, and by 1970, to just seven percent. Moreover, considering that Maddison's figures are all estimates based on purchasing power parity, China's position in hard-currency terms looks far worse. According to hard-currency statistics from the World Bank, between 1976 and 1994, Chinese GDP per capita was less than two percent of U.S. GDP per capita, and today it is still under ten percent.

In other words, China's massive economic growth over the past two decades has done nothing more—and perhaps much less— than return the country to its 1870 position (in terms of purchasing power parity). Optimists will see this as further evidence of China's potential: if China is at only 1870 levels, there is still plenty of room for further growth. But pessimists might note that if China could fall from this position in 1870, it might well fall from it again. There is no reason, on the face of it, to expect one outcome or the other; a conservative bet would be that China stays right where it is.

ONE-TIME BENEFITS

Another reason that economic models forecasting China's continuing rise are too simplistic is that they tend to ignore both the one-time boosts that helped propel the country in the past and the political, environmental, and structural obstacles that will limit its growth in the future. China is now in a much stronger political and military position vis-à-vis the West than it was in 1870 and seems very unlikely to descend into another century-long ordeal of repeated human and economic catastrophes. But does that necessarily mean it will grow to become the world's richest country?

China's dramatic rise over the past 20 years was propelled by two one-time bonuses: the population's declining fertility rate and its increasing urbanization. Both factors have led to massive increases in economic productivity, but they are finite processes and cannot be counted on in the future. China's fertility rate was already falling well before the first implementation of its draconian one-child policy in 1979. The decline in fertility in the 1970s meant that throughout the 1980s and 1990s, both families and the state could focus their limited resources on a relatively small number of children. Now, these children are in their mid-30s and are actively contributing to the development of the country's human capital and to its GDP. Future generations may be even better educated, but the major gains have already been made. More important, low fertility rates over the past few decades freed up adults, particularly women, to enter the formal labor market. Hundreds of millions of women who would have worked in the home or on the farm are now working in the money economy, boosting the county's GDP figures. This has given China a one-time boost—sustained higher output—but it will not help GDP continue to grow. There is little room for further fertility decline; China cannot move to a zero-child policy.

Moreover, there are today comparatively large numbers of workers born in the high-fertility 1950s, 1960s, and early 1970s making their way through their careers. Because their parents' generation is dying relatively young and because they have few children, these workers are largely unencumbered by either caregiving or child-rearing duties. Of all the generations of Chinese throughout history, this one is uniquely positioned to pursue work and create wealth. Future generations of Chinese workers will be smaller and will be saddled with the care of ever more elderly relatives. Moreover, fertility rates can only rise going forward, meaning that these workers may have more children to care for as well.

Increasing urbanization is the other one-time bonus that boosted China's economic growth during the past 20 years. Urbanization increases GDP because urban populations are generally more productive than rural ones and because city dwellers typically work outside the home in paid employment, whereas many people in the countryside engage in unpaid subsistence farming. But like fertility reduction, urbanization is a process with natural limits. China's level of urbanization is still well below that of the West, and urban expansion in China shows no signs of slowing down. (At current growth rates, urbanization in China will not catch up to urbanization in the West or Latin America until the 2040s.) But what form will this expansion take? Huge shantytowns are already forming on the edges of Beijing, Shanghai, and other Chinese megacities. The Chinese government bulldozes shanties by the hundreds of thousands every year, but it is unclear whether their residents are being relocated or just being made homeless. Whether or not the government wins its war against slum development, the days when urbanization was a boost to economic growth are gone.

STRUCTURAL STRICTURES

In addition, China is facing political, environmental, and structural barriers that will limit its economic growth in the future. For example, many analysts believe that China will not be able to move up the global value-added chain unless its politics open up. The argument is that high-value-added activities, such as branding, design, and invention, require a kind of free thinking possible only in democratic societies. China may educate hundreds of thousands of engineers, but if it continues to stifle their creativity, they will never succeed at the highest levels of the global economy. China will not reach the top ranks of the global economy (in terms of GDP per capita) until its schools, companies, and people learn to innovate more than they have in the past. This is happening, but China's stifling political culture is hindering the process. It is difficult to imagine a dynamic knowledge economy emerging in a politically repressive one-party state; none ever has before.

The environmental barriers to China's continued growth are better documented. The World Health Organization estimates that air pollution in China kills 656,000 people annually and water pollution another 95,600; China's own Ministry of Water Resources estimates that about 300 million people, two-thirds of them in rural areas, rely on water that contains "harmful substances." According to *The New York Times*, officials from China's State Council have said that the massive Three Gorges Dam is plagued by "urgent problems" that "must be resolved regarding the smooth relocation of residents, ecological protection, and geological disaster prevention." China is also now the world's largest emitter of greenhouse gases. The great drought and floods that have hit China so far this year may or may not be related to its environmental record, but it is clear that China's ability to monetize its environment to promote economic growth without regard for ecological devastation is coming to an end. China's future growth will have to be cleaner than its past growth; thus, it will be more expensive. Long a densely populated country, China has always had one of the most intensively exploited environments in the world. Today, it has little environment left to exploit.

Still, the greatest barriers to China's continuing rapid economic growth are structural. Until 1980, the country was effectively closed to the world; by 1992, nearly all of urban China had been incorporated into special economic zones open to private enterprise and foreign investment. The incredibly inefficient Maoist economy is gone and has been replaced by some of the most competitive firms in the world. Creating more value than did state industries during the Cultural Revolution was not very difficult. But creating more value than today's efficient Chinese firms do will be much harder.

This difficulty will be exacerbated by major structural changes in the economy. Since 1960, life expectancy in China has risen from 47 years to 74 years, but the number of children per family has declined from more than five to fewer than two. Today's little emperors will spend their most productive years taking care of their parents. And as they do, China's economic activity will have to move away from high-productivity manufacturing and toward low-productivity health services. This shift will further limit China's future growth prospects because productivity is harder to increase in service industries than in manufacturing, mining, or agriculture. In the past, to make the most of their comparative advantage, Chinese producers focused on manufacturing for the world's industrial market. In the future, Chinese service providers will have no choice but to focus on the domestic health-care market, without regard for getting an edge.

CAN-DO OR HAS-DONE?

Many commentators, most notably the political scientists George Gilboy and Eric Heginbotham, have warned recently of the "Latin Americanization" of China, specifically its rising income inequality. In 2003, China had just one billionaire (as measured in U.S. dollars); by 2011, according to Forbes magazine, it had 115. Yet China is still a poor country: GDP per capita in hard-currency terms is substantially lower in China (under $5,000) than in Brazil, Mexico, and Russia ($9,000-$10,000), the world's three big middle-income countries. But as China catches up to them, its inequality levels are also rising to levels close to theirs.

China shares many features with Brazil, Mexico, and Russia. Sociologists have identified these four countries as belonging to the "semi-periphery" of the world economy, a group of states that are not as rich and powerful as the developed democracies but not as poor as the small countries of Africa, Central America, and Southeast Asia. (Other examples include Indonesia and Turkey.) These countries are characterized by strong states with weak institutions, governments highly influenced by the richest citizens, and mass poverty.

At its current growth rates, China will likely catch up to Brazil, Mexico, and Russia around the year 2020 in terms of per capita GDP. At that point, all four states will have per capita national income levels between $10,000 and $15,000 (in today's dollars). All will also have similar levels of economic inequality—levels far higher than those in the developed countries. Their people will not experience serious hunger or malnutrition, but they will know mass squalor. About 40 percent of these countries' populations will live in large cities, and about 20 percent will live in rural areas, with the rest in small cities and towns. Their fertility rates will have fallen somewhat under replacement levels, and about two-thirds of their populations will be between the ages of 16 and 65. In the face of rapid aging, these countries will need to shift their economies away from growth industries and toward slow-growth health-care services.

All of which raises this question: If in 2020, China will almost certainly face structural conditions nearly identical to those in Brazil, Mexico, and Russia, why should anyone expect it to grow any faster than them? Brazil and Mexico have belonged to the middle-income league for generations. Russia was in that bracket in the early twentieth century and returned to it immediately after the collapse of communism. China was there in 1870, and it is back there again. Granted, China is bigger than those countries, but there is no reason to think that being big makes it different. Historical statistics show no correlation between a country's size and its economic growth.

The relative position of China in 2020 will look an awful lot like that of China in 1870 and of Brazil, Mexico, and Russia today. There is no particular reason to believe that the China of 2020 will be any more successful than these other states have been. Perhaps China's proactive attitude toward development will allow it to power through the middle ranks of the global income distribution despite a weak civil society, an aging population, and a devastated environment. And having already returned to its nineteenth-century position relative to the West, perhaps China might eventually regain its thirteenth-century superiority over the West. Structure is not destiny. And if China does overcome its limitations, it could provoke a complete realignment of the international system.

But it is more reasonable to see China's famous can-do attitude as more of a has-done attitude: a legitimate pride in recent accomplishments rather than a harbinger of future success. Like other middle-income countries, China will likely continue to grow slightly faster than Western countries, although not as fast as it did between 1990 and 2010 and with much more volatility. But its population will start to fall soon after 2020, whereas the U.S. population will keep rising. The overall size of China's economy is thus likely to remain roughly equal to that of the United States for the remainder of the twenty-first century. This is not to say that China will not become a major world player. Even if it reaches only parity with the United States in terms of overall GDP and attains only about one-quarter of U.S. GDP per capita, it will still be a power to be reckoned with. It will become the second indispensable country.

But given the United States' far greater alliance network and geostrategic position, U.S. hegemony is not threatened by the rise of China. The United States is encircled by long-standing allies (Canada and the countries of western Europe) or stable but weak noncompetitors (Latin America). China's neighbors are a rich and powerful Japan, rising South Korea and Vietnam, giant India and Russia, and a host of failed or failing states in Central and Southeast Asia. The United States reigns supreme over the oceans, the skies, and outer space; China struggles to maintain order within its own territory. China will, and legitimately should, play an increasing role in Asian and world politics, but it is in no position to dominate even Asia, never mind the world.

Pundits may relish the opportunity to speculate about a post-American future in which the world has to learn Mandarin, but the facts say not in this century. It is time to start treating China like a large but ordinary country. The rest of the world should neither relish nor fear the prospect of Chinese domination. Putting aside the hype and the panic, one should see in China a country that suffered terrible tragedy for 200 years and is finally returning to normal. This is a good thing—for China, for the United States, and for the world. If the international system comes to see China, and China comes to see itself, as an important but not all-powerful participant in the global system, irrational fears will diminish on all sides, and rightly so. Tomorrow's China is more likely to focus on meeting the needs of its own people than on establishing itself as the new global hegemon.

Indebted Dragon

The Risky Strategy Behind China's Construction Economy

Lynette H. Ong

For four decades, the Chinese economy has grown by between seven and ten percent each year. It is the envy of the world, despite its relatively sluggish recent performance. Visitors to Beijing, Shanghai, and other major Chinese cities are quickly awed by impressive skyscrapers, glittering shopping malls, new highways, and high-speed rail lines, all of which leave the impression that China is a developed economy—or at least well on its way to becoming one. Even in some smaller cities in inland provinces, government buildings make those in Washington and Brussels appear meager. In an area of Anhui Province that is officially designated an "impoverished county," the government office block looks exactly like the White House, only newer and whiter.

Underwriting the impressive facade, however, is an incredibly risky strategy. Governments borrow money using land as collateral and repay the interest on their loans using funds they earn from selling or leasing the same land. All this means that the Chinese economy depends on a buoyant real estate market to keep grinding. If housing and land prices fall dramatically, a fiscal or banking crisis would likely soon follow. Meanwhile, local officials' hunger for land has displaced millions of farmers, leading to 120,000 land-related protests each year.

LYNETTE H. ONG is Associate Professor of Political Science at the Munk School of Global Affairs at the University of Toronto. She is the author of Prosper or Perish: Credit and Fiscal Systems in Rural China.

RISKY BUSINESS

The recklessness can be traced to two things: First, local Chinese officials are evaluated for promotions and other rewards based on how well the economy they manage performs. Construction and real estate activities are among the most straightforward ways to stimulate growth. White-elephant construction projects thus offer eager officials a perfect opportunity to impress their political superiors, even if massive developments do not necessarily make any economic sense. Take, for example, the city of Ordos in Inner Mongolia: Its elaborate urban infrastructure and its sea of new flats and office blocks are nearly all unoccupied, making it China's largest ghost city.

Another factor was China's fiscal recentralization reform of 1994, in which the central government raised its own revenue by taking back power from local governments to levy some major taxes. The move lowered local governments' revenues but left their financial responsibilities—providing education, health care, subsistence allowances, and pensions—unchanged. So local officials had to find other ways to generate money.

In the wake of the tax reform, sales and business taxes on construction, real estate, and other service industries became the main source of tax revenue for municipal governments. Not surprisingly, in the 1990s, local authorities started to engineer real estate and construction booms. According to Chinese law, collectively owned farmland must be converted to state ownership before it is leased to private developers. Local governments were thus able to expropriate farmland from villagers and then rent it to private commercial ventures such as factory owners and real estate companies. According to a 2011 survey by Landesa, a Seattle-based nonprofit organization, local governments earn on average $740,000 per acre of land. That is 40 times the average amount they pay to displaced farmers.

The involvement of municipal governments in land sales goes beyond leasing. To entice property developers, officials also invest in infrastructure. Although they sometimes finance that development directly with land transfer revenue, more often they simply use the land as collateral to borrow from state-owned banks. They generally work through local-government-incorporated urban development and investment companies (UDICs, or chengtou gongsi) and local government financing platforms to skirt laws prohibiting such borrowing. To service interest payments, local governments typically draw from land transfer revenue, taxes, or user fees and charges.

Using bank loans to finance infrastructure investment is not necessarily bad or unusual. It has been common practice in the United States for years, and tax experts say it is a fair and efficient way of building public infrastructure. The problem with China's approach is that the local-government financing platforms are not regulated or subject to any disclosure standards. And although the law formally prohibits local governments from borrowing recklessly, the central government's financing practices encourage them to do so in a roundabout way.

SHOW XI THE MONEY

Until Beijing started conducting audits in mid-2009, neither the central government nor the banking regulator knew how much debt local governments had racked up. Since then, official estimates by the National Audit Office, the People's Bank of China, and the China Banking Regulatory Commission have put the size of local government debt at 5 trillion to 14.4 trillion yuan (803 billion to over two trillion dollars) 13 to 36 percent of GDP—as of the end of 2010. Private analysts often put the number much higher: between 50 and 100 percent of GDP, depending on whether local governments' contingent liabilities or indirect debts (debts owed by government-owned and government-related entities) are included.

On the surface, banks' balance sheets have remained healthy despite these debts, since banks tend to roll over or "ever green" loans by issuing new loans to help borrowers "repay" old ones. In addition, local governments have been able to make their interest payments using their land as collateral.

The banks' accounting tricks treat only a symptom of the problem. Eventually, banks will become unable to roll over loans because they will run out of fresh money. And officials' ability to pay off loan interest depends on the continued rise of real estate prices and a buoyant economy, neither of which can be taken for granted. Some analysts are already saying that China's real estate bubble has burst. That could be terrible, but as I have argued elsewhere, Beijing cannot and will not let banks that hold the savings of ordinary people go under. Bank runs would send millions of depositors into a panic and lead to widespread social unrest.

OUTSIDE THE BUBBLE

Even before it pops, China's real estate bubble is causing social harm. An inevitable effect of state-led urbanization is that farmers are forced to vacate their land. Close to 300,000 peasants are removed from their villages every year to make room for the construction of airports, highways, and buildings. Since 1980, more than 60 million peasants, roughly the population of the United Kingdom, have been moved.

The displaced are not usually consulted before relocation. Governments frequently force them to leave by suspending the supply of utilities, such as electricity, to their homes. Increasingly, local governments are even hiring or colluding with gangsters to intimidate villagers who refuse to move. Tellingly, in some villages, these mobsters are known as the "second government."

Compensation to farmers who do move is often inadequate, because negotiations over the value of their land take place without them. The opacity allows authorities to line their own pockets with funds meant for farmers. It is no surprise, then, that in a recent Landesa survey of nearly 1,800 rural households across 17 provinces, about 20 percent of the displaced (which made up 43 percent of the survey's sample) had not received any compensation. Of those who had received remuneration, 53.4 percent reported that they were "very dissatisfied" or "dissatisfied" with it, compared with 25 percent who were either "satisfied" or "very satisfied." When asked why, 80 percent complained of inadequate compensation, 47 percent said it was determined without their input,

38.4 percent said payment was insufficient to maintain their previous standard of living, 28.6 percent said they were unable to find nonagricultural income after having their land taken away, and 25 percent reported that compensation had been intercepted by local officials.

For Chinese farmers, farmland is both a livelihood and a form of social insurance. In bad times, when temporary work or factory jobs dry up in cities and towns, migrant workers can return to subsistence living in villages. By way of comparison, urban residents are entitled to state-provided social welfare, namely, subsistence allowance, unemployment insurance, and pensions.

Unsurprisingly, demolition, relocation, and land expropriation have become the leading causes of social unrest in China. Discontented peasants typically try to air their grievances using China's petition system, but when efforts through official channels prove futile, they take to the streets: The number of "mass incidents" in China continues to rise.

Given slower growth rates and falling real estate prices this year, the frequency of land expropriation is slowing down. But the truth remains that much of urbanization in China is a state-driven phenomenon, using resources drawn from the financial sector.

Although the central government recognizes the seriousness of the problem, it seems to lack any real resolve to tackle the issue head on. Muddling through seems to be so much easier. So until a major slowdown in the economy happens, the Chinese real estate market will continue on its current course.

An earlier verion of this article stated that 5 trillion to 14.4 trillion yuan is 800 million to over two billion dollars. In fact, it is 800 billion to two trillion dollars.

Austerity with Chinese Characteristics

Why China's Belt-Tightening Has More To Do With Confucius Than Keynes

John Delury

This year, to the consternation of the world's luxury-goods producers, "austerity" became one of Beijing's most prominent political buzzwords. Since becoming head of the Chinese Communist Party last November, Xi Jinping has announced a steady stream of belt-tightening measures: government officials have been barred from hosting lavish banquets and wearing designer watches, and the construction of government buildings has been banned for five years. It's only natural that Western commentators have been quick to interpret China's austerity drive in terms of their own long-running debate about macroeconomics: from Athens to Dublin to Washington, D.C., politicians and economists are arguing the economic merits and drawbacks of budget-cutting and deficit spending.

But it would be a big mistake to interpret Xi's ban on shark-fin soup as an extension of what Paul Krugman describes as the West's "turn to austerity" since 2010. Whereas Western austerity has been

JOHN DELURY is an Assistant Professor at Yonsei University's Graduate School of International Studies, in South Korea. He is the Co-Author, with Orville Schell, of *Wealth and Power: China's Long March to the Twenty-First Century*. Follow him on Twitter @JohnDelury.

an economic policy tool, in China its essence is primarily political. China has a long history of turning to frugality not to stimulate business confidence but, rather, to combat the disease of corruption. It's safe to say that Xi has been thinking less of Milton Friedman or John Maynard Keynes than of China's own political reform tradition, stretching from Confucius to the Communists.

In the formative period of Chinese politics, some 2,500 years ago, Confucius crafted a philosophy of government and social ethics that left a profound imprint on East Asian civilization. He admonished rulers to keep both taxation and spending to a minimum. The enlightened ruler, Confucius and his followers said, should embody a certain kind of moral austerity in his personal behavior and fiscal austerity in matters of state. The people—most of them farmers—would then follow the emperor "like grass bends in the wind." In other words, demonstrating one's political virtue through austerity, frugality, and simplicity would ensure popular legitimacy and dynastic stability.

The Confucian approach to ensuring virtuous government through frugality has been a consistent thread in Chinese politics well into the modern era. One early-eighteenth-century emperor, for example, declared a permanent freeze on tax rates as a show of Confucian thriftiness. (Although this policy eventually backfired: the tax ceiling hampered the government's ability to generate revenues for the remainder of its 200 years in power.) Campaigns against corruption—including arrests of senior ministers—were a regular feature of late imperial times. Even the major political upheavals of the twentieth century turned on questions of corruption and frugality. The Nationalist Party of Chiang Kai-shek, who took over as head of state of the Republic of China after Sun Yat-sen's death in 1925, quickly earned a reputation for corruption. Chiang responded by promoting neo-Confucian values as part of what he called his New Life movement, which made "simplicity and frugality" one of its core virtues. But he ultimately fell to Mao Zedong, who promoted an even more radical notion of the austere state. Mao demanded that Communist Party cadres reject the slightest hint of bourgeois comfort, including by wearing a uniform of a nondescript Mao suit. Although Mao ended up living more like a Roman emperor than a Spartan soldier, he was effective at creating the perception that the Communists were incorruptible, in stark contrast to the Nationalist Party's reputation for graft. As Confucius would have predicted, this helped the Communists win the "hearts and minds" of the people.

The old Confucian paragon of the "clean official" still resonates powerfully in today's half-capitalist, half-Communist, pseudo-Confucian China. The current austerity program is best understood as Xi's attempt to put his own stamp on that traditional notion of good governance. In particular, there are clear traces of Mao in Xi's program. Xi even recently praised Mao's list of "six nos" that barred officials from squandering the people's wealth, and he promised to renew Mao's old fight against "formalism, bureaucratism, and hedonism and extravagance."

But Xi has also been drawing on the unique language of the progressive reform tradition in Chinese political thought, which traces back to the nineteenth century. Its standard-bearer, Feng Guifen, called upon his countrymen to study Western countries' "techniques of wealth and power," including the democratic political system that ensured "closeness" between ruler and ruled. That influence is especially clear when Xi explains the goal of austerity in terms of preserving harmony between the Communist Party and the Chinese people. "If we don't redress unhealthy tendencies and allow them to develop," Xi cautioned earlier this year, "it will be like putting up a wall between our party and the people, and we will lose our roots, our lifeblood and our strength." This is a standard trope among Chinese reformers going back to Sun Yat-sen and Feng Guifen, who argued that elections and representative assemblies would reduce the distance between the people and the government, and thus tighten the bonds of the nation. Xi too wants to keep the people close to the Party, but to do so through austerity, not democracy.

It is clear, then, that Xi sees a lot more at stake than mere GDP growth; austerity implicates the very future of the polity. The Communist Party wants to win the "people's trust" with top-down anti-corruption campaigns based on austerity exhortations, as well as punishments for high-profile officials who get caught with their hand in the cookie jar. The most prominent conviction so far in the Xi Jinping era was of former Minister of Railways Liu Zhijun, and the much-awaited trial of disgraced leader Bo Xilai is expected soon. Xi is hoping that traditional forms of frugality and discipline of this sort can obviate the need for bottom-up political empowerment. To put it bluntly, whereas in the EU and United States the alternative to austerity is stimulus, in China austerity's alternative is democracy.

In this light, it is worth remembering that the last major challenge to Communist Party rule—when millions of Chinese occupied Tiananmen Square in the spring of 1989—centered on two popular demands: more democracy and less corruption. When those two goals become intertwined, the pillars of CCP legitimacy start to rattle and shake. This helps to explain the real significance of Communist Party austerity, and why Xi has made fighting corruption from the top down a centerpiece of his agenda.

In the short run, it may be easier for the party to try to discipline itself, and to regain public confidence by catching the "tigers and flies" who abuse power at the people's expense. But in the long run, Xi might find that the burdens of this top-down, self-policing approach are too much to bear for Beijing's most powerful. The only sustainable solution for deeply rooted corruption will likely be to strengthen democratic mechanisms and civil society organizations, and empower the media and the courts, so that top-down discipline is matched with bottom-up accountability. Whatever austerity's merits as an economic policy, as a method of political reform, it will probably soon reach its limits.

Where Have All the Workers Gone?

China's Labor Shortage and the End of the Panda Boom

Damien Ma and William Adams

I t became fashionable after the Soviet Union's collapse to say that breakneck economic growth was the only thing postponing the Chinese Communist Party's (CCP) day of reckoning. Communist ideology was discredited, went the argument, but as long as the economic pie kept growing, citizens would set aside broader concerns and take their piece. But what if growth were interrupted by, say, a global financial crisis, collapse of world trade, and mass layoffs on the Chinese factory floor? The music would stop, the masquerade party would end, and Jennifer Connelly would smash her way through David Bowie's bubble prison, so to speak.

Except that it didn't. The Chinese economy faced exactly this cataclysmic scenario in the final months of 2008. Collapsing confidence and worldwide financial dysfunction forced businesses to cancel orders en masse. It was a huge blow to the Chinese manufacturing industry, compounding the weaknesses of a domestic economy already fragile after months of government efforts to cool a real estate bubble and overheating inflation. Tens of millions of Chinese migrant workers

DAMIEN MA is a Fellow at The Paulson Institute. WILLIAM ADAMS is a Center Associate of the University of Pittsburgh Asian Studies Center. They are authors of *In Line Behind a Billion People,* from which this essay is adapted.

were laid off in the lead up to the Lunar New Year holiday in late January 2009. They returned to the countryside, passed the holiday with relatives, and waited for the crisis to abate.

Meanwhile, Zhongnanhai's poobahs began to sweat. The global economy was plunging into the worst recession since the 1930s. China responded hastily with an outsized stimulus package that boosted confidence, but was insufficient to create jobs for both the laid-off workers and the millions of college graduates and young migrant workers who had flocked to urban job markets every year for decades. Early in 2009, Chinese officials were openly worrying about maintaining social stability in the Chinese countryside.

The economy in 2009 was indeed shaky by Chinese standards, if not in comparison to the rest of the world. China's real GDP growth slowed to single digits—the lowest it had been in nearly a decade. Accordingly, the China bears rose from hibernation to swarm op-ed pages and talk show panels, predicting the collapse of the Chinese labor market, an economic crisis, and a political crisis.

Instead, the labor market overheated.

Over the next two years, China's economic policymakers flooded the economy with bank credit, funding countless new housing projects, amazing feats of infrastructure modernization, and some fantastical white elephants along the way. Migrant workers gravitated toward the millions of jobs created on construction sites, or back to the factories whose order books were filled by investment-led demand. By early 2010, job postings began to outnumber job-seekers for the first time since the start of China's resource-intensive economic boom at the beginning of the twenty-first century, a period we call the Panda Boom (after that cuddly creature's voracious habit of eating 10–15 percent of its body weight in bamboo each day). Suddenly, in 2010, it was a lack of workers rather than a lack of orders keeping factories from running at full tilt.

In the heat of the moment, it was unclear exactly what had saved the country from disaster. Did the massive stimulus program pull the economy from the brink of recession? Or did the crisis fundamentally transform the labor market in some unanticipated way?

With the benefit of several years' hindsight, it seems clear that the labor market had been transforming even before the crisis hit.

SOCIALIST EMPLOYERS PARADISE LOST

The structure of the Chinese labor force changed—and is still changing—much faster than Beijing had anticipated.

During the Panda Boom, all the major factors guiding Chinese labor relations had swung in employers' favor, the foremost being supply and demand. First came demographics: the country was enjoying a mini–baby boom that boosted the number of annual workforce entrants around the end of the twentieth century, an echo of the baby boom amid the relative peace and social stability of the decade following China's 1949 reunification. Second came urbanization: a massive movement of workers gravitated toward factory work on the coasts in the 1990s and 2000s after the earliest market-oriented reforms of the 1980s, which freed up farm laborers by dramatically increasing agricultural productivity per worker. And third came tens of millions of layoffs in state-owned enterprises in the late 1990s, which helped keep true unemployment in urban China (as opposed to what meaningless official unemployment statistics said) elevated for most of the 2000s. Add to this the millions of teenagers aging into the workforce each year, and you have an employer's paradise: workers needed jobs much more urgently than employers needed labor.

During China's demographic explosion, maintaining job growth was the government's paramount priority. Occupational safety, collective bargaining rights, and other costly labor protections were vastly less important, and summarily ignored. That started to change a little with the Chinese Labor Contract Law of 2008, the centerpiece of a stronger labor regulatory package that increased worker protections against layoffs, obliged employers to negotiate with the party-controlled unions over pay rates and benefits, and provided workers with new avenues to defend their rights against employers in courts. Fully enforced, the regulation's provisions were estimated to increase the cost of employing Chinese workers by some 10–20 percent. But at the time the law was enacted, no one gave that much thought. After all, there were still nearly 200 million migrants in the cities and millions more waiting to move off farms. As long as the supply remained abundant, the employer's paradise would endure.

By 2010, however, cracks were starting to show. They became most visible in a string of highly publicized wildcat strikes at foreign-owned factories that year. Multinational and Chinese manufacturers had cut wages during the downturn of 2008–2009 and had been slow to raise them as production began normalizing over the following year—even as inflation had taken off in a hurry.

It was a double shock for foreign employers. First, they were flummoxed that workers were emboldened to shut down production so soon after many manufacturers had been driven to the brink of bankruptcy. Managers were still twitching at the memories of 2008, when the economy was so bad that many owners in Shenzhen had snuck over the factory wall in the cover of night, leaving their unpaid workers behind. Second, that the strikes happened at all turned preconceived notions on their heads: China was not supposed to have strikes.

Double-digit wage increases eventually ended the strikes, but they didn't bring back the old labor market. Factory employers who were slow to keep wage increases in line with market rates quickly saw their workers walking away. Annual workforce turnover of half or more were not uncommon at some factories. After lagging behind GDP growth for the previous decade, average Chinese wages grew faster than GDP in 2011 and 2012, right alongside a major slowdown of the economy as a whole.

MIGRANTS CAME, SAW, AND LEFT

The recent labor drought revealed that the usual explanation of how the Chinese blue-collar labor market works is insufficient. It significantly overestimated the amount of excess labor. In particular, it misunderstood the dynamics of a large rural labor force that could have potentially entered the workforce as migrant workers. It was widely believed that Chinese would leave the farms, come to the cities where they would be vastly more productive, GDP would boom, and the countless underemployed laborers still idling on the farm would keep wages from rising.

But that story ignores an ugly truth of how the Chinese workforce functions, or at least how it functioned historically.

Many westerners have failed to recognize, for example, that the size of the Chinese labor market is significantly limited by Chinese prejudices. By Western standards, China would be considered a racist, ageist place. Nondiscrimination is a foreign legal concept to Chinese employers. During the previous decade of unrelenting growth, many factories would only hire female Han Chinese workers under the age of 25, because they were believed to be more easily managed than men and more energetic than older workers. For migrant workers over the age of 40, finding work was exponentially more difficult than it was for younger migrants (and sometimes impossible). Based on employers' preferences, if one wanted to understand the real supply of potential laborers for Chinese factories, it would have been unrealistic to include many potential workers in their 40s and 50s.

Analysts overestimated the blue-collar labor force in another important way, as well. It is true that, in the last decade, high schools graduated millions of students who might have gone straight to work. But many of them opted to go to college rather than to factories and construction sites. From 2000 to 2010, the number of young people enrolling in higher education programs rather than entering the workforce after high school tripled, growing from 2.2 million to 6.6 million. With so many young people hitting the books, the usual squeeze through the factory gates became less tight.

Chinese factory managers have more or less adapted, willingly or otherwise, to the new reality. Employers are, of course, increasing wages as necessary to keep their workers from walking off the line. Manufacturers are also shifting factories further inland, away from the largest Chinese cities where costs of doing business (and wages) are highest, and where they might find more willing migrants—those who would rather work six hours from their home village instead of 26 hours away in Guangdong.

A job close to home appeals not only to older migrant workers as a practical way to balance work and family obligations, but also to migrants of the post-1980s and 1990s generations, though for different reasons. The younger migrants tend to weigh lifestyle considerations heavily and approach the workforce with radically different expectations and attitudes than previous generations.

Early on in the post-1978 reform and opening period, migrant workers often left their parents and siblings (the one-child policy was not as strictly enforced in the countryside as in cities) for life in the factory town or the city. To be sure, the work they found in Chinese factories was tough and mind numbing, but still compared favorably to the exhausting rigors of farm life.

The new generation of migrant workers, by contrast, hardly worked on the farm, if ever at all, and often never saw their parents doing field labor either. Recent studies from Chinese think tanks have shown that these new migrants are less motivated by simple financial opportunities than by their own career advancement and individual interests. Moreover, they tend to put a premium on social justice and fair treatment. These lifestyle considerations make living closer to home, family, friends, and a familiar dialect and culture (which range as much in China as do the modern-day variations of Latin spoken in different corners of Europe) as important as their salary, if not more so in some cases.

SCHOOL OF HARD KNOCKS

The flip side of the dearth of blue-collar labor has been the glut of recent college graduates that scarcely qualify for work in China's competitive job market. During the beginning of the market economy era in the 1980s, less than three percent of Chinese young people received a four-year university education. This exclusive cabal of credentialed elites was placed into high flying careers and lived lifestyles befitting their social status.

That was then. College graduates now face a life that would be totally unrecognizable to those a generation earlier, who had the fortune of first-mover advantage. Tripling the size of the higher education system in only a decade has meant a rapid proliferation of new institutions, most of which provide educations—and professional prospects—that can't compare with those of the graduates of the top tier institutions. A massive riot in 2006 illustrated how different the prospects are for graduates of elite universities and those of newer ones: Some graduates of the satellite campus of a university in central China apparently went berserk when they discovered that their diplomas designated them graduates of the satellite, not of the parent university as they were originally promised.

In a situation that would sound familiar to Americans, graduates of new and lower-ranked universities have struggled to find good entry-level jobs. They live in small, crowded, shared apartments at the edge of major cities, scraping by to make rent. The plum jobs for university graduates at state-owned enterprises, in government, or at glitzy multinationals are no more attainable for these young people than for migrant laborers of the same age. And the college graduates won't take the manufacturing jobs, perhaps to their detriment: average starting wages for college graduates were actually lower than average migrant worker salaries in 2011. Without a good employer to secure their place in urban China, these young people do not simply struggle economically; in many ways, they can be as marginalized from the economic and social fabric of their urban life as are migrant workers.

WHAT NOW?

The consequences of China's transforming labor market are by no means all bad; in fact, they will make the task of managing the Chinese economy easier in several crucial ways. A simultaneous influx of college graduates and lack of blue collar workforce entrants will narrow the wage gap between more and less educated Chinese, and also between rural and urban households. It must be a relief for the government that a secular demographic change is narrowing inequality in a way that its own policies have not. However, the strains of a rapidly changing population also bring new and unfamiliar complexities. Growth is slowing as China's economy runs short of

---

underemployed laborers to power its export juggernaut and anchor the "China price" for which the country is so famously known.

These changes are quite visible in China's recent economic statistics. In nominal terms, GDP rose 9.8 percent from 2011 to 2012, but in a change for China, more of the gains from growth accrued to workers, thanks to a tight labor market, than to the owners of capital. Median urban disposable incomes rose by 15 percent. The corporate profits of industrial firms, by contrast, rose by only five percent. Rapidly rising wages accelerated the country's shift from an export-oriented to domestically focused economy. Economic underperformance in the United States, Europe, and Japan also did China no favors.

Yes, to a certain extent, China's demographic hangover and the country's transition to a consumption-based economy are actually good news. Overreliance on investment and exports is not exactly sustainable. But the process of transition will have winners and losers. Rebalancing means households living on their salaries get more of the economic pie. Entrepreneurs, "red capitalists," multinationals, and tax collectors, commensurately, will likely be left with less.

Meanwhile, governing and encouraging economic development will become considerably more challenging. Economic management is much easier with an enormous demographic gust blowing at a government's back, propelling its economy forward even if policies are less than optimal. As the wind dies, individual policies and economic decisions are starting to matter much more. Now, China will need to be a whole lot smarter and more creative in designing policy incentives.

Productivity growth (that is, growth in output per worker) is likely to slow markedly. This is partly because of a less productivity-friendly mix of economic activity. Expanding demand for services means that a larger share of Chinese GDP will be generated by the service sector. It is much harder to double GDP per person employed in these parts of the economy than it is in the manufacturing sector. Slower growth, in turn, will blunt some of the government's most effective tools at managing its hybrid market economy. Beijing has been incredibly successful at growing out of economic problems. The bad loans crippling the banking sector at the dawn of the hyper-growth era, which began in the early 2000s, weren't fully repaid, for example—they just shrank relative to the rest of the financial industry and gradually stopped being a systemic risk to the economy. China still has to deal with the fallout from the credit boom of 2009–2010, which will inevitably generate hefty bad loans; its old strategy of growing out of the problem may not be as effective in a post double-digit growth era.

There are also several challenges to companies, foreign and domestic. They are already moving factories inland and raising wages to adapt to the new balance of power between migrant workers and employers. Inevitably, many companies will also start incorporating business practices for managing a mature workforce, analogous to those adopted in the United States or Europe.

More broadly, corporate strategy has to adapt to the end of cheap Chinese labor. The shift matters most for multinationals, which allocate investment, R&D, and managerial resources between China and other markets. Some U.S. companies have contemplated bringing operations back to the United States, Mexico, or Vietnam. But a lower growth and more expensive China won't drive all the multinationals away. There is still value to being in proximity to the world's largest high-growth market, which contributes the most to global aggregate demand each year. Those that do stay, though, will likely opt for increased mechanization. As labor becomes more expensive, machines become relatively cheaper and a more attractive option for maximizing efficiency.

Finally, China's demographic hangover could coincide with a right-sizing of expectations about what China can do for a multinational business. Managers might become less willing to accommodate "Chinese characteristics"—the combination of regulatory uncertainty, intellectual property violations, and the risk of becoming embroiled in corruption scandals that seem much harder to avoid there than in a developed market. In other words, these dynamics might serve as a catalyst for the government to renew economic and institutional reforms as new enticements to attract foreign investment.

China's demographic hangover is here, and it is as unexpected and unpleasant as the morning after a 30th birthday. Given the facility with which the government has managed difficult economic transitions in the past 20 years—forcing the military out of the market economy in the 1990s and initiating the Panda Boom later that decade—the purely economic dimensions seem daunting, but no more so than the other feats the CCP has pulled off. Instead, it's the social and political dimensions of the demographic hangover that seem most perplexing.

Most obviously, the prospect of an independent labor movement, albeit a small one, holds the potential to trigger revolutionary changes. Much more so than a decade ago, Chinese workers, historically poorly represented in the country's politics, seem aware of their own interests and more vocal about their demands. If China's leaders want to keep the music playing, the emergence of labor as an interest group could well require them to rethink the grand bargain—growth in exchange for stability—they strike with the public they govern.

After the Plenum

Why China Must Reshape the State

Evan A. Feigenbaum and Damien Ma

In early November, as Beijing braced for the Communist Party's Third Plenum, the high-level conference that would decide major policies for the next decade, President Xi Jinping appeared to deliberately raise expectations for major economic reforms. He spoke of a "comprehensive" reform plan and invoked Deng Xiaoping, the man who changed history by overhauling China's economy and politics at an earlier Third Plenum, in 1978.

Yet no sooner had the plenum closed and the party released its initial communiqué than observers dismissed the meeting as a bust. Markets slumped. Hong Kong's Hang Seng Index dropped 1.9 percent, to its lowest level in ten weeks. The Shanghai Composite lost 1.8 percent. Many commentators argued that China's leaders, faced with their first big test, were disinclined—or else too timid—to undertake the sweeping economic reforms that Xi had promised.

But then the verdict abruptly shifted with the release of a follow-up 60-point decision document, which presented a sweeping economic reform agenda that included new commitments to financial liberalization, the repair of China's social safety net, new protections for property rights, and greater reliance on market forces. Across Asia, the markets shot upward.

Several factors explain this quick swing from pessimism to exuberance, not least of which is a volatile combination of high expectations for China as the world's second-largest economy and deep

EVAN A. FEIGENBAUM is vice chair of the Paulson Institute at the University of Chicago. DAMIEN MA is a fellow at the Paulson Institute.

cynicism about the Chinese leadership's intentions and political will to overcome vested interests that oppose reform. Many look to Beijing to change its investment-led growth model to one based on consumption and innovation. And many will continue, therefore, to see what they want to see in the plenum's reform agenda—both its promises and shortcomings.

But it is vital to assess the plenum's commitment to reform against the realities of China's political economy and the Chinese government's own goals. And, on that score, the plenum has reinvigorated a reform process that will, in time, make the Chinese economy more resilient, dynamic, and sustainable.

TO MARKET

A month removed, it is possible to be more reflective about the plenum, what it did, and what it failed to achieve.

The meeting's principal conceptual contribution was to replace the word "basic" with "decisive" in the 60-point "Decision on Major Issues Concerning Comprehensively Deepening Reforms" to describe the market's role in allocating resources. With that change, it is now clear that the Chinese government is committed to pursuing and executing market-based reforms, much as we predicted in *Foreign Affairs* last spring. From Beijing's perspective, this is an intellectual breakthrough because it means that Chinese leaders are prepared to allow the market to have a greater role in parts of the economy that have, until now, been mostly reserved for the state. One example is the allocation of capital, which has been concentrated in government-backed banks or else in informal lending channels. The plenum committed to boost the formal role of private capital.

Still, although this breakthrough is substantial, it would be a mistake to think that it is conclusive: to make the market decisive, the state must also retreat. That is why the question of the role of the state will define much of the reform challenge ahead. China's premier, Li Keqiang, has declared war on powerful "vested interests" that oppose market reforms. But the biggest vested interest in the Chinese economy is, in fact, the state itself.

So Beijing must change the state's relationship not only to the economy but also to Chinese society and individual citizens. Simply put, the state must transition from an "administrative" state to a "regulatory" one—in other words, it must become more of an umpire among contending interests than an active participant in an economy that referees itself.

None of that will be easy to do. Even after 35 years of economic reforms, ideologues remain. They instinctively distrust market forces and still prefer the government to manipulate and control the market. The plenum's outcome suggests that the state must surrender such roles if many of the reforms are to take hold.

Take prices—a fundamental market signal of the relationship between supply and demand. In China, three important prices have been controlled by the state or have been subject to the frequent interventions of Chinese bureaucrats: the exchange rate (the price of the Chinese yuan relative to other currencies); the interest rate (in simplest terms, the price of money); and energy and resource prices (input prices).

To reduce an expensive subsidy to export industries and encourage domestic consumption, China's currency was already appreciating before the plenum, and the eventual shift to a market-determined exchange rate seems almost certain over time. But the other two sets of prices—interest rates and energy prices—also appear poised to be further liberalized.

First, China has already liberalized lending interest rates, but it is likely to eventually liberalize deposit rates too. The Chinese central bank has outlined various steps, including testing the policies on an experimental basis in the newly established Shanghai Free Trade Zone and establishing deposit insurance, that should lead to market-based rates over the next several years.

Second, over the last decade or so, China has haphazardly liberalized the prices of some inputs but not others. In many cases, that has created complicated and distorted prices. For instance, although China imports crude oil at global market prices, the rate at the pump is controlled by the central government to protect consumers from inflation. This policy has led to regular hoarding of gasoline before anticipated price hikes and gripes from the oil industry about losses on their upstream investments. But during the recent plenum, China pledged to liberalize the price of commodities and scarce resources that have previously been subsidized, including oil, natural gas, and, over time, perhaps even water.

Subjecting these prices to market discipline will encourage more competition, allow banks to operate more like commercial ventures, and incentivize energy-intensive producers to become more efficient and invest based on a truer sense of costs. Market-based pricing will be a powerful tool for the government and companies to rationally and efficiently allocate resources and manage runaway resource consumption. To do so, however, the Chinese state must also be prepared to cede a long-standing pillar of its authority, reduce price controls, and perhaps tolerate a higher level of inflation.

SOCIAL CONTRACT

Millions of Chinese once relied on an explicit social contract with Beijing. For most of its contemporary history, the state provided virtually all aspects of job security, social security, and retirement security, usually delegated through state-owned enterprises (SOEs) and other work units *(danwei)*. That changed in the 1990s when SOEs, facing a "reform or die" moment, were forced to dramatically alter their functions. They became more commercially oriented and, in the process, shed many of their welfare obligations.

But since then, Beijing has largely failed to replace the old system with a new one of comparable quality and scope. Local governments, seduced by the lure of investment-led growth, spent liberally on infrastructure, housing, and other fixed assets rather than on welfare and retirement services. In some cases, local politicians shifted resources from social welfare to lucrative ventures such as real estate. One Politburo member, Chen Liangyu, was even indicted for pilfering some $4.8 billion from Shanghai's social security funds to line the pockets of property developers.

The plenum unambiguously articulated the need to repair China's social safety net, in part through fiscal transfers that will allow the central government to boost public spending on health care and pensions. It also encouraged the private sector to play a larger role in providing these services, particularly as an aging Chinese society demands more benefits. In an ironic twist, SOEs will likely be forced to partially resume their previous role as a source of social services funding. The dividends that they pay to Beijing will be raised two or three times to 30 percent by 2020, with the additional funds going to social welfare.

But to meet the public's needs and rising expectations, the state cannot simply rearrange resources and rebuild the social contract. It must also deal with the questions of property rights and mobility. The plenum decision began to address these by giving citizens, especially rural Chinese, more property rights. Although the state nominally "owns" all land, Chinese citizens living in cities are allowed to buy and sell property, and they have a mortgage market to help them do so. But rural farmers have virtually no right to sell, transfer, or develop their own land. The plenum pledged, albeit without a timetable, to permit rural land to be sold, rented, or leased with "equal rights" and "equal prices" to state-owned land. Allowing farmers to use land as collateral should soon follow. And that, in turn, should incentivize rural Chinese to move into cities and take jobs in more productive sectors.

The logical next step would be to reduce, and eventually remove, controls on mobility—the so-called *hukou* system that denies millions of Chinese equal access to social welfare benefits on grounds of "illegal" migration to the cities. The policy, enacted in a previous era to prevent a massive influx into cities, no longer makes much sense. China is now a majority urban country and the legions of migrants who intend to remain in the cities will not leave simply because the government denies them equal rights. There is a hint of change that the *hukou* policy may now be scrapped in townships and smaller cities—but it will come neither quickly nor easily.

STATE OF BEING

Ultimately, China will need to reorder the state's basic functions relative to the market, the social contract, and the citizen. But Beijing must also look to remake the state itself so that it is more capable of governance that will allow the market to work. That means the state must become more of an arbiter-like umpire than a pervasive and self-regulating participant in the economy.

Liberalizing prices is one step in the right direction because it will weaken bureaucracies whose current mandate permits them to use price controls to interfere with the market. Another step would be to ease market entry for private firms, which often face high administrative hurdles from local authorities. Already, the central government has taken modest steps with reforms that cut down on red tape and streamline project approvals at the local level. China has no dearth of rules and regulations, but there are few checks or balances on the state. Beijing could get back to basics by strengthening regulatory institutions and increasing enforcement capacity.

Yet surely many will wonder how the state can be remade if SOEs remain so dominant in the economy. The plenum's decision revealed no intention to either downsize or privatize the most important state-owned firms, but such expectations were unrealistic in the first place. The fact is that large-scale privatization is off the table for now.

Still, Beijing could help to discipline SOEs by exposing them to robust competition. If the sectors that they now dominate were opened to private firms and foreign entrants, SOEs would become less sheltered entities. The plenum document alluded to this, but the test is likely to come in trade and investment negotiations. Foreign competitors will insist that Beijing open more sectors to fair and equal competition, and this would ultimately benefit Chinese firms too. If SOEs cannot compete and survive, then the state would need to be prepared to let some of them fail, much as the Chinese government ostensibly tolerated in the 1990s.

Competition is an essential ingredient of well-functioning markets that shapes the behavior of a firm, whether it is public or private. Norway's Statoil is a state-owned firm that behaves like any private firm and has adopted global best practices. By contrast, the Chinese telecom giant Huawei is a nominally private firm that functions more like a state-backed national champion, often receiving state support in various guises. Even without privatization, then, Chinese SOEs could become more disciplined if they were exposed to greater domestic and foreign competition.

It is no small thing to restructure a $9 trillion economy, in which financial, labor, and industrial reforms are now inextricably interconnected. If reforms are to succeed, China needs not just to expand the market but also to refashion the state, even if a large state sector remains a fact of life. This is, ultimately, more of a political question than an economic one, and one that cannot be resolved overnight. So it is no surprise that Beijing gave itself until 2020—halfway through Xi's second term, when he is expected to be joined by five new colleagues on the seven-member Standing Committee, a wholesale turnover—to implement some of the toughest reforms. That will buy the Chinese leadership and its economy some breathing room as the country attempts such a massive rebalancing.

Many have bet long on Chinese growth over the last decade, believing that Beijing would continue to show a surprising capacity to adapt. The ambitious economic reform agenda that emerged from the Third Plenum suggests that their instinct was, on balance, right. Even amid a wave of bearish sentiment in recent years, it would be worthwhile to again bet long on reforms over the next decade.

The Great Leap Backward?

Elizabeth C. Economy

China's environmental problems are mounting. Water pollution and water scarcity are burdening the economy, rising levels of air pollution are endangering the health of millions of Chinese, and much of the country's land is rapidly turning into desert. China has become a world leader in air and water pollution and land degradation and a top contributor to some of the world's most vexing global environmental problems, such as the illegal timber trade, marine pollution, and climate change. As China's pollution woes increase, so, too, do the risks to its economy, public health, social stability, and international reputation. As Pan Yue, a vice minister of China's State Environmental Protection Administration (SEPA), warned in 2005, "The [economic] miracle will end soon because the environment can no longer keep pace."

With the 2008 Olympics around the corner, China's leaders have ratcheted up their rhetoric, setting ambitious environmental targets, announcing greater levels of environmental investment, and exhorting business leaders and local officials to clean up their backyards. The rest of the world seems to accept that Beijing has charted a new course: as China declares itself open for environmentally friendly business, officials in the United States, the European Union, and Japan are asking not whether to invest but how much.

ELIZABETH C. ECONOMY is C. V. Starr Senior Fellow and Director for Asia Studies at the Council on Foreign Relations and the author of The River Runs Black: The Environmental Challenges to China's Future.

Unfortunately, much of this enthusiasm stems from the widespread but misguided belief that what Beijing says goes. The central government sets the country's agenda, but it does not control all aspects of its implementation. In fact, local officials rarely heed Beijing's environmental mandates, preferring to concentrate their energies and resources on further advancing economic growth. The truth is that turning the environmental situation in China around will require something far more difficult than setting targets and spending money; it will require revolutionary bottom-up political and economic reforms.

For one thing, China's leaders need to make it easy for local officials and factory owners to do the right thing when it comes to the environment by giving them the right incentives. At the same time, they must loosen the political restrictions they have placed on the courts, nongovernmental organizations (NGOs), and the media in order to enable these groups to become independent enforcers of environmental protection. The international community, for its part, must focus more on assisting reform and less on transferring cutting-edge technologies and developing demonstration projects. Doing so will mean diving into the trenches to work with local Chinese officials, factory owners, and environmental NGOs; enlisting international NGOs to help with education and enforcement policies; and persuading multinational corporations (MNCs) to use their economic leverage to ensure that their Chinese partners adopt the best environmental practices.

Without such a clear-eyed understanding not only of what China wants but also of what it needs, China will continue to have one of the world's worst environmental records, and the Chinese people and the rest of the world will pay the price.

SINS OF EMISSION

China's rapid development, often touted as an economic miracle, has become an environmental disaster. Record growth necessarily requires the gargantuan consumption of resources, but in China energy use has been especially unclean and inefficient, with dire consequences for the country's air, land, and water.

The coal that has powered China's economic growth, for example, is also choking its people. Coal provides about 70 percent of China's energy needs: the country consumed some 2.4 billion tons in 2006—more than the United States, Japan, and the United Kingdom combined. In 2000, China anticipated doubling its coal consumption by 2020; it is now expected to have done so by the end of this year. Consumption in China is huge partly because it is inefficient: as one Chinese official told Der Spiegel in early 2006, "To produce goods worth $10,000 we need seven times the resources used by Japan, almost six times the resources used by the U.S. and—a particular source of embarrassment—almost three times the resources used by India."

Meanwhile, this reliance on coal is devastating China's environment. The country is home to 16 of the world's 20 most polluted cities, and four of the worst off among them are in the coal-rich province of Shanxi, in northeastern China. As much as 90 percent of China's sulfur dioxide emissions and 50 percent of its particulate emissions are the result of coal use. Particulates are responsible for respiratory problems among the population, and acid rain, which is caused by sulfur dioxide emissions, falls on one-quarter of China's territory and on one-third of its agricultural land, diminishing agricultural output and eroding buildings.

Yet coal use may soon be the least of China's air-quality problems. The transportation boom poses a growing challenge to China's air quality. Chinese developers are laying more than 52,700 miles of new highways throughout the country. Some 14,000 new cars hit China's roads each day. By 2020, China is expected to have 130 million cars, and by 2050—or perhaps as early as 2040—it is expected to have even more cars than the United States. Beijing already pays a high price for this boom. In a 2006 survey, Chinese respondents rated Beijing the 15th most livable city in China, down from the 4th in 2005, with the drop due largely to increased traffic and pollution. Levels of airborne particulates are now six times higher in Beijing than in New York City.

China's grand-scale urbanization plans will aggravate matters. China's leaders plan to relocate 400 million people—equivalent to well over the entire population of the United States—to newly developed urban centers between 2000 and 2030. In the process, they will erect half of all the buildings expected to be constructed in the world during that period. This is a troubling prospect considering that Chinese buildings are not energy efficient—in fact, they are roughly two and a half times less so than those in Germany. Furthermore, newly urbanized Chinese, who use air conditioners, televisions, and refrigerators, consume about three and a half times more energy than do their rural counterparts. And although China is one of the world's largest producer of solar cells, compact fluorescent lights, and energy-efficient windows, these are produced mostly for export. Unless more of these energy-saving goods stay at home, the building boom will result in skyrocketing energy consumption and pollution.

China's land has also suffered from unfettered development and environmental neglect. Centuries of deforestation, along with the overgrazing of grasslands and overcultivation of cropland, have left much of China's north and northwest seriously degraded. In the past half century, moreover, forests and farmland have had to make way for industry and sprawling cities, resulting in diminishing crop yields, a loss in biodiversity, and local climatic change. The Gobi Desert, which now engulfs much of western and northern China, is spreading by about 1,900 square miles annually; some reports say that despite Beijing's aggressive reforestation efforts, one-quarter of the entire country is now desert. China's State Forestry Administration estimates that desertification has hurt some 400 million Chinese, turning tens of millions of them into environmental refugees, in search of new homes and jobs. Meanwhile, much of China's arable soil is contaminated, raising concerns about food safety. As much as ten percent of China's farmland is believed to be polluted, and every year 12 million tons of grain are contaminated with heavy metals absorbed from the soil.

WATER HAZARD

And then there is the problem of access to clean water. Although China holds the fourth-largest freshwater resources in the world (after Brazil, Russia, and Canada), skyrocketing demand, overuse, inefficiencies, pollution, and unequal distribution have produced a situation in which two-thirds of China's approximately 660 cities have less water than they need and 110 of them suffer severe shortages. According to Ma Jun, a leading Chinese water expert, several cities near Beijing and Tianjin, in the northeastern region of the country, could run out of water in five to seven years.

Growing demand is part of the problem, of course, but so is enormous waste. The agricultural sector lays claim to 66 percent of the water China consumes, mostly for irrigation, and manages to waste more than half of that. Chinese industries are highly inefficient: they generally use 10–20 percent more water than do their counterparts in developed countries. Urban China is an especially huge squanderer: it loses up to 20 percent of the water it consumes through leaky pipes—a problem that China's Ministry of Construction has pledged to address in the next two to three years. As urbanization proceeds and incomes rise, the Chinese, much like people in Europe and the United States, have become larger consumers of water: they take lengthy showers, use washing machines and dishwashers, and purchase second homes with lawns that need to be watered. Water consumption in Chinese cities jumped by 6.6 percent during 2004–5. China's plundering of its ground-water reserves, which has created massive underground tunnels, is causing a corollary problem: some of China's wealthiest cities are sinking—in the case of Shanghai and Tianjin, by more than six feet during the past decade and a half. In Beijing, subsidence has destroyed factories, buildings, and underground pipelines and is threatening the city's main international airport.

Pollution is also endangering China's water supplies. China's ground water, which provides 70 percent of the country's total drinking water, is under threat from a variety of sources, such as polluted surface water, hazardous waste sites, and pesticides and fertilizers. According to one report by the government-run Xinhua News Agency, the aquifers in 90 percent of Chinese cities are polluted. More than 75 percent of the river water flowing through China's urban areas is considered unsuitable for drinking or fishing, and the Chinese government deems about 30 percent of the river water throughout the country to be unfit for use in agriculture or industry. As a result, nearly 700 million people drink water contaminated with animal and human waste. The World Bank has found that the failure to provide fully two-thirds of the rural population with piped water is a leading cause of death among children under the age of five and is responsible for as much as 11 percent of the cases of gastrointestinal cancer in China.

One of the problems is that although China has plenty of laws and regulations designed to ensure clean water, factory owners and local officials do not enforce them. A 2005 survey of 509 cities revealed that only 23 percent of factories properly treated sewage before disposing of it. According to another report, today one-third of all industrial wastewater in China and two-thirds of household sewage are released untreated. Recent Chinese studies of two of the country's most important sources of water—the Yangtze and Yellow rivers—illustrate the growing challenge. The Yangtze River, which stretches all the way from the Tibetan Plateau to Shanghai, receives 40 percent of the country's sewage, 80 percent of it untreated. In 2007, the Chinese government announced that it was delaying, in part because of pollution, the development of a $60 billion plan to divert the river in order to supply the water-starved cities of Beijing and Tianjin. The Yellow River supplies water to more than 150 million people and 15 percent of China's agricultural land, but two-thirds of its water is considered unsafe to drink and 10 percent of its water is classified as sewage. In early 2007, Chinese officials announced that over one-third of the fish species native to the Yellow River had become extinct due to damming or pollution.

China's leaders are also increasingly concerned about how climate change may exacerbate their domestic environmental situation. In the spring of 2007, Beijing released its first national assessment report on climate change, predicting a 30 percent drop in precipitation in three of China's seven major river regions—around the Huai, Liao, and Hai rivers—and a 37 percent decline in the country's wheat, rice, and corn yields in the second half of the century. It also predicted that the Yangtze and Yellow rivers, which derive much of their water from glaciers in Tibet, would overflow as the glaciers melted and then dry up. And both Chinese and international scientists now warn that due to rising sea levels, Shanghai could be submerged by 2050.

COLLATERAL DAMAGE

China's environmental problems are already affecting the rest of the world. Japan and South Korea have long suffered from the acid rain produced by China's coal-fired power plants and from the eastbound dust storms that sweep across the Gobi Desert in the spring and dump toxic yellow dust on their land. Researchers in the United States are tracking dust, sulfur, soot, and trace metals as these travel across the Pacific from China. The U.S. Environmental Protection Agency estimates that on some days, 25 percent of the particulates in the atmosphere in Los Angeles originated in China.[1] Scientists have also traced rising levels of mercury deposits on U.S. soil back to coal-fired power plants and cement factories in China. (When ingested in significant quantities, mercury can cause birth defects and developmental problems.) Reportedly, 25–40 percent of all mercury emissions in the world come from China.

What China dumps into its waters is also polluting the rest of the world. According to the international NGO the World Wildlife Fund, China is now the largest polluter of the Pacific Ocean. As Liu Quangfeng, an adviser to the National People's Congress, put

---

1   The original Associated Press story that was the source for the statement was mistaken and has been corrected. In fact, the EPA, citing a model saying that Asia contributes about 30 percent of the background sulfate particulate matter in the western United States, estimates that Asia contributes about one percent of all particulate matter in Los Angeles.

it, "Almost no river that flows into the Bo Hai [a sea along China's northern coast] is clean." China releases about 2.8 billion tons of contaminated water into the Bo Hai annually, and the content of heavy metal in the mud at the bottom of it is now 2,000 times as high as China's own official safety standard. The prawn catch has dropped by 90 percent over the past 15 years. In 2006, in the heavily industrialized southeastern provinces of Guangdong and Fujian, almost 8.3 billion tons of sewage were discharged into the ocean without treatment, a 60 percent increase from 2001. More than 80 percent of the East China Sea, one of the world's largest fisheries, is now rated unsuitable for fishing, up from 53 percent in 2000.

Furthermore, China is already attracting international attention for its rapidly growing contribution to climate change. According to a 2007 report from the Netherlands Environmental Assessment Agency, it has already surpassed the United States as the world's largest contributor of carbon dioxide, a leading greenhouse gas, to the atmosphere. Unless China rethinks its use of various sources of energy and adopts cutting-edge environmentally friendly technologies, warned Fatih Birol, the chief economist of the International Energy Agency, last April, in 25 years China will emit twice as much carbon dioxide as all the countries of the Organization for Economic Cooperation and Development combined.

China's close economic partners in the developing world face additional environmental burdens from China's economic activities. Chinese multinationals, which are exploiting natural resources in Africa, Latin America, and Southeast Asia in order to fuel China's continued economic rise, are devastating these regions' habitats in the process. China's hunger for timber has exploded over the past decade and a half, and particularly since 1998, when devastating floods led Beijing to crack down on domestic logging. China's timber imports more than tripled between 1993 and 2005. According to the World Wildlife Fund, China's demand for timber, paper, and pulp will likely increase by 33 percent between 2005 and 2010.

China is already the largest importer of illegally logged timber in the world: an estimated 50 percent of its timber imports are reportedly illegal. Illegal logging is especially damaging to the environment because it often targets rare old-growth forests, endangers biodiversity, and ignores sustainable forestry practices. In 2006, the government of Cambodia, for example, ignored its own laws and awarded China's Wuzhishan LS Group a 99-year concession that was 20 times as large as the size permitted by Cambodian law. The company's practices, including the spraying of large amounts of herbicides, have prompted repeated protests by local Cambodians. According to the international NGO Global Witness, Chinese companies have destroyed large parts of the forests along the Chinese-Myanmar border and are now moving deeper into Myanmar's forests in their search for timber. In many instances, illicit logging activity takes place with the active support of corrupt local officials. Central government officials in Myanmar and Indonesia, countries where China's loggers are active, have protested such arrangements to Beijing, but relief has been limited. These activities, along with those of Chinese mining and energy companies, raise serious environmental concerns for many local populations in the developing world.

SPOILING THE PARTY

In the view of China's leaders, however, damage to the environment itself is a secondary problem. Of greater concern to them are its indirect effects: the threat it poses to the continuation of the Chinese economic miracle and to public health, social stability, and the country's international reputation. Taken together, these challenges could undermine the authority of the Communist Party.

China's leaders are worried about the environment's impact on the economy. Several studies conducted both inside and outside China estimate that environmental degradation and pollution cost the Chinese economy between 8 percent and 12 percent of GDP annually. The Chinese media frequently publish the results of studies on the impact of pollution on agriculture, industrial output, or public health: water pollution costs of $35.8 billion one year, air pollution costs of $27.5 billion another, and on and on with weather disasters ($26.5 billion), acid rain ($13.3 billion), desertification ($6 billion), or crop damage from soil pollution ($2.5 billion). The city of Chongqing, which sits on the banks of the Yangtze River, estimates that dealing with the effects of water pollution on its agriculture and public health costs as much as 4.3 percent of the city's annual gross product. Shanxi Province has watched its coal resources fuel the rest of the country while it pays the price in withered trees, contaminated air and water, and land subsidence. Local authorities there estimate the costs of environmental degradation and pollution at 10.9 percent of the province's annual gross product and have called on Beijing to compensate the province for its "contribution and sacrifice."

China's Ministry of Public Health is also sounding the alarm with increasing urgency. In a survey of 30 cities and 78 counties released in the spring, the ministry blamed worsening air and water pollution for dramatic increases in the incidence of cancer throughout the country: a 19 percent rise in urban areas and a 23 percent rise in rural areas since 2005. One research institute affiliated with SEPA has put the total number of premature deaths in China caused by respiratory diseases related to air pollution at 400,000 a year. But this may be a conservative estimate: according to a joint research project by the World Bank and the Chinese government released this year, the total number of such deaths is 750,000 a year. (Beijing is said not to have wanted to release the latter figure for fear of inciting social unrest.) Less well documented but potentially even more devastating is the health impact of China's polluted water. Today, fully 190 million Chinese are sick from drinking contaminated water. All along China's major rivers, villages report skyrocketing rates of diarrheal diseases, cancer, tumors, leukemia, and stunted growth.

Social unrest over these issues is rising. In the spring of 2006, China's top environmental official, Zhou Shengxian, announced that there had been 51,000 pollution-related protests in 2005, which amounts to almost 1,000 protests each week. Citizen complaints about the environment, expressed on official hotlines and in

Elizabeth C. Economy

letters to local officials, are increasing at a rate of 30 percent a year; they will likely top 450,000 in 2007. But few of them are resolved satisfactorily, and so people throughout the country are increasingly taking to the streets. For several months in 2006, for example, the residents of six neighboring villages in Gansu Province held repeated protests against zinc and iron smelters that they believed were poisoning them. Fully half of the 4,000–5,000 villagers exhibited lead-related illnesses, ranging from vitamin D deficiency to neurological problems.

Many pollution-related marches are relatively small and peaceful. But when such demonstrations fail, the protesters sometimes resort to violence. After trying for two years to get redress by petitioning local, provincial, and even central government officials for spoiled crops and poisoned air, in the spring of 2005, 30,000–40,000 villagers from Zhejiang Province swarmed 13 chemical plants, broke windows and overturned buses, attacked government officials, and torched police cars. The government sent in 10,000 members of the People's Armed Police in response. The plants were ordered to close down, and several environmental activists who attempted to monitor the plants' compliance with these orders were later arrested. China's leaders have generally managed to prevent—if sometimes violently—discontent over environmental issues from spreading across provincial boundaries or morphing into calls for broader political reform.

In the face of such problems, China's leaders have recently injected a new urgency into their rhetoric concerning the need to protect the country's environment. On paper, this has translated into an aggressive strategy to increase investment in environmental protection, set ambitious targets for the reduction of pollution and energy intensity (the amount of energy used to produce a unit of GDP), and introduce new environmentally friendly technologies. In 2005, Beijing set out a number of impressive targets for its next five-year plan: by 2010, it wants 10 percent of the nation's power to come from renewable energy sources, energy intensity to have been reduced by 20 percent and key pollutants such as sulfur dioxide by 10 percent, water consumption to have decreased by 30 percent, and investment in environmental protection to have increased from 1.3 percent to 1.6 percent of GDP. Premier Wen Jiabao has issued a stern warning to local officials to shut down some of the plants in the most energy-intensive industries—power generation and aluminum, copper, steel, coke and coal, and cement production—and to slow the growth of other industries by denying them tax breaks and other production incentives.

These goals are laudable—even breathtaking in some respects—but history suggests that only limited optimism is warranted; achieving such targets has proved elusive in the past. In 2001, the Chinese government pledged to cut sulfur dioxide emissions by 10 percent between 2002 and 2005. Instead, emissions rose by 27 percent. Beijing is already encountering difficulties reaching its latest goals: for instance, it has failed to meet its first target for reducing energy intensity and pollution. Despite warnings from Premier Wen, the six industries that were slated to slow down posted a 20.6 percent increase in output during the first quarter of 2007—a 6.6 percent jump from the same period last year. According to one senior executive with the Indian wind-power firm Suzlon Energy, only 37 percent of the wind-power projects the Chinese government approved in 2004 have been built. Perhaps worried that yet another target would fall by the wayside, in early 2007, Beijing revised its announced goal of reducing the country's water consumption by 30 percent by 2010 to just 20 percent.

Even the Olympics are proving to be a challenge. Since Beijing promised in 2001 to hold a "green Olympics" in 2008, the International Olympic Committee has pulled out all the stops. Beijing is now ringed with rows of newly planted trees, hybrid taxis and buses are roaming its streets (some of which are soon to be lined with solar-powered lamps), the most heavily polluting factories have been pushed outside the city limits, and the Olympic dormitories are models of energy efficiency. Yet in key respects, Beijing has failed to deliver. City officials are backtracking from their pledge to provide safe tap water to all of Beijing for the Olympics;

they now say that they will provide it only for residents of the Olympic Village. They have announced drastic stopgap measures for the duration of the games, such as banning one million of the city's three million cars from the city's streets and halting production at factories in and around Beijing (some of them are resisting). Whatever progress city authorities have managed over the past six years—such as increasing the number of days per year that the city's air is deemed to be clean—is not enough to ensure that the air will be clean for the Olympic Games. Preparing for the Olympics has come to symbolize the intractability of China's environmental challenges and the limits of Beijing's approach to addressing them.

PROBLEMS WITH THE LOCALS

Clearly, something has got to give. The costs of inaction to China's economy, public health, and international reputation are growing. And perhaps more important, social discontent is rising. The Chinese people have clearly run out of patience with the government's inability or unwillingness to turn the environmental situation around. And the government is well aware of the increasing potential for environmental protest to ignite broader social unrest.

One event this spring particularly alarmed China's leaders. For several days in May in the coastal city of Xiamen, after months of mounting opposition to the planned construction of a $1.4 billion petrochemical plant nearby, students and professors at Xiamen University, among others, are said to have sent out a million mobile-phone text messages calling on their fellow citizens to take to the streets on June 1. That day, and the following, protesters reportedly numbering between 7,000 and 20,000 marched peacefully through the city, some defying threats of expulsion from school or from the Communist Party. The protest was captured on video and uploaded to YouTube. One video featured a haunting voice-over that linked the Xiamen demonstration to an ongoing environmental crisis near Tai Hu, a lake some 400 miles away (a large bloom of blue-green algae caused by industrial wastewater and sewage dumped in the lake had contaminated the water supply of the city of Wuxi). It also referred to the Tiananmen Square protest of 1989. The Xiamen march, the narrator said, was perhaps "the first genuine parade since Tiananmen."

In response, city authorities did stay the construction of the plant, but they also launched an all-out campaign to discredit the protesters and their videos. Still, more comments about the protest and calls not to forget Tiananmen appeared on various Web sites. Such messages, posted openly and accessible to all Chinese, represent the Chinese leadership's greatest fear, namely, that its failure to protect the environment may someday serve as the catalyst for broad-based demands for political change.

Such public demonstrations are also evidence that China's environmental challenges cannot be met with only impressive targets and more investment. They must be tackled with a fundamental reform of how the country does business and protects the environment. So far, Beijing has structured its environmental protection efforts in much the same way that it has pursued economic growth: by granting local authorities and factory owners wide decision-making power and by actively courting the international community and Chinese NGOs for their expertise while carefully monitoring their activities.

Consider, for example, China's most important environmental authority, SEPA, in Beijing. SEPA has become a wellspring of China's most innovative environmental policies: it has promoted an environmental impact assessment law; a law requiring local officials to release information about environmental disasters, pollution statistics, and the names of known polluters to the public; an experiment to calculate the costs of environmental degradation and pollution to the country's GDP; and an all-out effort to halt over 100 large-scale infrastructure projects that had proceeded without proper environmental impact assessments. But SEPA operates with barely 300 full-time professional staff in the capital and only a few hundred employees spread throughout the country. (The U.S. Environmental Protection Agency has a staff of almost 9,000 in Washington, D.C., alone.) And authority for enforcing SEPA's mandates rests overwhelmingly with local officials and the local environmental protection officials they oversee. In some cases, this has allowed for exciting experimentation. In the eastern province of Jiangsu, for instance, the World Bank and the Natural Resources Defense Council have launched the Greenwatch program, which grades 12,000 factories according to their compliance with standards for industrial wastewater treatment and discloses both the ratings and the reasons for them. More often, however, China's highly decentralized system has meant limited progress: only seven to ten percent of China's more than 660 cities meet the standards required to receive the designation of National Model Environmental City from SEPA. According to Wang Canfa, one of China's top environmental lawyers, barely ten percent of China's environmental laws and regulations are actually enforced.

One of the problems is that local officials have few incentives to place a priority on environmental protection. Even as Beijing touts the need to protect the environment, Premier Wen has called for quadrupling the Chinese economy by 2020. The price of water is rising in some cities, such as Beijing, but in many others it remains as low as 20 percent of the replacement cost. That ensures that factories and municipalities have little reason to invest in wastewater treatment or other water-conservation efforts. Fines for polluting are so low that factory managers often prefer to pay them rather than adopt costlier pollution-control technologies. One manager of a coal-fired power plant explained to a Chinese reporter in 2005 that he was ignoring a recent edict mandating that all new power plants use desulfurization equipment because the technology cost as much as would 15 years' worth of fines.

Local governments also turn a blind eye to serious pollution problems out of self-interest. Officials sometimes have a direct financial stake in factories or personal relationships with their owners. And the local environmental protection bureaus tasked with guarding against such corruption must report to the local governments, making them easy targets for political pressure. In recent years, the Chinese media have uncovered cases in which local officials have put pressure on the courts, the press, or even hospitals to prevent the wrongdoings of factories from coming to light. (Just this year, in the province of Zhejiang, officials reportedly promised factories with an output of $1.2 million or more that they would not be subjected to government inspections without the factories' prior approval.)

Moreover, local officials frequently divert environmental protection funds and spend them on unrelated or ancillary endeavors. The Chinese Academy for Environmental Planning, which reports to SEPA, disclosed this year that only half of the 1.3 percent of the country's annual GDP dedicated to environmental protection between 2001 and 2005 had found its way to legitimate projects. According to the study, about 60 percent of the environmental protection funds spent in urban areas during that period went into the creation of, among other things, parks, factory production lines, gas stations, and sewage-treatment plants rather than into waste-or wastewater-treatment facilities.

Many local officials also thwart efforts to hold them accountable for their failure to protect the environment. In 2005, SEPA launched the "Green GDP" campaign, a project designed to calculate the costs of environmental degradation and pollution to local economies and provide a basis for evaluating the performance of local officials both according to their economic stewardship and according to how well they protect the environment. Several provinces balked, however, worried that the numbers would reveal the extent of the damage suffered by the environment. SEPA's partner in the campaign, the National Bureau of Statistics of China, also undermined the effort by announcing that it did not possess the tools to do Green GDP accounting accurately and that in any case it did not believe officials should be evaluated on such a basis. After releasing a partial report in September 2006, the NBS has refused to release this year's findings to the public.

Another problem is that many Chinese companies see little direct value in ratcheting up their environmental protection efforts. The computer manufacturer Lenovo and the appliance manufacturer Haier have received high marks for taking creative environmental measures, and the solar energy company Suntech has become a leading exporter of solar cells. But a recent poll found that only 18 percent of Chinese companies believed that they could thrive economically while doing the right thing environmentally. Another poll of business executives found that an overwhelming proportion of them do not understand the benefits of responsible corporate behavior, such as environmental protection, or consider the requirements too burdensome.

NOT GOOD ENOUGH

The limitations of the formal authorities tasked with environmental protection in China have led the country's leaders to seek assistance from others outside the bureaucracy. Over the past 15 years or so, China's NGOs, the Chinese media, and the international community have become central actors in the country's bid to rescue its environment. But the Chinese government remains wary of them.

China's homegrown environmental activists and their allies in the media have become the most potent—and potentially explosive—force for environmental change in China. From four or five NGOs devoted primarily to environmental education and biodiversity protection in the mid-1990s, the Chinese environmental movement has grown to include thousands of NGOs, run primarily by dynamic Chinese in their 30s and 40s. These groups now routinely expose polluting factories to the central government, sue for the rights of villagers poisoned by contaminated water or air, give seed money to small newer NGOs throughout the country, and go undercover to expose multinationals that ignore international environmental standards. They often protest via letters to the government, campaigns on the Internet, and editorials in Chinese newspapers. The media are an important ally in this fight: they shame polluters, uncover environmental abuse, and highlight environmental protection successes.

Beijing has come to tolerate NGOs and media outlets that play environmental watchdog at the local level, but it remains vigilant in making sure that certain limits are not crossed, and especially that the central government is not directly criticized. The penalties for misjudging these boundaries can be severe. Wu Lihong worked for 16 years to address the pollution in Tai Hu (which recently spawned blue-green algae), gathering evidence that has forced almost 200 factories to close. Although in 2005 Beijing honored Wu as one of the country's top environmentalists, he was beaten by local thugs several times during the course of his investigations, and in 2006 the government of the town of Yixing arrested him on dubious charges of blackmail. And Yu Xiaogang, the 2006 winner of the prestigious Goldman Environmental Prize, honoring grass-roots environmentalists, was forbidden to travel abroad in retaliation for educating villagers about the potential downsides of a proposed dam relocation in Yunnan Province.

The Chinese government's openness to environmental cooperation with the international community is also fraught. Beijing has welcomed bilateral agreements for technology development or financial assistance for demonstration projects, but it is concerned about other endeavors. On the one hand, it lauds international environmental NGOs for their contributions to China's environmental protection efforts. On the other hand, it fears that some of them will become advocates for democratization.

The government also subjects MNCs to an uncertain operating environment. Many corporations have responded to the government's calls that they assume a leading role in the country's environmental protection efforts by deploying top-of-the-line environmental technologies, financing environmental education in Chinese schools, undertaking community-based efforts, and raising operating standards in their industries. Coca-Cola, for example, recently pledged to become a net-zero consumer of water, and Wal-Mart is set to launch a nationwide education and sales initiative to promote the use of energy-efficient compact fluorescent bulbs. Sometimes, MNCs have been rewarded with awards or significant publicity. But in the past two years, Chinese officials (as well as local NGOs) have adopted a much tougher stance toward them, arguing at times that MNCs have turned China into the pollution capital of the world. On issues such as electronic waste, the detractors have a point. But China's attacks, with Internet postings accusing MNCs of practicing "eco-colonialism," have become unjustifiably broad. Such antiforeign sentiment spiked in late 2006, after the release of a pollution map listing more than 3,000 factories that were violating water pollution standards. The 33 among them that supplied MNCs were immediately targeted in the media, while the other few thousand Chinese factories cited somehow escaped the frenzy. A few Chinese officials and activists privately acknowledge that domestic Chinese companies pollute far more than foreign companies, but it seems unlikely that the spotlight will move off MNCs in the near future. For now, it is simply more expedient to let international corporations bear the bulk of the blame.

FROM RED TO GREEN

Why is China unable to get its environmental house in order? Its top officials want what the United States, Europe, and Japan have: thriving economies with manageable environmental problems. But they are unwilling to pay the political and economic price to get there. Beijing's message to local officials continues to be that economic growth cannot be sacrificed to environmental protection—that the two objectives must go hand in hand.

This, however, only works sometimes. Greater energy efficiency can bring economic benefits, and investments to reduce pollution, such as in building wastewater-treatment plants, are expenses that can be balanced against the costs of losing crops to contaminated soil and having a sickly work force. Yet much of the time, charting a new environmental course comes with serious economic costs up front. Growth slows down in some industries or some regions. Some businesses are forced to close down. Developing pollution-treatment and pollution-prevention technologies requires serious investment. In fact, it is because they recognize these costs that local officials in China pursue their short-term economic interests first and for the most part ignore Beijing's directives to change their ways.

This is not an unusual problem. All countries suffer internal tugs of war over how to balance the short-term costs of improving environmental protection with the long-term costs of failing to do so. But China faces an additional burden. Its environmental problems stem as much from China's corrupt and undemocratic political system as from Beijing's continued focus on economic growth. Local officials and business leaders routinely—and with impunity—ignore environmental laws and regulations, abscond with environmental protection funds, and silence those who challenge them. Thus, improving the environment in China is not simply a matter of mandating pollution-control technologies; it is also a matter of reforming the country's political culture. Effective environmental protection requires transparent information, official accountability, and an independent legal system. But these features are the building blocks of a political system fundamentally different from that of China today, and so far there is little indication that China's leaders will risk the authority of the Communist Party on charting a new environmental course. Until the party is willing to open the door to such reform, it will not have the wherewithal to meet its ambitious environmental targets and lead a growing economy with manageable environmental problems.

Given this reality, the United States—and the rest of the world—will have to get much smarter about how to cooperate with China in order to assist its environmental protection efforts. Above all, the United States must devise a limited and coherent set of priorities. China's needs are vast, but its capacity is poor; therefore, launching one or two significant initiatives over the next five to ten years would do more good than a vast array of uncoordinated projects. These endeavors could focus on discrete issues, such as climate change or the illegal timber trade; institutional changes, such as strengthening the legal system in regard to China's environmental protection efforts; or broad reforms, such as promoting energy efficiency throughout the Chinese economy.

Another key to an effective U.S.-Chinese partnership is U.S. leadership. Although U.S. NGOs and U.S.-based MNCs are often at the forefront of environmental policy and technological innovation, the U.S. government itself is not a world leader on key environmental concerns. Unless the United States improves its own policies and practices on, for example, climate change, the illegal timber trade, and energy efficiency, it will have little credibility or leverage to push China.

China, for its part, will undoubtedly continue to place a priority on gaining easy access to financial and technological assistance. Granting this, however, would be the wrong way to go. Joint efforts between the United States and China, such as the recently announced project to capture methane from 15 Chinese coal mines, are important, of course. But the systemic changes needed to set China on a new environmental trajectory necessitate a bottom-up overhaul. One way to start would be to promote energy efficiency in Chinese factories and buildings. Simply bringing these up to world standards would bring vast gains. International and Chinese NGOs, Chinese environmental protection bureaus, and MNCs could audit and rate Chinese factories based on how well their manufacturing processes and building standards met a set of energy-efficiency targets. Their scores (and the factors that determined them) could then be disclosed to the public via the Internet and the print media, and factories with subpar performances could be given the means to improve their practices.

A pilot program in Guangdong Province, which is run under the auspices of the U.S. consulate in Hong Kong, provides just such a mechanism. Factories that apply for energy audits can take out loans from participating banks to pay for efficiency upgrades, with the expectation that they will pay the loans back over time out of the savings they will realize from using fewer materials or conserving energy. Such programs should be encouraged and could be reinforced by requiring, for example, that the U.S.-based MNCs that worked with the participating factories rewarded those that met or exceeded the standards and penalized those that did not (the MNCs could either expand or reduce their orders, for example). NGOs and the media in China could also publicize the names of the factories that refused to cooperate. These initiatives would have the advantages of operating within the realities of China's environmental protection system, providing both incentives and disincentives to encourage factories to comply; strengthening the role of key actors such as NGOs, the media, and local environmental protection bureaus; and engaging new actors such as Chinese banks. It is likely that as with the Greenwatch program, factory owners and local officials not used to transparency would oppose such efforts, but if they were persuaded that full participation would bring more sales to MNCs and grow local economies, many of them would be more open to public disclosure.

Of course, much of the burden and the opportunity for China to revolutionize the way it reconciles environmental protection and economic development rests with the Chinese government itself. No amount of international assistance can transform China's domestic environment or its contribution to global environmental challenges. Real change will arise only from strong central leadership and the development of a system of incentives that make it easier for local officials and the Chinese people to embrace environmental protection. This will sometimes mean making tough economic choices.

Improvements to energy efficiency, of the type promoted by the program in Guangdong, are reforms of the low-hanging-fruit variety: they promise both economic gains and benefits to the environment. It will be more difficult to implement reforms that are economically costly (such as reforms that raise the costs of manufacturing in order to encourage conservation and recycling and those that impose higher fines against polluters), are likely to be unpopular (such as reforms that hike the price of water), or could undermine the Communist Party's authority (such as reforms that open up the media or give freer rein to civil society). But such measures are also necessary. And their high up-front costs must be weighed against the long-term costs to economic growth, public health, and social stability in which the Chinese government's continued inaction would result. The government must ensure greater accountability among local officials by promoting greater grassroots oversight, greater transparency via the media or other outlets, and greater independence in the legal system.

China's leaders have shown themselves capable of bold reform in the past. Two and half decades ago, Deng Xiaoping and his supporters launched a set of ambitious reforms despite stiff political resistance and set the current economic miracle in motion. In order to continue on its extraordinary trajectory, China needs leaders with the vision to introduce a new set of economic and political initiatives that will transform the way the country does business. Without such measures, China will not return to global preeminence in the twenty-first century. Instead, it will suffer stagnation or regression—and all because leaders who recognized the challenge before them were unwilling to do what was necessary to surmount it.